THE AMERICAN LIBERTY POLE

THE REVOLUTIONARY AGE
Francis D. Cogliano and Patrick Griffin, Editors

# The American Liberty Pole

*Popular Politics and the Struggle
for Democracy in the Early Republic*

SHIRA LURIE

UNIVERSITY OF VIRGINIA PRESS
*Charlottesville and London*

University of Virginia Press
© 2023 by Shira Lurie
All rights reserved
Printed in the United States of America on acid-free paper

*First published 2023*

9 8 7 6 5 4 3 2 1

Library of Congress Cataloging-in-Publication Data

Names: Lurie, Shira, author.
Title: The American liberty pole : popular politics and the struggle for democracy in the early Republic / Shira Lurie.
Description: Charlottesville : University of Virginia Press, 2023. | Series: The revolutionary age | Includes bibliographical references and index.
Identifiers: LCCN 2023013861 (print) | LCCN 2023013862 (ebook) | ISBN 9780813950105 (hardcover) | ISBN 9780813950112 (paperback) | ISBN 9780813950129 (ebook)
Subjects: LCSH: United States—Politics and government—1775–1783. | United States—Politics and government—1783–1865. | Liberty poles—United States—History. | Democracy—United States—History. | Political culture—United States—History—18th century. | Political culture—United States—History—19th century.
Classification: LCC E302.1 .L87 2023 (print) | LCC E302.1 (ebook) | DDC 306.2097309/033—dc23/eng/20230629
LC record available at https://lccn.loc.gov/2023013861
LC ebook record available at https://lccn.loc.gov/2023013862

*Cover art: Scenes from the American Revolution: Fifth Liberty Pole on the New York Commons, Charles MacKubin Lefferts, c. 1910. (New York Historical Society; gift of Charles MacKubin Lefferts, 1920.130)*

*For*
*Mom and Dad*
*Nothing without you*

## ❖ CONTENTS ❖

| | |
|---|---|
| *Preface* | ix |
| *Acknowledgments* | xi |
| Introduction: Politics at the Poles | 1 |

### I. Origins

| | |
|---|---|
| 1. The New York City Liberty Poles | 15 |
| 2. Regulation, Ratification, and the Right to Resist | 31 |

### II. Contests

| | |
|---|---|
| 3. Debating Dissent in the Whiskey Rebellion | 47 |
| 4. The Federalist Popular Politics of Assent | 64 |
| 5. "Wandering Apostles of Sedition": Itinerant Republican Activists | 84 |

### III. Transformations

| | |
|---|---|
| 6. From Poles to Polls: The Elections of 1799 and 1800 | 105 |
| 7. Partisan Politics and Poles in the Nineteenth Century | 125 |
| Epilogue: "Forgetting While Remembering" | 143 |

| | |
|---|---:|
| *Appendix: Recorded Liberty Poles Raised, 1766–1799* | 149 |
| *Notes* | 155 |
| *Essay on Sources* | 191 |
| *Bibliography* | 199 |
| *Index* | 217 |

❖ PREFACE ❖

If history is to be creative, to anticipate a possible future without denying the past, it should, I believe, emphasize new possibilities by disclosing those hidden episodes of the past when, even if in brief flashes, people showed their ability to resist, to join together, and occasionally to win.
—Howard Zinn

The recent American past has exposed the nation's troubling relationship with protest. Americans have fought in the streets, courtrooms, legislatures, and media over how and when a person can protest, who is allowed to protest, where a protest can take place, and how long it can last. Some protests have occurred without incident, while others have turned deadly. Some have issued heroic calls for justice, while others, like many of the movements in this book, have supported causes distinctly less righteous. This fight is, at its heart, about political power—who has access, when, and to how much.

My book reveals the origins of that struggle. It shows that the founding era did not provide a stable or unanimous understanding of the citizen's political role in American democracy. Americans fought then, as they do now, about how ordinary people can and should exercise their political power. Instead of taking the norms and traditions of American political culture for granted, my book reveals the many conflicts over them. It suggests that future reforms are not a renunciation of some sacred founding vision, but rather a needed next phase of an ever-evolving, ever-contested political system.

Writing history is often a depressing endeavor, but I believe it is fundamentally a practice of hope. It is the act of revealing what the past has taught us and what we still need to learn. It is the exercise of exploring how we got here and how we can do better. And so, my book is a work of optimism. It is grounded in the belief that the next era of American politics can be made fairer than the last. I write it in honor of all those rising against the forces of oppression, deprivation, and injustice. They are the place where history and hope rhyme. May they lead us to a future worthy of them.

❖ ACKNOWLEDGMENTS ❖

You can't raise a liberty pole alone. And you can't write a book about them alone, either. I am grateful to so many people, the first of whom are the generous teachers and mentors I have had the good fortune to encounter throughout my education. Especial thanks to Rob MacDougall, Nancy Rhoden, Alan Taylor, and Elizabeth Varon. The latter two offered essential guidance as I wrote the first draft of this book as my PhD dissertation at the University of Virginia. Thanks also to Brian Balogh, Joanne Freeman, and Sidney Milkis for the advice and expertise they provided as members of my dissertation committee.

I have presented portions of this book at too many conferences, workshops, and seminars to mention. Those experiences were generative and inspiring and greatly enhanced this project, as well as my time spent working on it. As such, I wish to give a blanket thank you to the early Americanist community for their endless generosity and thoughtful suggestions. In particular, the feedback I received from my long-distance writing group of Kristen Beales, Jackie Beatty, and Lauren Duval was critical in transforming my dissertation into this book.

I am thankful for financial support from the following institutions: the American Philosophical Society, the Bankard Fund for Political Economy, the David Library of the American Revolution, the Dilworth Fund at the Historical Society of Pennsylvania, the Jack Miller Center, the New England Regional Fellowship Consortium, the Omohundro Institute of Early American History and Culture, the Social Sciences and Humanities Research Council of Canada, and the University of Virginia's Office of the Vice President for Research and the Power, Violence, and Inequality Collective. I also wish to acknowledge the assistance I received from the staffs of the many archives and libraries I visited.

I am immensely grateful for a two-year postdoctoral fellowship from the University of Toronto that made this book possible. Thank you to the wonderful people at U of T's University College whose support and encouragement gave me a soft place to land after graduate school. The fellowship also enabled me to come home to my family after many years away. I will always treasure that time together.

I am thrilled to now call Saint Mary's University my intellectual home. I could not have asked for kinder, more welcoming, or more supportive colleagues than those in SMU's Department of History. They are everything academia should strive to be, and I feel immensely proud and fortunate to be one of them. SMU students are some of the most hardworking, curious, and humble people I have ever met. I have learned so much from them (and they are included in these acknowledgments not just because some of them asked to be mentioned!).

I wish every first-time author an editor as perceptive, thoughtful, and enthusiastic as Nadine Zimmerli. She has been a true joy to collaborate with and has improved this book in countless and essential ways. My thanks as well to everyone at the University of Virginia Press for their faith in this project and their work in shepherding it across the finish line.

I have been accompanied on this book's journey of nearly a decade by some of the smartest and funniest friends one could ever hope to find. Many have given crucial advice on this project, others have helped less directly—but either way, their influence is all over this work. Thanks to Miranda Beltzer, Clayton "Old Fuss" Butler, Lindsay Chervinsky, Benji Cohen, Jon Cohen, Mary Draper, Erik Erlandson, Simon Fisher, Jack Furniss, Alexi Garrett, Katie Gorick, Susan Joudrey, Alice King, Mark Lore, Cecilia Márquez, Emma McClure, Claire Meyers, Brian Neumann, Abbey Plein, Nicole Schroeder, Brett Turner, Chris Whitehead, and Cecily Zander. Especial thanks to Rachael Bell, a bosom friend who when needed most is right on time, and Melissa Gismondi, my writing soulmate.

I could not have achieved this long-held ambition to publish a book without the people who have supported me since I first dared to dream it. Thank you to the Davis, Friedman, Kaplan, Kossowsky, Lowenstein, Shevil, and Todes families and to Lynette Deutsch for surrounding me with a loving community. And thanks to my extended "Fam-Jam" who have cheered me from afar.

The last and most important thanks go to my extremely hilarious, endearingly eccentric, and all-around wonderful family. My siblings, Asher, Dani, and Lisa, and my siblings-in-law, Jen and Shael, are the people with whom I share the deepest bonds. Theirs is always my favorite company, and it is a privilege to make my way through life alongside them. My nieces, Avery and Hallie, are the best story writers, joke tellers, dance partners, pretend players, game inventors, and hand holders that I know. They have filled my world with endless magic, wonder, and surprise, and I am so proud of who they are and who they are becoming.

I carry in my heart the memories of my grandparents, Harry, Pat, Rose, and Victor, and my Aunt Melanie. They lived lives of quiet courage, and each in their own way faced down darkness with love and laughter. By their examples, I have learned the truest meaning of freedom.

History is often a study of the worst of humanity. I am so lucky to have parents who represent its best. Anyone who has met David and Lynne Lurie can attest to the ways in which their goodness ripples through their corners of the world, the very embodiment of the Jewish principle *Tikkun Olam*. There is not a day of my life when they have failed to make me laugh, feel loved, or taught me something new. Mom, I know you will read this book from cover to cover. Dad, I know you will try your hardest to make it through the first twenty pages. Both are fine with me. You can do with it whatever you like, because it's for you.

Portions of this book first appeared in "Liberty Poles and the Contested Right of Protest in America's Founding Era," in *Protest in the Long Eighteenth Century*, edited by Yvonne Fuentes and Mark R. Malin (New York: Routledge, 2021), and "Liberty Poles and the Fight for Popular Politics in the Early Republic," *Journal of the Early Republic* 38, no. 4 (Winter 2018): 673–97 (© 2018 Society for Historians of the Early American Republic; reprinted with permission of the University of Pennsylvania Press).

I wrote this book on the lands of the Monacan, Huron-Wendat, Seneca, Mississaugas of the Credit River, and Mi'kmaq First Nations. I am grateful to have lived and worked on these parts of Turtle Island.

# THE AMERICAN LIBERTY POLE

❖ INTRODUCTION ❖

# Politics at the Poles

It is often said that "the sovereign and all other power is seated in the people." This idea is unhappily expressed. It should be "all power is derived from the people." They possess it only on the days of their elections. After this, it is the property of their rulers.
　—Benjamin Rush, 1787

On September 11, 1794, Jacob Heydrick of Carlisle, Pennsylvania, swaggered into the town square brandishing his gun and ranting against a new tax on whiskey levied by the federal government. As he scoured the square, Heydrick spied two workmen paving a path next to a church. He confronted them, forcibly taking their pick and shovel. He had grander purposes than a mere walkway. Joined by two compatriots, Heydrick left for a nearby farm, where he paid the owner to cut a tall pole from a tree and help them carry it into town.[1]

That evening, two hundred people gathered in the square to take part in one of the scores of anti-tax demonstrations in Pennsylvania, Maryland, and Virginia known as the Whiskey Rebellion. Using the stolen pick and shovel, a group of men dug a hole, placed the bottom of the pole in it, and, using the strength of the crowd, hoisted it up to stand vertically. The throng celebrated the feat with cheers, gunfire, and liberal swigs of whiskey. One man affixed a board to the pole that read "Liberty and Equality." The next night, the crowd reassembled at the pole, lit a bonfire, and burned an effigy of the state's chief justice. Their actions recalled the liberty poles of the Imperial Crisis, when

Patriots raised poles to protest Parliament's taxes and the presence of British soldiers in their communities.²

But Heydrick and his crew's work was not yet done. They organized an armed watch to guard their pole at night. Heydrick warned any potential assailants that "he had a good gun and could shoot damned straight." Another pole-raiser vowed that "he would be damned if some lives should not be lost if attempts were made" to interfere with the pole. Even perceived antipathy proved enough to earn the pole-raisers' ire. "The people who appeared on Thursday [to raise the pole]," reported one inhabitant, "seem to shun the conversation of any person who they thought was opposed to their proceeding, and it was thought advisable to say but little to them." Tension hung over the town like a fog.³

Such agitation over a wooden pole may seem foolish, but the pole-raisers were far from paranoid. The pole that Heydrick and his neighbors raised on September 11 was actually a replacement. A few days earlier, residents of Carlisle had erected a pole in the town square that read "Liberty and No Excise, O Whiskey," only to find it prostrate in the dirt the next morning. Under cover of darkness, a dissenting group had cut down the pole.⁴

An editorial in the *Carlisle Gazette* provides some insight into what may have prompted the nocturnal assault. The pseudonymous "A Yellow Breeches Farmer" complained bitterly that his fellow townsmen so brazenly opposed Congress's will with their pole, thereby attacking the foundation of self-government. "What, gentlemen, is the great principle of our government? Certainly that the majority have the right of making laws both for themselves and the minority," he explained. Whether or not individual Americans disliked certain laws, they had an obligation to obey them. He expressed astonishment that those who had so recently fought a war for the right of the people to rule could "oppose the laws which we ourselves have made." The display in the town square implied that the pole-raisers and their supporters would not submit to Congress's, and hence the people's, authority to govern. They were enemies of the American Revolution and the republic it had conceived.⁵

But the pole-raisers believed that their actions aligned with the Revolution and its promises. To them, government by the people meant government was answerable to the people. One newspaper explained, "An interest in the approbation of the people, and a strong sense of accountability to them, in all official conduct, is the greatest or rather the only effectual security against abuses in those who exercise the powers of government." And when their elected representatives acted unjustly, the people had a right to oppose the government's actions, just as they had done as colonists subject to Parliament's authority. The liberty pole offered ordinary people a way to critique government and organize local opposition to tyrannical laws.[6]

There was more at stake in the Carlisle conflict than a mere tax law and a wooden pole. The town divided over the very meaning of self-government. Americans based their new governing system on the principle of popular sovereignty, the notion that the government derives its power from the will of the people. Due to the impracticalities of a pure democracy, in which all citizens have a direct say in government, the Constitution's framers opted for a republic, in which citizens elect officials to govern on their behalf. But while these concepts of popular sovereignty and representation seem like axioms to modern readers, they are actually rather shaky foundations upon which to form a government.[7]

The popular will does not truly exist. It is an abstract term meant to give definition to that which is undefinable—the opinion of the entire body of citizens—and so relies on an imagined homogeneity and unity that can never be realized. Since the basis of political authority is unlocatable, it is constantly claimed. As we will discover, governments, communities, protestors, and counter-protestors have all justified their actions by asserting that they embodied the popular will. Just as "the people" can never be fully constituted, they can also never be wholly represented. Instead, representation, Edmund S. Morgan famously argued, is a "fiction" in which we "make believe that the representatives of the people *are* the people." The distance between the facts and fictions of representation sparked the struggles over legitimate political expression in the early republic. Americans clashed over what constituted sufficient representation and what to do when "the people" disagreed with their representatives.[8]

During the 1790s, Americans raised over one hundred liberty poles and scores of skirmishes broke out as others tore them down. These conflicts reveal the difficulties Americans experienced in translating the abstract principles of self-government into practice. Was majority rule paramount, or did minority voices have a right to dissent? Did elections provide sufficient means for citizens to influence politics, or should they have a more regular, participatory role? What political power did citizens yield to their representatives through the act of election, and what did they retain as individuals?

Underpinning these questions was a larger one about the implications of transitioning from a colonial political system to a republican one. As colonists, the people had enjoyed a central political role in their communities, sometimes mobilizing in support of authority and other times using crowd action to resist unpopular policies. But the advent of popular sovereignty and representative government challenged the compatibility of these older practices with a new political order. Some argued that republican government required the people's traditional scrutiny of officials and resistance to unjust laws, and that such methods had been given renewed sanction by the American Revolution. But others insisted that Americans no longer needed colonial methods of political expression now that they elected their own governing officials. Popular organizing and resistance were relics of an imperial system that lacked representative government's institutional accountability. In stressing rupture, not continuity, this position articulated a novel, narrower vision for popular political participation that emphasized electing and instructing representatives. Benjamin Rush explained, "It is often said that 'the sovereign and all other power is seated in the people.' This idea is unhappily expressed. It should be 'all power is derived from the people.' They possess it only on the days of their elections. After this, it is the property of their rulers."[9]

The liberty pole became a flashpoint in this struggle. Critics of the federal government, who eventually formed the Republican party, raised liberty poles to protest legislation and rally resistance. They viewed popular action as the bedrock of American liberty and a critical safeguard against concentrations of power. Representative government, like all methods of government, required tried-and-true popular resistance methods to ensure that it did not descend into tyranny. As in Carlisle, they used their poles to evoke the Imperial Crisis and position themselves as true Patriots. Federalists, those in support of government, viewed liberty poles as an improper form of political expression because they undermined elected officials. They argued that colonial liberty poles had been acceptable, but republican government rendered such methods illegitimate. Thus, while usually understood as conservative, the Federalists, in fact, advanced a radical new vision for American politics that advocated an abrupt break with the past and the wholesale adoption of a new system. The Republicans, for their part, rejected the Federalists' new model for a more submissive, acquiescent citizenry as a scheme to weaken the people's political power. But to the Federalists, Republican insistence on a traditional understanding of politics marked them as conservatives who clung to outdated methods and beliefs.

Grassroots Federalists tore down liberty poles to weaken popular opposition and reassert the supremacy of majority rule. Pole-raisers often fought back by re-erecting their poles and organizing armed guards to defend them. Occasionally, tensions boiled over into violence. The impact of the conflicts then reverberated outward as the partisan press spread these stories across the country, politicians struggled to deal with popular protests without alienating voters, and pole-raisers and their allies mobilized to win elections at the local, state, and national levels. As a result, the raising and destroying of liberty poles fueled a national conversation over the citizen's power in the young republic.

As the first book-length study of liberty poles, *The American Liberty Pole* spans the period from the American Revolution to the Civil War but focuses on the 1790s. It centers grassroots partisans and the significance of local conflict to the development of early American political culture and the First Party System. While most scholarship confines popular politics to Republicans, liberty poles reveal a pattern of grassroots Federalist activity that contested Republican claims to the public sphere. Federalists created their own style of popular politics that used crowd action to bolster the government's authority, enforce majority rule, and implement their vision for republican politics. The resulting clashes between pole-raisers and destroyers sharpened partisan divisions as Republicans and Federalists defined themselves against their opponents' ideas and actions. These local conflicts ballooned into national issues that hardened partisan identities, challenged elite leaders, and shaped electoral strategies and outcomes.

To fully grasp why liberty pole conflicts proved so inflammatory, we must forget what we already know—that the United States, of course, survived the challenges of its early years. Instead, we must imagine the overwhelming uncertainty of the period. The new republic seemed to teeter on a high wire, with two opposing forces threatening to topple it in either direction. Pole-raisers and their allies feared that the federal government would grow too powerful, beyond popular influence and control. Insulated from the people, the government would oppress its citizens. In contrast, Federalists worried that an overactive citizenry would undermine government authority and fatally weaken the force of law, causing a descent into chaos. The dual spectres of tyranny and anarchy haunted almost every political debate of the era.

Early Americans worried that the triumph of either force would doom not only the United States but also the rest of the world to the shackles of monarchy. In 1788, John Jay exhorted his fellow New Yorkers to "be mindful that the cause of freedom greatly depends on the use we make of the singular opportunities we enjoy of governing ourselves wisely." For if their experiment in self-government should fail, "the minds of men everywhere will insensibly become alienated from republican forms." Americans believed that humanity's hopes for liberty were pinned to their success. Such was their burden (and hubris), and such is the prism through which a wooden pole became a tinderbox.[10]

The field of political culture in the early republic is exceedingly rich. For decades, innovative scholars have expanded politics beyond stuffy legislatures and dry vote tallies and taken us instead to dueling grounds, mock executions, town gatherings, illicit parties, street riots, rowdy taverns, militia musters, religious services, and union meetings, to name just a few. This work has changed not only where we look for politics, but also what we look for. Historians have shown how even the mundane, like clothing and food, or internal, like emotion and honor, informed and reflected the politics of the early republic.[11]

This scholarship has yielded a robust literature on Republican popular political culture. Historians have investigated organized opposition movements, like the Whiskey Rebellion, Fries's Rebellion, and the Democratic-Republican Societies. They have also explored widespread backlash to Federalist legislation, as well as the foundational importance of Republican festive culture to the formation and growth of the party. This work has been critical in solidifying our understanding of the Republicans' popular politics of dissent—crowd action that opposed unjust legislation and Federalist overreach.[12]

This book builds on this scholarship by revealing the centrality of liberty poles to Republican organizing, identity, and expression. Early American protestors used liberty poles as their primary method of voicing dissent because of their symbolic resonance and mobilizing power. As recognizable icons, liberty poles connected movements across time and space. The early republic's liberty poles most obviously referenced the Imperial Crisis, but they also linked together the various protests of the 1790s. In doing so, the poles signaled the legitimacy of popular opposition as a regular political practice employed by a variety of Americans. They also confirmed widespread support for a particular cause. For instance, a pole-raiser during the

Whiskey Rebellion cited liberty poles in other areas as his inspiration, and explained that his community's pole stood "in support of their brethren" elsewhere.[13]

But while the symbol of the pole connoted a general right to protest, the signs and flags of each one communicated pole-raisers' specific messages. Most often, these banners denounced particular laws, invoked Revolutionary slogans, or issued ominous promises—"WE WILL DEFEND OUR RIGHTS" read a pole in Small Lotts, New Jersey. Pole-raisers also individualized their poles with patriotic symbols, like flags and eagles, which further identified their poles as an American emblem, or liberty caps, which linked their poles to France and the spirit of revolution.[14]

Crucially, liberty poles marked public space. Pole-raisers usually placed their poles in communal areas, like the town square. In doing so, they claimed to represent the community's opinions and values and implied popular support for their pole's message. The poles' height, often between seventy and ninety feet, further strengthened this symbolism. By towering over the area, the pole inserted a new, striking, and dominant visual onto the town's landscape that dwarfed other community markers, like the local church, school, or tavern. The size of the pole also meant that its erection required a team of people—raising a liberty pole was no individual act. In all of these ways, the liberty pole implied popular approval from the community in which it stood.[15]

Most often, pole-raisings were big celebrations in which crowds accompanied the erection with feasts, gunfire salutes, and bonfires. The communal, extra-institutional nature of these events created a space for those excluded from the suffrage to engage in politics. For White women, children, the poor, immigrants, and occasionally people of color, pole-raisings offered an opportunity to express political beliefs, ally with certain ideological currents, and claim the right to check government power. Still, it would be foolish to ascribe general motivations to a diverse set of actors. Some participants may have viewed these events as an important vehicle of political expression, while others may have joined out of a sense of excitement and community belonging. Regardless of motivation, pole-raisings provided politically marginalized people with the chance to participate in politics and embody a form of political behaviour that was less exclusive and regulated than voting.[16]

Once raised, the liberty pole operated as a staging ground for all kinds of traditional resistance activities. Neighbors gathered at the pole to burn effigies, drink toasts, sign pledges of noncompliance, and threaten their opponents. The pole formed the center of community organizing and action, and in between, its looming presence reminded onlookers, especially potential dissenters, of the community's commitment to the cause. The liberty pole was both symbolically and operationally powerful and melded seamlessly with older organizing and resistance methods.

Of most importance, the liberty pole often signaled pole-raisers' engagement in regulation—crowd action designed to protect local communities from oppressive legislation while simultaneously pressuring government officials to amend or repeal. Regulators' methods included closing courts and auctions, intimidating and attacking officials, and barricading roads. As regulators, pole-raisers made a claim to a political role outside of government institutions and mechanisms, one in which communities had significant local control over federal law. As an extra-institutional process, regulation empowered the citizenry with a political function beyond electing and instructing representatives. Indeed, regulation offered a method of adjusting a policy *after* it became law.[17]

And so, the liberty pole operated simultaneously as a powerful symbolic marker of public space, a rallying point for related resistance activities, and a mode of political practice. As mentioned, liberty pole customs contained elements of traditional festive culture, public justice rituals, and crowd action. They created a space for communities to organize and engage in these activities. But unlike a public meeting, effigy burning, festival, or riot, the liberty pole blended claims to sovereignty and legitimate, extra-institutional political process with visible, lasting, and imposing physical demonstrations of popular support. This potent combination helps explain why dissatisfied early Americans regularly turned to liberty poles to enact their dissent.

Grassroots pole-raisers forced Republican elites to walk a fine line between distancing themselves from liberty poles and regulations and still stoking popular disapproval of the Federalists. While eager to capitalize on the backlash against the Federalists' legislation, Thomas Jefferson and James Madison feared that radical ideas and actions within the growing opposition movement would strengthen Federalist accusations of Republican anarchy. They performed an awkward dance, signaling their general approval of resistance while scapegoating a handful of leaders for going too far. The Republican press reinforced this messaging by criticizing certain regulations but upholding the legitimacy of liberty poles and condemning the Federalists for attacking them.

Liberty pole destructions provide an untapped window into grassroots Federalist political activity. While a rich scholarship exists on Republican popular politics of dissent, work on Federalist reactions to Republican opposition tends to focus on elites. Often, the narrative jumps from Republican activity on the ground to the frustrated figures of Washington, Hamilton, and Adams denouncing the radicals and planning their responses. Rarely do these works consider how local Federalists countered Republican activity in their communities, even when they do make brief mention of liberty poles. As a result, these studies imply that Republicans monopolized popular mobilization during the 1790s.[18]

Those who have examined Federalist popular politics emphasize participants' use of street theatre to give ritual assent to government. During the struggle for ratification and the Washington administration's early years, Federalists used celebrations and their coverage in the press to demonstrate popular backing of the new regime. As scholars like David Waldstreicher and Simon P. Newman have shown, by attending and participating in parades, festivals, feasts, and toasts in celebration of the Constitution and George Washington, Federalists performed their allegiance and loyalty, demonstrating that the federal government had the citizenry's approval. In later years, when the Republicans began to organize displays of opposition, Federalists responded with counter-demonstrations of support. As Todd Estes and Jeffrey L. Pasley have revealed, Federalists held meetings, wrote letters, and passed resolutions in favor of the federal government's actions.[19]

While foundational, this work gives the impression of a Federalist popular politics that was almost entirely confined to scheduled celebrations and that existed in isolation from that of the Republicans. In these accounts, partisans largely hosted their own events and reported on them in the press, vying to appear as the true manifestation of the popular will. But popular politics was more than just a shouting match between rival groups. Attention to grassroots Federalists' reactions to liberty poles reveals a dynamic and spontaneous popular politics that went beyond public celebration and counter-demonstration and instead developed through in-person confrontations with Republicans.

Federalists tore down liberty poles and denounced regulations as dangerous uprisings. They did so to enforce their new vision for politics and uphold the will of the majority, as expressed in Congress. To them, liberty poles threatened representative government, and so destroying the poles constituted a defense of the Revolution and its promises. Wary of the poles' symbolic power, Federalists not only toppled them, they also used the press to counter pole-raisers' messages of legitimacy and popular approval. Federalist newspapers decried the icons as "sedition poles" and "anarchy poles" and (often falsely) claimed that only a small number of people participated in their erections.

By attacking liberty poles and pole-raisers, Federalists created a popular politics of assent that used crowd action to defend the government's authority and enforce its will on unruly populations. In this way, Federalists enacted a political role for citizens in which they vigilantly defended representative government by attempting to silence its critics. This aggressive and often violent aspect of the Federalists' popular politics prompted Republican backlash—in person, in the press, at the poles, and at the ballot box. The politics of assent and dissent clashed repeatedly as grassroots Republicans and Federalists developed their ideas and actions through battles triggered by the local liberty pole. As conflicts escalated, partisan divisions grew increasingly entrenched. The First Party System developed on the ground dialectically, and so the stories of Republican and Federalist popular politics must be told together.

In 1832, the residents of Jonestown, easterly neighbors of Carlisle, raised a one-hundred-foot-tall liberty pole. But it was different than the Carlisle pole of 1794. Rather than a critique of legislation, the pole's decorations proudly displayed the names of locally favored politicians, including gubernatorial candidate Joseph Ritner. The people of Jonestown used their pole to signal their partisan preferences, not to engage in dissent and regulation. As such, readers understood press reports of the Jonestown example "being followed in several other places" as a predictor of future electoral results and not the rumblings of a growing resistance movement. Four decades after the Carlisle pole, liberty poles still dotted American communities, but their meaning had transformed.[20]

As the First Party System gave way to the Second, grassroots Republicans increasingly accepted the Federalist concept of politics. After Jefferson's election, many Republicans abandoned the protest tradition and instead raised liberty poles in support of the administration. In the nineteenth century, the consolidation of the two-party system and the corresponding extension of the franchise for White men further marginalized the earlier decentralized model of political participation. Electoral politics largely replaced extra-institutional resistance as White Americans elevated voting as the key form of political participation and raised poles, like the people of Jonestown, only in support of their candidates. Similarly, most reformers and activists relied on institutional methods, like petitions and resolutions, to seek change. In doing so, they sacrificed the more expansive, traditional version of American politics that pole-raisers had previously envisioned—one in which institutional politics constituted one option within a much broader catalog through which Americans practiced politics. Despite their electoral losses, the Federalists' vision won.

By limiting acceptable political expression to institutional politics, antebellum political culture pushed the unenfranchised further to the margins and reduced traditional resistance methods to the desperate resort of those outside the "real" political community. As a result, the arc of the liberty pole reveals important and uncomfortable truths about the limits of American democracy, both then and now. Delegitimizing extra-institutional modes of political participation limits the mechanisms of political change to those designed by and for elites, leaving the barriers to a full and free process as formidable in the twenty-first century as they were in the eighteenth.

But the early republic, of course, was no halcyon era. Liberty poles and regular popular resistance made for a messy, unstable, and frequently violent political culture that failed to achieve any major victories for those on the political and social margins. This is not a story of a lost golden age. It is a story of one imperfect system replacing another, each with its own benefits and costs. More importantly, it is a story about contingency and contestation. The American founding did not generate a single, stable, consensual, or universal understanding of how self-government should operate in practice. Americans fought for years over their differing visions. There is nothing predetermined or inherently righteous about the way American politics functions—it is the product of choices made at particular moments. Every day brings a new opportunity to choose again.

❖ I ❖

# Origins

This monument is erected in terrorem not only to the tories of the present, but of future generations.
—*Massachusetts Spy,* November 3, 1774

❖ 1 ❖

# The New York City Liberty Poles

Cutting this Post down can only be done with a Design to affront all the *Sons of Liberty* in this Place, [and] the Perpetrators would do well to consider the Consequences.
—*New York Gazette, or Weekly Post Boy*, March 26, 1767

On the night of January 13, 1770, British soldiers stationed in New York City snuck onto the Common to destroy the liberty pole that stood there. But it would not be an easy job. The city's pole-raisers had encircled the pole's base with iron rings to prevent assailants from chopping it down. By moonlight, the soldiers quickly and quietly bored a hole in the pole and filled it with gunpowder. They planned to blow it to pieces. But before they could light the fuse, men on their way to the nearby Montayne's Tavern, headquarters of the Sons of Liberty, spotted the suspicious silhouettes around their pole. They ran inside and raised the alarm. Frustrated, the soldiers turned their destructive energies on the tavern, smashing the front windows and several bowls and lamps and cutting the forehead of a patron inside. This done, they beat a hasty retreat to their barracks.[1]

The commotion on the night of the thirteenth was just one of many clashes between redcoats and colonists over the city's liberty pole. Between 1766 and 1770, residents replaced their pole four times after redcoats destroyed each one amid escalating scenes of violence. Despite its benign appearance, the liberty pole proved a potent source of conflict because it contained multiple layers of meaning. New Yorkers had raised the first American liberty pole in 1766 to commemorate the Stamp Act's repeal. On the surface, the pole celebrated colonists' membership in an empire of liberty and their thankfulness to the king and Parliament. But it also signified their commitment to popular mobilization in defense of their rights and their wariness of Parliament's power. The latter meaning grew increasingly pronounced when newly arrived redcoats attacked the pole that summer, viewing it as an audacious affront to imperial authority. The soldiers' actions triggered a back-and-forth of erecting and destroying poles that disrupted city life for years. The struggle in New York City transformed the liberty pole into an emblem of colonial defiance. And as the imperial relationship crumbled during the mid-1770s, liberty poles sprang up in other colonies as powerful symbols of the Patriot cause.

The liberty pole grew out of the traditional rituals of Anglo-American culture. Throughout the colonial era, communities practiced a diverse range of political activities in which crowds gave sanction to official power structures, punished transgressors, and pressured officials. During the 1760s and 1770s, Patriots drew upon these tactics and used crowd action to resist imperial legislation. The liberty pole emerged as the perfect symbol for expressing and organizing Patriot opposition—to those both within and outside the community it strongly signaled popular resistance, while also serving as a rallying point for further political activity. When British soldiers, like those in New York City, targeted liberty poles for destruction, their assaults both revealed and reinforced the liberty pole's potency.[2]

Liberty poles came to symbolize the enactment and defense of a system of politics in which the people played a central role. As a result, pole-raisers equated attacks on their liberty poles with attacks on their liberty itself. And so, a seemingly harmless wooden pole became the flashpoint for conflict in New York City and spread across the colonies as Americans prepared to declare their independence.

To early Anglo-Americans, politics was a community affair. They congregated, marched, feasted, rioted, heckled, vandalized, cheered, stomped, and thrashed to enact their views about power and control its operation in their lives. These were not merely symbolic displays or excuses for entertainment.

Colonists mobilized with intention, sometimes to achieve targeted political goals and other times to enact traditions that expressed political beliefs and legitimized collective action. Each occasion when people gathered and acted together, they testified to the strength of the crowd and the power that mobilization held in their communities.

In colonial America, when officials enacted unpopular policies, the people responded. Boston residents repeatedly vandalized ships to prevent the exportation of grain from the colony. Virginians and Marylanders destroyed tobacco plants to control production after their legislatures failed to do so. In 1764, a New York City crowd protested impressment by seizing the barge of a British press gang, carrying it to the Common, and burning it. Similar examples pervaded every colony as communities organized to defend themselves from unjust or unresponsive authority. Crowds also attacked private property. In several instances, angry colonists pulled down the houses of local officials whose policies appeared to threaten the public good. In extreme cases, colonists physically attacked those in power, like in 1730 when residents of New Hampshire assaulted the new assistant governor in retribution for his enforcement of the royal lumber monopoly. Colonists legitimized these direct actions according to traditional Whig theories of resistance in which the community had a right to challenge and correct government when it functioned improperly.[3]

But colonists also mobilized in support of authority. When officials ordered criminals to the stocks or pillory or paraded through the streets, community members played their part by jeering and pelting the transgressors. Local rites of public justice also assumed unofficial forms. Drawn from the English tradition of "rough music," sometimes known as skimmington or charivari, colonists punished those suspected of violating community norms by making noise outside the offenders' windows at night, vandalizing their property, beating them, parading them through town, or forcing them to ride a wooden rail.[4]

Celebration, too, offered colonists avenues of political expression. To mark official holidays like the King's Birthday or Accession Day, local elites organized processions, cannon salutes, bonfires, illuminations, and food and drink for the masses. By attending and participating, colonists offered their tacit consent to the political system and those who exercised its power. But the colonial calendar also contained regional "plebeian holidays," like Pope's Day in Boston and New York, which commemorated the anniversary of Guy Fawkes's foiled plot to blow up Parliament in 1605. Each November 5, the lower orders temporarily ruled the city by invading the streets, burning effigies, and levying an unofficial tax on the wealthy to fund the day's refreshments. Through this ritual, colonists voiced their anti-popery and loyalty to the Hanovers, but also implied hostility to any monarch who appeared warm to Catholicism.[5]

Colonial crowd action, public justice rituals, and festive culture often involved participants from across social classes, races, genders, and ages. The extra-institutional nature of these activities, that they occurred outside of formal institutions, allowed all kinds of groups to attend and take part. Of course, not all demographics participated equally and in all cases. Still, colonists regularly referred to these crowds as "the people," implying that they represented the broader community. To early Americans, politics was a group event in which neighbors joined together to enforce collective notions of justice, power, and liberty through public action and display.[6]

During the Imperial Crisis, these traditions took on heightened importance as colonists used them to express their opposition to Parliament's legislation and its colonial executors. For instance, crowds in New York City echoed their annual Pope's Day celebrations by parading and burning effigies of Lieutenant Governor Cadwallader Colden to protest the Stamp Act. In the late 1760s, colonists began tarring and feathering customs officials and informants. Drawn from maritime culture and evocative of traditional public justice rituals, tarring and feathering involved forcibly stripping the victim, covering them in pine tar, rolling them in feathers, and parading or carting them through the streets. In Boston, crowds intimidated merchants who refused to comply with non-importation by tarring and feathering their property. Colonists also relied on familiar methods of rough music. For instance, in June 1776, New Yorkers attacked several Tories in the city, forcing them to strip and ride the rail.[7]

Angry colonists also turned to popular rituals of destruction to hamper the enforcement of Parliament's legislation and protest its injustices. To prevent the Stamp Act's execution, colonists destroyed stamp offices and papers, as well as the property of stamp officers and other officials. In the summer of 1765, Bostonians pulled down Lieutenant Governor Thomas Hutchinson's house. The most famous ritual of destruction, of course, was the Boston Tea Party, in which 150 men boarded East India cargo ships and threw forty-five tons of tea overboard while thousands of spectators lined the docks. After the colonies officially declared independence from Britain in the summer of 1776, colonists initiated a wave of popular destruction and vandalism of monarchical symbols to ritualistically break the bonds of Crown and subject. Across the colonies, crowds burned portraits, toppled statues, and destroyed effigies of the king. These actions reinforced the strength and legitimacy of crowd action in the colonies.[8]

The liberty pole combined the popular power of community celebration, resistance, and public justice traditions into one striking symbol. Colonists came together to make and raise their poles—often accompanying the erections with traditional festivities. They then used their poles not only as a visual representation of their commitment to opposition, but also as the center of their political organizing. Disaffected colonists met at their liberty poles to plan and launch other forms of protest. They also used them as the site of intimidation and punishment, either calling those with questionable loyalty to the poles or burning officials in effigy at their base. Once raised, colonists mobilized to defend their poles from redcoat and Loyalist attacks. These assaults testified to the liberty pole's symbolic and operational significance—by marking the emblems as worthy of destruction, they enhanced the poles' power. This phenomenon originated with the first liberty poles of New York City, when conflict with British soldiers transformed the liberty pole from a celebratory symbol to an icon of resistance.

In May 1766, news reached New York City that Parliament had repealed the Stamp Act. A cacophony of sound burst through the city as residents rang church bells, lit fireworks, and fired guns and cannons to convey their joy. All manner of city dwellers flooded the Common, the open green area in lower Manhattan also referred to as the Fields. Relishing the mild spring weather, the crowd washed down freshly roasted ox with liberal swigs of beer, rum, and punch. They cheered their victory, but also their membership in an empire of liberty—one in which the king and Parliament had abandoned an unjust policy in the face of reasonable resistance. And so, this celebration echoed the festivities that accompanied official holidays, when colonists' merriment signaled their approval of those in power. But it also affirmed the efficacy and legitimacy of popular mobilization to achieve political results.[9]

The highlight of the day occurred when the crowd raised a tall pine mast.

Four prominent members of the city's Sons of Liberty led the effort: Joseph Allicocke, a mixed-race man; John Lamb, the son of an Englishman; Alexander McDougall, a Scotsman; and Isaac Sears, originally from Connecticut. In their backgrounds, they represented different parts of the English-speaking British Empire. But they were united through their strong ties to shipping and seafaring, having made their fortunes as merchants despite humble origins. Sears, for instance, the son of an oysterman, had won riches as a privateer during the Seven Years' War before becoming a prosperous and influential merchant in the city. Although wealthy, all four retained close bonds with the city's sailors, dockworkers, and artisans. Their mast evoked these connections.[10]

The men affixed to the pole a sign that read "George 3rd, Pitt—and Liberty." By naming the king and William Pitt, a former prime minister beloved for his opposition to the Stamp Act, alongside the word "Liberty," the pole-raisers acknowledged that the British Crown and government maintained the freedom of all subjects. A few weeks later, on the king's birthday, city residents added a flag with the St. George's Cross. But the pole also stood as a reminder of the people's power to affect political change. A local paper pronounced it "a Monument of Gratitude to his Majesty, and the British Parliament who repealed the Act, and to those worthy Patriots, by whose Influence the repeal was obtain[e]d." So although General Thomas Gage, commander-in-chief of the British Army in North America, described the pole as the means by which the people "testif[ied] their Joy and Thankfulness," the New York City liberty pole also represented New Yorkers' belief that they had a role to play in the politics of empire.[11]

The pole conveyed this secondary meaning to onlookers because wooden poles, as icons, connoted liberty to Anglo-Americans. Derived from the wand and cap used to grant enslaved Ancient Romans their freedom, British artists depicted both Britannia and the Roman goddess of liberty carrying a long pole with a cap on top. Anglo-American paintings, political cartoons, and coins used the image of a liberty cap balanced on a pole to signify freedom. During the War of Independence, the Continental Congress, the *Pennsylvania Magazine*, and several military units all displayed the device—likely a reference to both the ancient symbolism and the colonists' physical poles.[12]

European tradition offered further connections between wooden poles and the struggle for freedom. During the seventeenth century, rural men and women raised maypoles on festival days, especially the first of May, or

*Britannia*, engraving by Francesco Bartolozzi after Giovanni Battista Cipriani, 1768. (Library of Congress)

May Day, the celebration of spring. May Day featured the relaxation of social norms, including feasting and sexual license. Europeans also associated maypoles with the carnivalesque's ritualistic social inversion. The New York City liberty pole drew upon these traditions to signify liberty and the reversal of political hierarchy. After all, maypoles could also be political. During the English Civil Wars, Royalists had adopted maypoles as an icon of their cause, using them to register defiance of the Puritan Parliamentarians' opposition to traditional festive culture as popish. Similarly, in seventeenth- and eighteenth-century France, peasants raised maypoles as rallying signs when they rioted against their landlords. Maypoles gradually made their way to colonial North America, appearing in many celebrations of the Tammany Society, a club devoted to celebrating May Day in the colonies.[13]

Onlookers may have also drawn a connection to Boston's Liberty Tree, a large elm near the Boston Common. Beginning in the summer of 1765, Bostonians centered their political expression around the tree, using it to post messages, suspend lanterns, and raise flags. Colonists also used it as a gathering place for their meetings and demonstrations, as well as a site of public justice. Bostonians led victims of tarring and featherings to the Liberty Tree and called officials to "Liberty Hall," the space around the foot of the tree, to resign their commissions. And by stringing up effigies on its branches, colonists used the Liberty Tree as their own symbolic gallows—a popular alternative to the real gallows located just half a mile away. From 1765 to 1776, at least thirteen other communities adopted the symbol and designated their own liberty trees. The majority were in New England, but the practice spread south to Maryland, South Carolina, and Georgia.[14]

Boston's Liberty Tree predated the New York City liberty pole by a year, making it a possible source of inspiration. At the very least, those in New York likely related the two emblems and saw in their pole the same opportunities for community organizing and resistance. Still, the liberty pole possessed several symbolic features that distinguished it from the liberty tree. The New Yorkers' manmade pole suggested a more anthropocentric, deliberate view of liberty, one in which freedom was produced and defended by the people, rather than springing naturally from the ground. The liberty pole was also more visually striking than a tree and more versatile—it towered over the landscape and could be created, modified, moved, and decorated as desired.[15]

The material and location of the New York City liberty pole imbued it with further meaning by referencing points of contention within the imperial relationship. New Yorkers fashioned their pole out of a ship's mast made from white pine. The British navy valued white pine for its slender, straight build and light weight, making it the perfect wood for masts, beams, and bowsprits. Beginning in the 1690s, Parliament monopolized the harvesting of white pines for naval use by fining colonists one hundred pounds for felling a white pine over twenty-four inches in diameter. Outraged colonists protested these laws for decades by stealing white pine logs from British officials. By using a white pine mast for their pole, New Yorkers challenged the monopoly and reminded onlookers of the long-existing frictions between city residents and imperial officials.[16]

By erecting their pole on the Fields, the Sons of Liberty chose a location that encapsulated the tensions between city residents and British regulars that had simmered since the Seven Years' War. The British victory in that conflict brought enormous territorial gains in North America, including Canada, Florida, and all French-claimed land east of the Mississippi River. Anxious over the security of their newly enlarged empire and a £133 million war debt, imperial officials kept nearly ten thousand men in North America and demanded that the colonists help pay for their upkeep. But the colonists balked at the expense and at Parliament's efforts to tax them without the consent of their colonial legislators. Despite the concern of imperial officials, American colonists felt secure, having ousted the French from the continent. They viewed the lodging and provisioning of a peacetime standing army as at best unnecessary and at worst as a threat to their liberty.[17]

New York City served as the British army's headquarters on the continent and so housed two regiments, which residents resented. The colonial Assembly at first refused to supply the troops, but gave in after Parliament threatened to suspend the legislature. The Sons of Liberty then took up the cause, stirring up opposition at meetings and in writing. After the Assembly's passage of the Supply Act, which taxed colonists to provision the garrison, Alexander McDougall censured the legislators: "And what makes the Assembly's granting this Money the more grievous, is, that it goes to the Support of Troops kept here, not to protect, but to enslave us." Of all city residents, the laborers who worked along the docks felt particularly aggrieved because off-duty soldiers often undercut them by accepting lower wages.[18]

The Fields provided a geographic microcosm for this conflict. The Upper Barracks for the British soldiers stood at one end, and Abraham Montayne's Tavern, the headquarters of the city's Sons of Liberty, lay at the other. New Yorkers chose to place their pole right between the two. Their choice of location is perhaps unsurprising, as the Fields was the natural gathering point for city dwellers. But it also held deeper implications. New Yorkers occupied and marked a fraught space with a prominent emblem that testified to their enthusiasm and numerical strength. In doing so, they added another layer of symbolism to their pole—one that asserted colonists' control and authority in the city despite the presence of hundreds of British troops.[19]

The liberty pole towered over the landscape—a reminder that the people of New York City were loyal to the empire but watchful of its power. Still, the pole was not yet a revolutionary symbol. The summer, however, would bring warmer temperatures and hotter tempers as the 28th Regiment of Foot, a unit notorious for clashes with civilians, arrived from Quebec. They lodged in the Upper Barracks, just a stone's throw from the liberty pole. But the soldiers did not, in fact, throw stones at it. They tore it down.[20]

On August 10, after waiting for nightfall, the men quietly snuck out of their barracks and felled the pole. Their actions suggest that despite the pole's monarchical trappings, the redcoats understood its additional connotations of freedom and resistance. As a result, they viewed the emblem as an impudent assertion of the colonists' right to resist Parliament's will and so an affront to imperial authority. Ironically, the soldiers' actions conferred deeper significance to the pole than if they had just allowed it to remain standing. The *New York Gazette* explained that New Yorkers initially viewed their pole as a "Trifle" and would not have worried if "it had fallen by natural Decay." But after "being destroyed by Way of Insult, we could not but consider it as a Declaration of War against our Freedom and Property, and resent it accordingly." The regiment's attack increased the pole's symbolic power by marking it as a threat warranting destruction. It also stripped away the pole's endorsement of king and Parliament and in doing so initiated the liberty pole's transformation into an unambiguous symbol of the colonists' struggle against tyrannical exercises of imperial power.[21]

The next day, an estimated three thousand colonists gathered at the site of their fallen pole and defiantly raised another one, reasserting their control over the Fields. Of course, their actions drew the attention of the nearby troops, and both sides readied for a fight. Pole-raisers' bats and pistols clashed with the redcoats' bayonets as grunts and cries filled the air—a perverse inversion of the shouts of delight that had rung out from the same spot just three months earlier. Now, rather than the remnants of celebration littering the ground, the injured lay scattered across the Fields, a testament to how much had changed between the first and second poles. Eventually, the 28th Regiment's commanding officer and General Gage's aide-de-camp ushered the regulars back to their barracks. Fortunately, no one died.[22]

But both sides dug in, and the fracas in August proved just the first in a series of battles over the city's liberty poles. In September, the soldiers of the 28th Regiment cut down the pole raised in August. When the colonists erected a third pole, the soldiers again destroyed it. New Yorkers once more erected a replacement, but this time took deliberate measures to defend it. On March 19, 1767, they sunk their new pole deep into the ground and rein-

*Liberty Pole*, 1770. (Library Company of Philadelphia)

forced it with iron around its base. In doing so, the colonists attested to their changing view of the liberty pole. They intended it to be a permanent fixture of the landscape. The pole was certainly no longer a "Trifle" or evocative of short-lived maypoles. Colonists now wanted their liberty pole to have staying power, and their defensive actions conveyed their committed opposition to the outrageous behavior of the redcoats in the city.[23]

The soldiers made several unsuccessful attempts on the new pole over the next few weeks, including an initial plan to fill it with gunpowder and blow it up. In the wake of these events, the *New York Gazette* published a defiant denunciation of the 28th Regiment's actions: "Cutting this Post down can only be done with a Design to affront all the *Sons of Liberty* in this place, [and] the Perpetrators would do well to consider the Consequences." The paper reminded the redcoats of the colonists' successful mobilization to defeat the Stamp Act: "for they may know, that such a Body of People who would not yield to be enslaved by the most august Body on Earth, will not tamely submit to such a mean low-lived Insult on their Liberty, as this is." The reference attested to the strength of New Yorkers' resistance and surely intended to strike a nerve.[24]

But before the soldiers could retaliate, Gage transferred the 28th Regiment to Ireland and brought in the 16th Regiment of Foot to replace them.

Despite this attempt to defuse tensions, the city's residents continued to chafe under what they deemed needless military occupation. Likewise, the new soldiers inherited their predecessors' frustrations with the restless populace who met frequently at the liberty pole to denounce them. "People seem distracted everywhere," Gage wrote to a colleague in London. "It is now as common here to assemble on all occasions of public concern at the Liberty Pole and Coffee House as for the ancient Romans to repair to the Forum. And orators harangue on all sides." His words reveal how entrenched the liberty pole had become as a site of politics to those in the city.[25]

As described earlier, violence once again broke out on the night of January 13, 1770, when the 16th Regiment tried in vain to blow up the liberty pole and attacked Montayne's Tavern in retaliation. John Lamb circulated a broadside denouncing the assault and connecting it to the injustices of the Supply Act. "All the Money that you have hitherto given them," he vented, "has only taught them to despise and insult you." Lamb called for a meeting at the liberty pole at noon on January 17 to discuss opposition to the soldiers.[26]

On the eve of the meeting, the soldiers succeeded in toppling the pole and left it in pieces on Montayne's doorstep—a new level of insult. Three thousand colonists gathered the next day at the Fields and resolved to find and punish those responsible. They vowed to treat all soldiers out at night as "Enemies of the Peace of this City." They further affirmed that the multiple attempts to destroy their "Memorial of Freedom" offered "incontestable Proof, that [the soldiers] are not only Enemies to the Peace and good Order of this City; but that they manifest a Temper, devoted to destroy the least Monument, raised to shew the laudable Spirit of Liberty, that prevails among the Inhabitants." The redcoats' actions proved their intent to "enslave" city residents and confirmed their reputation as the "mortal Enemies to all that is dear and valuable to Englishmen." In this way, the liberty pole operated as the impetus for popular action, as well as its organizational center. Even in its absence, the pole served as the gathering point for community members to collectively voice their opinions and plan their next moves.[27]

The 16th Regiment rebutted Lamb's broadside and the subsequent resolutions in a broadside of their own. They denied destroying the pole and mocked the Sons of Liberty for their complaints: "observe, how chagrined those pretended S[ons] of L[iberty] look as they pass thro' the streets; especially as these great heroes thought their freedom depended in a piece of wood." The soldiers blamed the recent disturbances on the Sons of Liberty who "in defiance of the laws and good government of our most gracious sovereign . . . openly and r[iotousl]y assemble in multitudes, to stir up the minds of his Majesty's good subjects to sedition." The broadside criticized the colonists' popular action and insisted that the people could restore peace in the city if they simply acquiesced to the soldiers' authority and stopped inciting unrest.[28]

Harsh words turned into violent deeds when a handful of soldiers began posting their broadside along city streets. Isaac Sears and Walter Quackenbos, a baker, confronted them. Sears grabbed one of the soldiers by the collar and demanded to know "what Business he had to put up Libels against the Inhabitants?" As the soldier squirmed in Sears's grip, Quackenbos seized the man carrying the broadsides. A third soldier drew his bayonet and Sears struck him on the head. The remaining soldiers ran to the barracks for reinforcements. The two colonists took their captives to Mayor Whitehead Hicks's residence, carrying out, in their minds, the community's resolutions of a few days prior. The commotion drew a crowd outside the mayor's house of city residents eager to see the soldiers brought to justice. Meanwhile, the redcoat reinforcements arrived and pushed their way to the front. They drew their weapons and demanded the release of their men. In response, several colonists pulled rungs from some nearby sleighs, ready to defend the house from attack. The mayor emerged just in time and ordered the soldiers to go back to their barracks.[29]

But the conflict did not end there. The disgruntled soldiers walked to the top of nearby Golden Hill, so named for its "golden" grain, followed by an angry group still wielding sleigh rungs and more than likely shouting a few choice taunts. The soldiers turned on the crowd, with one among the number ordering the group to "cut your way through them." They raced down the hill with their weapons drawn, allegedly crying, "Where are your Sons of Liberty now?" As the two sides clashed, forty more soldiers appeared at the bottom of the hill, opening a second front. But soon Hicks and several officers arrived, and the "Battle of Golden Hill" ended with injuries on both sides but no casualties.[30]

The escalating violence demonstrates how significant the liberty pole had become. It intensified the imperial conflict in New York City and operated as the focal point for the struggle. Colonists and soldiers understood the pole's importance as both the center of the Sons of Liberty's resistance and the symbol of their cause. Every time redcoats attacked the pole and those who raised it, they further confirmed its power. Every time New Yorkers replaced their pole and clashed with the soldiers, they affirmed the connection between the pole and the larger movement against imperial authority. The Battle of Golden Hill testified to the ever-increasing stakes of this conflict. It also foreshadowed another violent outburst between colonists and soldiers that would occur just six weeks later: the Boston Massacre.

Smaller scuffles continued in New York City for several weeks afterward. Residents hurled insults and stones at the soldiers, who threatened them with bayonets, allegedly cutting a few. "We are all in confusion in this city," lamented one inhabitant. That March, Gage sent the 16th Regiment to Florida. With their assailants gone, the Sons of Liberty applied to the mayor to raise a replacement pole on the Fields. But the City Corporation refused, believing a new pole would spark further disorder. The Sons of Liberty seethed: "We question whether this Conduct can be paralleled by an Act of any Corporation in the British Dominions, chosen by the Suffrages of a free People." Sears circumvented the authorities by purchasing a private lot near the Fields where the group raised their tallest pole yet—eighty-eight feet—topped with a gilded vane and flag that both read "Liberty." They preempted would-be assailants by surrounding the base with iron, nails, and metal hoops. [31]

As the Imperial Crisis intensified, the liberty pole's symbolism extended beyond just conflict with redcoats to include denunciations of all representations of British authority and allegiance in the city. In 1774, New Yorkers met at the pole to celebrate colonists' destruction of a tea ship's cargo. In 1775, a crowd of two hundred men attacked a pair of Loyalists for refusing to kneel to the liberty pole and curse the king—a strong indication of the centrality of the pole to the symbolic, ritualistic, and emotional break with the Crown. The pole also operated as a site where those with suspicions could test loyalty to the Patriot cause. Rather than a declaration of the colonists' rights within the empire, the pole now firmly symbolized New Yorkers' defiance of and hostility to imperial power. The pole stood until the fall of 1776, when British governor William Tryon denounced it as a "monument of insult to the Government" and ordered its removal.[32]

As newspapers spread word of the conflict in New York City throughout the colonies, residents in other areas raised scores of liberty poles. The bulk of them followed the Coercive Acts of 1774, which closed the port of Boston, suspended its charter, and imposed a new Quartering Act in retribution for the Boston Tea Party. By June 1775, liberty poles had reached as far as Savannah, Georgia. However, most poles were confined to the Northeast, likely reflecting southern anxieties about raising an emblem of freedom in a slave society. While unhesitant to use the language of slavery in their rhetoric, most southerners perhaps viewed a visual representation of liberty and resistance as too great a security risk.[33]

Like their counterparts in New York, colonial pole-raisers used their liberty poles as staging grounds for demonstrations against British policies, embedding the poles within familiar rites of crowd action and asserting their commitment to popular resistance. For instance, Patriots in Farmington, Connecticut, raised a liberty pole and burned at its base an effigy of Massachusetts royal governor Thomas Hutchinson and a copy of the Boston Port Act, which closed the port of Boston. The people of Hanover, Massachusetts, raised a liberty pole "as a lasting monument, in praise and commendation, of that glory of patriotism and love of this country, which not long since have taken possession of the worthy inhabitants of this county." In the *Massachusetts Spy*, the pole-raisers stated boldly, "This monument is erected in terrorem not only to the tories of the present, but of future generations." They threatened potential assailants with "the flaming vengeance of the majesty of the people." With this wording, the pole-raisers transferred the "majesty" of the king to "the people" and so asserted that they would treat their opponents as traitors.[34]

Despite such warnings, or perhaps because of them, redcoats and Loyalists regularly attacked liberty poles and those who raised them. As in New York City, such actions galvanized Patriots to re-erect their poles and vigorously defend them as emblems of their commitment to popular resistance. This was the case in Boston after British troops hacked down the Liberty Tree in the wake of the Battles of Lexington and Concord. The Sons of Liberty responded by raising a liberty pole to replace the tree that August, on the anniversary of the Stamp Act's repeal. In Sandwich, Massachusetts, after three Loyalists tore down the local liberty pole, the community erected a replacement and forced the guilty persons to apologize and pay £5 each in damages. British officials, soldiers, and Loyalists continued to mock the Patriot obsession with liberty poles. One Tory taunted that "Liberty," to Patriots, "is the *Happiness of Assembling in the open Air*, and performing *Idolatrous* and *vociferous* Acts of Worship, *to a Stick of Wood*, called a Liberty Pole."

But to the Patriots, the liberty pole held profound meaning, and each time their opponents attacked their "stick of wood," it gained further significance as an emblem of colonial resilience and defiance in the face of tyranny.[35]

The Imperial Crisis gave birth to the American liberty pole, but it grew organically out of longstanding Anglo-American political culture. Liberty poles blended the symbolic and festive elements of community celebrations, the intimidation and popular authority of public justice rituals, and the organization and resistance of crowd action. Communities gathered to raise poles, defend them, and re-raise them. In doing so, they drew upon the people's traditional role in politics.

In New York City, when redcoats attacked the liberty pole, colonists saw it as not only an attempt to stifle their political expression, but also, and more fundamentally, an assault on their power. Little wonder that they fought back so vigorously. The years-long conflict transformed liberty poles into emblems of resistance to tyrannical encroachment, as well as symbols of this way of doing politics—in which the people had a crucial part in the formation, execution, enforcement, and adjustment of the law. As liberty poles spread and pole-raisers encountered similar attacks from local soldiers and Loyalists, the poles' symbolic significance continued to intensify and pole-raisers cast their assailants as enemies of the Revolution and the people's role in politics.

And so, the liberty pole connoted much more than just a vague notion of freedom. Indeed, it stood for a specific political system that empowered ordinary citizens to check unjust exercises of authority, as well as a history of popular mobilization in defense of one's community and the Patriot cause. All of these elements made the liberty pole a powerful icon for future protestors who aimed to secure a significant political role for the citizenry in the new republic.

❖ 2 ❖

# Regulation, Ratification, and the Right to Resist

That all power being originally inherent in, and consequently derived from, the people; therefore all officers of government, whether legislative or executive, are their trustees and servants, and at all times accountable to them.
—Pennsylvania State Constitution, 1776

As displays of opposition gave way to actual fighting, reports of liberty pole–raisings dwindled away. Several possibilities may account for the poles' disappearance from the historical record during the War of Independence. Perhaps communities felt resistance activities and symbolic displays were less imperative now that they had declared independence and war had broken out. Perhaps the occupation of British troops made pole-raisings too dangerous in certain areas. Perhaps Americans continued to raise liberty poles, but the press was too preoccupied with the war's progress to report on them. Likely, a combination of factors explains their absence.

But liberty poles reappeared in the 1790s, after the ratification of the Constitution specified how, at least in structural terms, the new government would be organized. Dissenters returned to the liberty pole as the key method to organize and express their resistance under this system. Often, they also drew upon another tradition that became increasingly visible during the 1770s and 1780s: regulation. These decades crushed rural Americans under the combined pressures of new taxes, mounting debt, a lack of circulating currency, and restrictive land policies. Drawing on colonial rituals of crowd action, communities banded together to protect their indebted neighbors from speculators, creditors, and tax collectors. By closing courts and auctions, intimidating and attacking officials, and barricading roads, they sealed their towns off from external intrusions, thereby preventing the enforcement of economic policies they could not afford. These regulations aimed to protect vulnerable communities while simultaneously pressuring government officials to amend or repeal oppressive legislation.

After independence, regulators adapted imperial forms of crowd action to an American system of government. As a result, the regulations of the 1780s raised questions about the compatibility of these older methods with a new political structure. While some argued that the Revolution solidified the people's role in politics, others insisted that it marked a rupture with the past. As officials cracked down on community regulations, they imposed new legislative, judicial, and constitutional constraints on the people's role in politics. These conflicts formed the foundation for the early republic's struggle over how, when, and whether citizens could engage in politics beyond electing representatives.

Colonial traditions, the experience of the Imperial Crisis and the American Revolution, and the pressures of the Confederation Era placed two competing visions for American politics on a collision course. The regulators of the 1790s revived the liberty pole and insisted that longstanding precedent guaranteed the place of popular politics in the new nation. But critics argued that representative government obviated the need for such displays and instead required the acquiescence of the citizenry to the decisions of their elected representatives. As the new republic dawned, the nation lacked consensus on where "the people" fit within the new political order.[1]

This chapter, along with the previous one, sets the stage for the ensuing conflict. It reveals the wide-ranging catalog of political behavior embedded in regulation and charts the emerging debate over the future of those methods in the American republic.

The first regulation occurred in North Carolina, where backcountry residents felt overburdened by mounting debt, cash scarcity, and rising taxes. "Currency of all kinds has becom[e] so very Scarce, it is believed by the most Knowing that the whole of it now within this County . . . would not be

Sufficiant to pay the Taxes only," declared a 1766 petition to Royal Governor William Tryon and the colony's General Assembly. Frustrated by a lack of response from those in power, colonists from Orange County formed the Sandy Creek Association in August of that year to coordinate their resistance. Encouraged by the recent widespread opposition to the Stamp Act, the association urged other communities to organize and nullify their colonial government's oppressive policies.[2]

In April 1768, the Sandy Creek Association combined with colonists from Rowan, Anson, and Mecklenburg Counties to form the Regulators, a term derived from mid-seventeenth-century England referring to people who corrected government abuses.[3] Inspired by the Sons of Liberty, the Regulators pressured the colonial government to correct course and respond to the needs of the people. But Tryon scoffed at their pretense of legitimacy and demanded that they stop referring to themselves with "the borrowed Title of Regulators assuming to themselves Powers and Authorities unknown to the Constitution." The people, in his eyes, had no grounds to organize outside of government channels.[4]

Nevertheless, the Regulators continued their efforts, turning to the time-tested methods of public justice to oppose harmful policies. They first took direct action against a Hillsborough sheriff who had seized a colonist's horse as payment for the man's back taxes. More than seventy Regulators confronted the sheriff, tied him up, and carried him to the village. Some in the procession also shot at the home of Edmund Fanning, a hated Orange County judge. The Regulators then returned the mare to its owner. Fuming at the "traitorous" and "rebellious" behavior, Fanning appealed to Tryon for assistance. The royal governor issued two proclamations denouncing the Regulators for "Confederat[ing] together to oppose the just Measures of Government." He ordered the colony's militia to Orange County to assist in the restoration of law and order.[5]

That May, the Regulators issued a petition to the royal governor blaming the recent trouble on corrupt officials and reiterating their earlier complaints of harsh taxes and a lack of specie to pay them. Tryon remained unmoved. "The Grievances complained of by no means Warrant the extraordinary steps [taken]," he countered. Tempers flared again in the fall of 1769 when Tryon dissolved the Assembly following the election of four Regulators to the legislature. In response, many farmers refused to pay their taxes. Meanwhile, the courts ruled against the Regulators in a series of cases. On September 24, Regulators took out their frustrations on county officials, beating two justices, a law clerk, and Fanning. The following day, they pulled down Fanning's house and broke the windows of several stores.[6]

Tryon called the Assembly into session to pass a new riot act for "preventing tumultuous & riotous Assemblies." The law provided for the retroactive prosecution of anyone who had interfered with an official's discharge of his duty. On March 15, 1771, a Special Court of Oyer and Terminer indicted sixty-one Regulators for rioting under the new law. At the same time, the royal governor organized a military expedition to suppress the Regulators. On May 16, Tryon and 1,100 men faced down 2,500 poorly armed Regulators at Alamance Creek. The resulting battle yielded 29 fatalities and 150 wounded, almost all on the Regulator side. Lingering for a week, Tryon's forces set fire to Regulators' homes, destroyed their crops, and requisitioned supplies. Overawed and humbled, 6,400 men signed an oath of allegiance, promising to obey the law and pay their taxes. Twelve Regulators stood trial under the new riot law, and six were hanged on June 19. With the North Carolina Regulation finally over, Tryon accepted the promotion to become royal governor of New York, a larger and richer colony.[7]

Soon after he began his new position, Tryon faced another regulation, this time in northeastern New York. During the 1760s, the governors of New Hampshire and New York had granted the same land to two different sets of people. The New Hampshire speculators sold their lots to settlers at low prices, hoping to solidify their claim through occupation and improvement. But the New York government declared the New Hampshire claim invalid and warned the settlers that to avoid eviction, they had to purchase New York land titles. Led by Ethan Allen and calling themselves the Green Mountain Boys, the settlers formed a local government and militia to resist and oust New York claimants. The Green Mountain Boys blocked sheriffs from serving eviction notices, set fire to the property of New York title holders, and violently intimidated officials from surveying the settled land. Allen insisted that the only legitimate form of possession was "sealed and confirmed with the Sweat and Toil of the Farmer." Tryon issued a warrant for Allen's arrest and put a bounty on his head, but the Green Mountain Boys avoided capture. Vermont, as the area came to be known, declared independence in 1777 as an autonomous republic.[8]

The North Carolina Regulation and the Green Mountain Boys' actions blended with the larger Patriot struggle of the 1770s. Like the pole-raisers in New York City and the many other Patriot efforts elsewhere, the regulators in North Carolina and Vermont employed traditional popular political practices in their battles against imperial officials and policies. To them, community mobilization and, often, extra-legal action constituted legitimate political practices and the obvious responses to unjust exercises of imperial power.

But after the War of Independence, regulators targeted American officials, not imperial governors. In this new context, regulation and the crowd action associated with it became controversial. A series of postwar regulations revealed uncertainty over whether the expansive popular political culture of the colonial era was compatible with a republican form of government. Many began voicing an alternative vision, one in which the principle of representation required the people to surrender their former active involvement in politics and adopt a more submissive and passive role.[9]

This conflict first emerged during the 1780s as state governments tried to finance the war with new taxes and higher land prices. To fund the army and pay down its share of the war debt, the Massachusetts legislature implemented nine different direct taxes from 1780 to 1786. Rural communities petitioned the legislature to lighten the load. "The Taxes ... the last twelve months is more than the full improved Value of all the property of Said Town," explained the residents of Mount Washington in Berkshire County. The tax burden would "reduce the said Town to desperation & ruin." To make matters worse, in 1781 the state repealed the tender status of paper money, making scarce specie the sole means to pay taxes and debts. The state's constitution also severely limited poorer residents' rights to political participation. The constitution implemented a £60 property qualification to vote and a £200, £300, and £1,000 property qualification to serve as a legislator, senator, and governor respectively.[10]

Matters came to a head in 1786 when the legislature passed the largest direct tax yet and demanded that residents pay one-third of it in specie. In response, communities organized a series of county conventions throughout the Massachusetts countryside. The conventions issued petitions and addresses calling for a more democratic constitution, paper money as legal tender, lower taxes and legal fees, and reduced government salaries. But elites in Boston dismissed the conventions as resulting from "British emissaries" or "wicked and unprincipled men," and the legislature ignored the complaints. That summer, fifteen hundred armed men of Hampshire County barricaded the county's court of common pleas and declared their intent to close the court until officials addressed "the present Circumstances of the good People of this Commonwealth & also consider[ed] the great Scarcity of Cash." The court did not reopen that session. Shortly afterwards, hundreds of Worcester County men closed their local courthouse, despite a proclamation from Governor James Bowdoin warning against such action as rebellion. Similar court closings followed in Concord, Middlesex, Taunton, and Berkshire.[11]

Like their North Carolina counterparts, the Massachusetts court-closers called themselves Regulators. They hoped to achieve through direct action what they had failed to gain through petition: reforms by an insensitive government, especially with regard to tax and debt relief. In the short term, they provided relief themselves by preventing the courts from prosecuting public and private debtors. "I had no intention to destroy the government but to have the courts suspended to prevent such abuses as have late taken place," a leading Regulator later explained. Their direct action protected their communities, while pressuring officials to institute legislative changes.[12]

But those in power, led by Bowdoin, denounced them as rebels who disturbed the peace and threatened law and order. Government supporters rejected the legitimacy of regulation, insisting instead that citizens had to obey the decisions of their elected officials. Unresponsive representatives should be voted out of office, not extorted into action by illegal displays of mob rule. Even Samuel Adams, a one-time champion of the people's right to organize and overthrow tyrannical government, maintained that while "County Conventions and popular committees served an excellent purpose when they were first in practice [during the Revolution]," they were currently unnecessary. "As we now have constitutional and regular governments and all our men in authority depend upon the annual, free elections of the people, we are safe without them." In other words, representative government replaced popular mobilization. The methods of the past were now illegitimate.[13]

The two sides met in September at the Springfield courthouse, where eight hundred militiamen confronted twelve hundred Regulators who intended to prevent the Supreme Judicial Court from opening its quarterly session. Among them was Daniel Shays, a farmer and War of Independence veteran. Shays and six others wrote a petition to the judges asking them to refrain from issuing any indictments for the court closings until the legislature addressed their grievances. After several failed attempts to empanel grand juries, the court adjourned.[14]

When the legislature convened a few days later in Boston, thirteen communities submitted petitions reiterating rural concerns. Meanwhile, Regulators continued to shut down courthouses. The legislature passed several modest reforms, including the acceptance of some tax payment in goods, rather than specie, and the extension of the tax payment deadline by four months. Still, representatives did not embrace paper money, the Regulators' chief demand. The legislators also passed a riot act that empowered local officials to prosecute assembled persons who failed to disperse when ordered, as well as bystanders who refused to assist in suppressing resistance. Most ominously, the act shielded from prosecution any official who harmed a rioter resisting arrest. On November 15, the legislature offered clemency to Regulators if they ceased their activities and took an oath of allegiance by January 1. Otherwise, they faced prosecution. The legislature declared that it would not "indulg[e]" an attitude of "unreasonable Jealousy & a complaining Temper." They had heard the people's complaints, and now the people must submit to the law.[15]

Unbowed, the Regulators continued to close county courts in western Massachusetts. An infuriated Bowdoin mobilized 4,400 men and ordered them to Springfield to block Regulators' plans to close the court there. In late January, about 2,000 Regulators led by Shays marched on the Springfield arsenal, defended by Bowdoin's militiamen. The government forces opened fire, killing four Regulators and injuring many more. The Regulators broke and fled. They reorganized in the hilly town of Pelham to the north of Springfield. The Regulators and militia stared each other down in a two-day stalemate. On February 4, the Regulators retreated further north to Presham, where the militiamen, shielded by a snowstorm, overwhelmed the camp in a surprise attack. The government force arrested 150 Regulators. Most of the remaining number, including Shays, fled to New York, New Hampshire, and Vermont. Smaller skirmishes continued in nearby areas as the militia captured more men, resulting in four more deaths.[16]

The Massachusetts legislature sought to make an example of many involved in the so-called "Shays's Rebellion." On February 16, the legislators passed the Disqualification Act, which mandated that anyone who had mobilized against the government or given aid to the Regulators lost his civil rights and must apply for a pardon. The law barred any pardoned man from voting, standing for office, working as a teacher, or selling alcohol for up to three years. All told, 790 men received a pardon. The Supreme Judicial Court indicted sixty Regulators for treason, convicted five and sentenced them to death. But the government reversed course after the electorate delivered a strong rebuke in the spring election. Most incumbents, including Governor Bowdoin, lost reelection. The new legislature restored the civil rights of those pardoned and stayed the executions of the condemned men, eventually pardoning them as well. During the summer of 1788, the legislature even pardoned Shays, but he never returned to Massachusetts.[17]

Shays's Rebellion revealed the fractures of the postwar political settlement. Americans lacked consensus on whether their success in the War of Independence guaranteed the survival of colonial popular politics or replaced it with representative government. Regulators could point to not only the long history of community mobilization during the colonial era, but also the widespread popular organizing and resistance that powered the American Revolution. These events further solidified the legitimacy of crowd action, and it appeared nonsensical to abandon that system just as it had proven its ultimate value. But critics viewed the advent of popular sovereignty as a turning point—a crucial break with the past. Community mobilization had been a necessary and desperate correction to a system whose power lay outside of the people's hands. It was no longer needed. Moreover, by holding on to previous practices, regulators weakened the new system by undermining faith in government. As more regulations followed, these competing understandings continually pulled at the threads of America's experiment in self-government, threatening to unravel it entirely.

Although less centrally organized than their counterparts in Massachusetts, rural Pennsylvanians also launched regulations in response to heavy taxes, cash scarcity, and mounting debt during the 1780s. To prevent the collection of harsh taxes, many county tax officials defaulted, believing that the people could not afford to pay. "The payment of the present Taxes is an intolerable grievance & altogether beyond our power to comply with," explained Westmoreland County commissioners. Justices of the peace, locally elected per Pennsylvania's constitution, often allied with their communities by stalling tax-related suits. Occasionally, county sheriffs and constables also joined the resistance by refusing to deliver arrest warrants or hold foreclosure auctions.[18]

When they could not count on cooperative officials, civilians organized more defiant measures. To prevent the sale of foreclosed property, locals crowded auction sites but refused to bid. "It is in vain to expose the Goods of Inhabitants for Sale," explained a Northampton commissioner, "for there are none to be purchasers." Communities also used rough music to intimidate officials into either resigning or neglecting their duties. For instance, during the spring of 1786, farmers accosted a Washington County tax collector. The men broke his pistol, ripped up his papers and threw them in the mud, cut off his hair, and marched him through town, forcing him to drink a shot of whiskey at every tavern they passed. By 1785, resistant Pennsylvanians had cost state revenues $1.2 million in unpaid taxes.[19]

Between 1786 and 1787, scattered regulations also occurred in Maryland, New Hampshire, New Jersey, South Carolina, Vermont, and Virginia. Rural communities plagued by economic injustice banded together to close courts, stop foreclosure sales, and violently intimidate officials. In Greenbrier County, Virginia, for instance, farmers formed an anti-tax association, freed arrested debtors by force, and set fire to the local jail. In New Jersey, angry residents boarded up several county courthouses and impaled an effigy of the governor after he opposed paper money as legal tender. In Charles County, Maryland, regulators disrupted court proceedings against a slate of debtor defendants. In attendance that day, Alexander Hamilton later explained the disturbances in Charles County and elsewhere as the product of "some radical Deffect in our Constitution" that required repair. Otherwise, "by aiming at too much Liberty we shall lose it all together." The regulations had to be stopped.[20]

Many conservatives agreed with Hamilton about the need to restrain the popular impulse towards mobilization and resistance. Elites sought to replace the Articles of Confederation with a stronger national constitution that would check state power and limit popular influence on government. The resulting document, drafted at the Philadelphia Constitutional Convention in the summer of 1787, empowered the federal government to enforce tax collection by mobilizing state militias, prevented states from issuing their own paper money or forcing creditors to accept it in payment, and created large electoral districts to the House of Representatives. The delegates created a system designed to benefit creditors, prevent future regulations, and, above all, empower elites. Hamilton declared that the new Constitution enjoyed "the good will of most men of property in the several states who wish a government of the union able to protect them against domestic violence and the depredations which the democratic spirit is apt to make on property." The Constitutional Convention required that at least nine states ratify the Constitution in their own ratifying conventions.[21]

The proposed Constitution divided public opinion. The Federalists, those who supported ratification, declared that the Constitution would give the new republic the strength and stability needed for its survival. Anti-Federalists, those who opposed ratification, countered that the document concentrated power in the hands of an elite few. They feared that enormous congressional districts, a powerful executive elected by the electoral college, senators chosen by the state legislature, and presidentially appointed federal judges all placed government beyond the reach and influence of ordinary Americans. "Liberty! What is liberty? The power of governing yourselves. If you adopt this constitution, have you this power?" warned a South Carolina Anti-Federalist. "No: you give it into the hands of a set of men who live one thousand miles distant from you." But the wealth and influence of the Federalists won them the majority in most state conventions and the advantage in the public sphere. Indeed, the Federalists enjoyed the support of eighty of the existing ninety-two newspapers in the United States.[22]

Each time a new state ratified the Constitution, local Federalists took to the streets in celebration. To express their joy, they employed the traditional festive elements of bonfires, illuminations, toasts, and feasts. Some areas planned elaborate processions, the most famous of which occurred in Philadelphia. The Philadelphia Grand Federal Procession contained five thousand people and stretched for over a mile. The banners, structures, and displays sold the Constitution as the natural culmination of the American Revolution, and the huge number and variety of participants gave popular sanction to this narrative. As one witness astutely observed, "Its design was to express public approbation of the new constitution, by all classes of the community, from the day labourer to the highest functionary of the commonwealth." The Federalists' celebrations, and their subsequent narration in the press, created an illusion of unanimous approval of the Constitution and a sense of ratification's inevitability.[23]

The Anti-Federalists understood the symbolic power of Federalist demonstrations and fought back. For instance, on December 26, 1787, the Federalists of Carlisle, Pennsylvania, met in the town square to celebrate their state's ratification of the federal Constitution. But as the crowd awaited the cannon salute, a group of Anti-Federalists descended on the gathering. The two sides exchanged blows, and the Anti-Federalists managed to destroy the cannon before it could fire. The Federalists reconvened the next day and successfully hailed ratification with an artillery salute and a series of toasts. But the Anti-Federalists refused to be outdone. They paraded effigies of two Federalist state officials through the town, which they repeatedly whipped to the delight of the crowd. The Anti-Federalists completed their demonstration by hanging the effigies and then burning them. A similar conflict occurred in Huntingdon County, Pennsylvania, a few months later. Anti-Federalists posted petitions throughout the town voicing their concerns, which the local Federalists promptly tore down. In response, the Anti-Federalists paraded effigies of local Federalists through town on horseback. Officials arrested the demonstrators, but the crowd "assembled and liberated the sons of liberty ... who passed down the jail steps, under loud huzzahs and repeated acclamations of joy from a large concourse of people." By referring to themselves as the "sons of liberty," the Anti-Federalists emphasized that the proposed Constitution was not the culmination of the Revolution, but rather its undoing.[24]

Despite such dissenting displays, by July 1788 eleven states had ratified the Constitution, making it the law of the land. The Anti-Federalists' popular politics could not combat the Federalists' advantage where it mattered most: the state ratifying conventions. Ratification dealt a blow to those intent on safeguarding the traditional role for people in politics. Upon hearing the news, Anti-Federalists in South Carolina held a mock funeral for liberty, complete with a coffin that they led in a procession and then solemnly buried.[25]

After ratification, Pennsylvania officials cracked down on community regulation. In March 1788, the legislature passed a new law that stiffened penalties for reluctant tax collectors and constables, including harsh fines and imprisonment. In 1790, the state ratified a new constitution that granted the governor the power to appoint justices of the peace, ending the tradition of local elections and thereby making justices much less responsive to their communities. The new constitution also gave the governor more oversight over sheriff elections, allowing him to choose between the two candidates who received the most votes. State officials sought to break the alliances between local officials and their neighbors by increasing both the rewards for obedience and the penalties for noncompliance.[26]

In response, communities developed a more desperate protection strategy: they barricaded the roads leading into their towns to isolate themselves from the outside world. The road closures occurred in two major waves in 1788 and 1792, both following increased prosecution of tax collectors. Pennsylvanians piled up logs and stones, dug ditches, and built fences on roads to thwart access to county courthouses and stop outsiders from entering their communities. With newly intrusive state and federal governments, communities tried to prevent unjust policies from reaching their towns by walling themselves off from external threats.[27]

In the District of Maine, settlers used similar tactics to ensure local autonomy. These so-called "Liberty Men" aimed to claim and hold land by improving it, rather than buying exorbitant titles from wealthy speculators, the "Great Proprietors." Liberty Men defended their homesteads by violently preventing surveyors, sheriffs, and proprietor agents from entering their communities. "Every avenue to their settlement was strictly guarded to prevent the approach of any officer," reported a deputy sheriff of Winslow, "and [they] emphatically declared they would kill any officer who should serve any writs of ejectment or upon whom any such writs were found." Liberty Men shored up internal solidarity by destroying the properties of those suspected of siding with external elites. Like the Pennsylvania road closures, these efforts sealed off communities from official intervention, thereby thwarting proprietor attempts to establish control through eviction, lawsuit, or arrest.[28]

In each case, whether regulators wrested legislative concessions or suffered costly defeats, their actions revealed significant disagreement about how republican government should function. The ratification of the Federal Constitution failed to determine whether the Revolution guaranteed the survival of the colonial era's popular political forms or marked their necessary end point. At its heart, it was a question about what it meant to be a citizen in a republic. And that question was deeply embedded in the contrasting fears of tyranny and anarchy. For those anxious about government power, community mobilization offered an essential defense mechanism. But for those wary of disorder, crowd action portended the violent overthrow of law and order, and so the collapse of the United States. Both pinned the future hopes of republicanism to their vision of American politics.

For the Anglo-Americans who lived through the American Revolution, the transition from a monarchical to republican form of government must have been jarring. To transform from a subject into a citizen required the abrupt termination of a lifelong political relationship and its replacement with a new one. But the practice of politics in colonial America had always been about more than just who held power and how they attained it. As such, early Americans emerged from their Revolution without consensus on whether their republic would mark a continuation or a rupture with the political culture of the past.

While the regulations of the 1780s revealed these two conflicting concepts, the Whiskey Rebellion of the early 1790s initiated a national debate over these issues. For the first time, rural regulators raised liberty poles and declared themselves the true defenders of American liberty and independence—a development that pitted neighbors, officials, and politicians against each other in the fight to determine the power of citizens in the new nation.

❖ II ❖

# Contests

The mere act of raising a liberty pole is, in itself, a harmless thing; the question is, what is the meaning of it.
—Alexander Addison, 1794

❖ 3 ❖

# Debating Dissent in the Whiskey Rebellion

It was said by the whole of the people that liberty poles were raised last war and they ought to be raised now.
—Henry Lebo, 1794

In January 1795, Daniel Montgomery, justice of the peace for Northumberland County, Pennsylvania, viewed a courtroom from an unfamiliar vantage point—the defendant's chair. Montgomery appeared in court to answer accusations that he had failed in his duty as justice of the peace by letting opponents of the whiskey excise law raise a liberty pole on his watch. Liberty poles were "the avowed standards of rebellion," argued the prosecution—raising one constituted a riot. The community relied on justices of the peace to suppress such activities, but although called upon by Justices William Wilson and John MacPherson to intervene, Montgomery had done nothing. The defense countered by claiming that "the mere erection of a liberty pole was innocent in itself." No official had the right to impede an act of peaceful political expression.[1]

The court's decision rested on whether the erection of a liberty pole constituted a legitimate form of politics. While the judges conceded that raising a wooden pole in the town square was legal in principle, the symbolism of the liberty pole rendered it potentially seditious. "The mere act of raising a liberty pole is, in itself, a harmless thing," Alexander Addison, president judge of the Fifth Judicial District of Pennsylvania, wrote later. "[T]he question is, what is the meaning of it."[2]

During the 1790s, Americans debated the meaning of the liberty pole as they struggled to determine the people's role in their new system of government. The question of whether citizens could apply the resistance methods and symbols developed under a monarchical system to a republican one—whether such actions were patriotic or treasonous—divided the nation. Beginning in small communities like Northumberland and reverberating outward, liberty poles triggered a national conversation over the power of the citizen in the American republic.

The Northumberland pole was one of thirty-nine liberty poles raised by those protesting the whiskey excise of 1791, which taxed whiskey production. Opposition to the excise, including refusals to pay the tax and attacks on collectors, began in 1791 in the western counties of Pennsylvania—Allegheny, Fayette, Washington, Westmoreland, and Bedford—among those who believed it disproportionately burdened western farmers. By 1794, resistance had spread to parts of central Pennsylvania, Kentucky, Maryland, and western Virginia. This movement constituted the first major regulation under the new Constitution. The Washington administration knew, as Fisher Ames put it, "governments are oftenest lost by flinching from trial." After much cajoling from Alexander Hamilton, Washington sent an army of fifteen thousand into western Pennsylvania and Maryland in the fall of 1794 to restore law and order.[3]

The Whiskey Rebellion, as it came to be known, revealed the failure of the Revolutionary settlement to specify how and when citizens could engage in politics. In response to the crisis, some argued that self-government required citizens to peaceably acquiesce to the decisions of elected officials. The extra-institutional politics of the earlier era were not just inappropriate, they were dangerous. Popular criticism and resistance weakened public confidence in government and so undermined federal authority, jeopardizing the republic's survival.[4]

But the tax resisters argued that representative government's flaws echoed the injustices of the colonial era and so required the same methods of community redress. They employed traditional tactics ranging from noncompliance to violence to locally nullify the law, sheltering their communities from its effects until they secured legislative changes. They raised liberty poles to signal the links between their opposition to the excise and the Patriots' struggle against taxation without representation—both relied on crowd action to resist unjust legislation. This association legitimized their efforts.

It also painted the Washington administration as monarchists who levied burdensome taxes and ignored calls for relief. Meanwhile, their critics condemned the poles for encouraging opposition to federal law and intimidating those in support of government.[5]

This debate occurred at all levels of American society, including within communities at the core of the resistance movement. Most scholars explain the Whiskey Rebellion as either an economic protest by poor farmers against wealthy elites or a regional struggle by western frontiersmen opposing eastern officials. In both cases, historians depict western Pennsylvanians as united in opposition. But conflicts over liberty poles reveal significant disagreement within communities over the legitimacy of popular resistance in a republican system.[6]

The Whiskey Rebellion brought widespread attention to the questions about popular political participation in a representative government first raised during the 1770s and 1780s. As Americans fought over these issues, they advanced differing interpretations of the citizen's role in republican politics. The Whiskey Rebellion was about much more than taxes or regional alienation. To all involved, it offered a critical test of what it meant to be a citizen of the United States.

Northumberland County constable William Bonham led the raising of the local liberty pole in September 1794. Bonham's grievances echoed those held throughout central and western Pennsylvania: the excise disproportionately burdened poor farmers. These men traveled difficult miles over bad roads to carry their produce to eastern markets. To ease their journey and maximize profits, they reduced their bulky grains to higher value and more potable whiskey. A targeted tax on whiskey, argued Bonham, was "oppressive on the poor people" whose location and livelihood required distilling. Moreover, rather than taxing the sale of whiskey, the excise applied to production, meaning that a distiller had to absorb the cost up front with no guarantee of a return. If he produced more whiskey than he could sell, he could not recoup the already paid tax. The law also stipulated that violators had to appear before a federal court in Philadelphia, some three hundred miles away.[7]

Bonham and his neighbors instead favored a land tax as a more just revenue raiser. Unlike the excise, a land tax could address the urgent issue of land scarcity in the west by encouraging speculators to sell some of their large holdings. The past ten years had brought increasing class stratification to Pennsylvania. By 1794, 60 percent of the taxable population in the west owned no land. To Bonham, the whiskey excise proved that "the officers of Government and the Land Jobbers were engrossing all the property of the country." They meant to enrich themselves by impoverishing ordinary people. Instead, "The Land Jobbers should pay the taxes."[8]

Clearly, Bonham argued, the federal government was abusing its power. "Government ha[s] carried themselves to[o] high and must be taken down," he proclaimed. Like-minded Pennsylvanians turned to regulation, a strategy that some had previously employed during the 1780 road closures. In fact, Pennsylvanians had already used such tactics, particularly the intimidation of tax collectors, to avoid paying a state excise tax on whiskey passed in 1784. In 1791, they secured a repeal of the law when the state legislature conceded it was unenforceable. Encouraged by this victory, disillusioned Pennsylvanians used the same methods in their efforts to defeat the federal excise. To them, this struggle was but the latest in a series of popular actions against burdensome taxation policies.[9]

Beginning in 1791, communities throughout western and central Pennsylvania mobilized to stymie enforcement of the federal excise and pressure the government for repeal. Regulators organized meetings where they pledged their noncompliance with the law and issued petitions and remonstrances to Congress. They also used violence and vandalism to harass and intimidate excise collectors and their local supporters. Some crowds drew direct connections with the American Revolution by tarring and feathering those attempting to execute or comply with the law. "They did not consider it *immoral*, or treasonable, to resist in every way a particular law by 'intemperate resolutions,' and even by direct acts of violence," the son of a regulator later explained. "They had examples before them of their British ancestors, in Hamden, Cromwell and Pym, and more recently in the Patriots of the Revolution." The Pennsylvania regulators acted as heirs to a tradition of community action that obstructed the enforcement of unjust laws.[10]

But others viewed popular resistance as incompatible with a republic. When a delegation of regulators meeting in Pittsburgh vowed to pursue "every other legal measure that may obstruct the operation of the Law until we are able to obtain its total repeal," Hamilton scoffed at what he called a "contradiction in terms": "The idea of pursuing *legal* measures to *obstruct* the *operation* of a *Law* needs little comment. . . . The *operation* (or what is the same thing, the *execution*) of a *law* cannot be *obstructed* after it has been constitutionally enacted without illegality and crime." In other words, the principle of representative government rendered regulation an illegitimate, and so illegal, form of politics.[11]

Likewise, other officials drew distinctions between old and new political systems. With the formation of the republic, the United States had replaced extra-institutional action with electoral politics. In 1792, Chief Justice Thomas McKean denounced the regulators' application of resistance methods developed under a monarchy to the politics of a republic: "They quarrel with a constitution and government purchased at the expense of much blood and treasure, and framed by themselves; they despise the rulers of their own choice, and trample on laws of their own making." Furthermore, a system that countenanced resistance could not properly function. Any disgruntled citizen could simply disobey a law with which they disagreed. "If you permit [the law] to be resisted or overthrown, with impunity, on any pretext, you in effect set an example to violate them on every pretext," Governor Thomas Mifflin explained. The fledgling nation could not survive regular challenges to the government's authority—citizens needed to support their representatives' decisions and accept that even measures they personally disliked served the common good.[12]

Citizens unhappy with legislation could elect new representatives and, in the meantime, petition their representatives for amendment or repeal. They could not, however, simply choose which laws to obey and which to disregard. "As Freemen, let us always remonstrate against actual wrongs," cautioned Mifflin, "but, as Citizens let us always obey existing Laws." Addison also encouraged obedience in all cases, warning that violent opposition would never bring political change because it would set too dangerous a precedent: "if one law is repealed, at the call of armed men, government is destroyed; no law will have any force; every law will be disobeyed, in some part of the union." Compliance, not regulation, provided the best way forward: "We have reason to believe, that our remonstrance would be listened to more effectually, if, by obedience we put ourselves in a capacity of being heard." Dissenters had to express their grievances through institutional channels and, in the meantime, pay their taxes.[13]

In Northumberland, Bonham and his neighbors had the same debate. "We made the laws ourselves, through our Representatives," explained one man in rebuttal to Bonham's complaints, and so the whiskey excise was "our own." "If the law [is] a bad one let us petition against it," he reasoned, but he could not support outright resistance. Another insisted that "people were exceedingly wrong in taking up arms in opposition to any law when they had a constitutional mode of redress." Bonham countered that "there had been remonstrances from the westward but they had been treated disrespectfully." Clearly, the new system was not protecting ordinary people's interests, no matter how many petitions Pennsylvanians sent. They may have elected their own representatives, but it did little good if Congress still proved insensitive to their needs. To Bonham, the failures of representative government were readily apparent and required the same strategies of popular mobilization that had been successful in the past.[14]

The stakes of these disagreements increased as resistance to the excise escalated in the summer of 1794. Crowds set fire to the home of the federal excise inspector for southwestern Pennsylvania, and an exchange of gunfire during the fracas left a popular Revolutionary War veteran dead. Eleven days later, regulators robbed the mail sent from Pittsburgh to Philadelphia, hoping to reveal local traitors who secretly advocated for federal intervention to supress the resistance. Finding incriminating letters, a crowd seven thousand strong gathered to march on Pittsburgh. Before embarking, they raised a liberty pole, the first reported pole of the Whiskey Rebellion. At the top flew a flag bearing six stripes, one for each of the six counties in the regulation: Washington, Westmoreland, Fayette, and Allegheny Counties in Pennsylvania and Ohio and Monongalia in Virginia. The liberty pole signaled the group's legitimacy by linking their actions to those of the Revolution. The crowd then marched on Pittsburgh, but did so peacefully after residents promised that they had banished the letters' authors.[15]

News of the mass action convinced Washington and his cabinet that they needed to act decisively to supress a rebellion against federal authority. On August 7, the president issued a proclamation ordering the "rebels" to disperse by the first of September or he would send in federalized militia. He also appointed three federal commissioners to meet with a committee of regulators and offer amnesty and absolution for previous unpaid taxes in exchange for pledges of loyalty and future obedience to the law. When the commissioners arrived, they found liberty poles outside of their accommodations and meeting grounds. The regulators had sent a clear message: their cause was one of liberty against tyranny, and they had the numerical strength and determination to defend it.[16]

But the commissioners pressed on with their negotiations, hoping for a submission to federal law and order. On August 22, they submitted a proposal to the committee of regulators offering a general pardon in exchange for a declaration of submission. A vote by secret ballot revealed a majority of thirty-four to twenty-three in favor of the terms, but the commissioners rejected the result. Dissatisfied with the slim majority and secrecy, they called for a public declaration of submission. On September 11, every citizen would sign a loyalty oath at their polling place or risk war with the United States.[17]

In preparation, Washington ordered federalized units of state militias to assemble at Carlisle, Pennsylvania, and Cumberland, Maryland. He would decide whether to send them further west once he had received the results of the September 11 vote. Militia captains, however, struggled to fill their quotas. Many men in central Pennsylvania and western Maryland and Virginia refused to serve, citing their discomfort in marching "against their countrymen, who were oppressed and could no other way obtain redress but by resort to arms." The men of Hagerstown, Maryland, "beat their officers from the field" after an attempted draft and erected a liberty pole bearing the motto "Liberty or Death," a reference to Patrick Henry and the Revolution.[18]

The Washington administration faced similar disappointment with the September 11 vote. While some western townships submitted, violence and intimidation reigned in others. For instance, in Franklin Township, Pennsylvania, a band of regulators stormed the polling place and demanded the list of signatories, but an official destroyed it to protect the men who had signed the oath. In neighboring Strabane Township, regulators raised a liberty pole outside of the polling place as a warning to those who considered voting for submission. Those in Carlisle likewise raised a pole on the day of the submission vote. Addison bemoaned these displays as irrational and anarchic. "What is the liberty, which those pole-raisers wanted?" he fumed. "A liberty to be governed by no law . . . a liberty to do what mischief they pleased."[19]

Over the next few weeks, regulators erected dozens of liberty poles. Citing these as examples, Bonham proposed to his neighbors that they raise their own "in support of their brethren." Some hesitated, again wondering if "a petition to Congress was the best way if they wanted to get a repeal." But Bonham insisted that a strong display of resistance would do the most good. "These poles [will] be of service," he told his neighbors, "[a]nd the disturbances to the westward [will] bring about a repeal." Popular mobilization would show the government that "the people [are] uneasy under" the excise tax. Those in power would be unable to ignore their actions, as they had their petitions.[20]

On September 20, Bonham and several supporters went to a nearby mill and made a pole by cutting down a tree and stripping its branches. They brought it to the town square, where they met a large crowd. The group surged forward as hands and shoulders eagerly braced the pole and raised it to stand tall. They cheered their success with huzzahs and large servings of whiskey. Amid the merriment, someone added a flag to the pole bearing the initials "L.E.," for liberty and equality. All in attendance understood the reference. The local innkeeper reported: "It was said by the whole of the people that liberty poles were raised last war and they ought to be raised now."[21]

The pole-raisers staked their claims to legitimacy not only in their Revolutionary heritage, but also in the placement of their pole. The town square was the center of the community. By marking the space, the crowd implied that the liberty pole represented the town's sentiments and had unanimous support. It signaled to the area's residents and all who passed through that the people of Northumberland believed in popular resistance to the whiskey excise tax. This forced those who disagreed into a difficult position: allow the pole to stand and risk undermining republican government and inviting federal retribution, or destroy the pole and risk a fight with their neighbors. Some opted for the latter. Led by William Perry Brady, a cabinet-maker, a handful of men cut down the pole, deeming it an inappropriate method of voicing dissent.[22]

Brady's actions did not surprise Bonham, as a few weeks prior he had confronted Brady about the liberty pole. Brady declared that he would cut down the pole and "not think it a crime if the pole was put there in opposition to Government." Bonham taunted Brady to do so "if you dare," for Bonham would whip him if he tried. Brady countered that he would drag Bonham and his fellow rebels to Philadelphia by his horse's tail to face federal justice. Bonham departed with a final promise: if Brady cut down the pole, they would raise "a better one with Liberty, Equality, Change of Ministers, and No Excise" written on the flag. He proved true to his word.[23]

Shortly after Brady's attack, Bonham and fifty others met at a local tavern and unanimously vowed to erect a replacement. The meeting put to a vote every detail of the pole-raising—who would cut the pole, who would dig the hole for it, and who would assemble the crowd. They even voted on whether Brady and his gang should be tarred and feathered (this motion failed). The meeting's votes gave the illusion of unanimous popular backing for the pole, but that was only part of the process.[24]

Bonham also engaged in a campaign of intimidation, traveling house to house and threatening retribution against anyone who refused to assist with the pole-raising. Doctor Benjamin F. Young reported that when he objected to the second pole, Bonham warned that he was "liable to be punished" for such cowardice "by way of ducking." Others threatened Young with a tarring and feathering. Bonham cautioned another man not to voice opposition or he would burn down his house. Some critics left town on the day of the pole-raising to avoid being called upon to assist. Bonham had plenty of supporters, and he could have easily raised the second pole without these men. His efforts indicate the importance of shoring up community support and creating, at least in appearance, a united movement. Bonham worried that infighting would weaken the cause by making the crowd's actions seem less threatening to officials. Their power lay in their numbers and conviction.[25]

As Bonham and his men prepared the new pole, Judges William Wilson and John MacPherson caught wind of the plan and rode to town to avert the raising. They called upon Daniel Montgomery as the local justice of the peace, but he refused to help, warning, "We might as well pretend to turn the Susquehanna [River], as to stop them, for they [are] determined to have their grievances redressed, and our going there would answer no good end." Montgomery agreed to accompany Wilson and MacPherson, but he offered no assistance when the posse arrived at the town square and found a crowd of sixty gathered around their newly raised liberty pole. Wilson asked the group their intentions, to which Bonham replied that their pole stood for "Liberty, Equality, and support of Government." The entire assembly huzzaed in agreement. Unconvinced, Wilson declared that they pursued these goals in a "very improper manner." He then read the riot act and ordered them to disperse.[26]

The crowd left the pole, but many went to the local tavern, where more trouble ensued. There, the pole-raisers met Young and some others who had rebuffed Bonham's requests for help with the pole. Bonham and an opponent came to blows as Bonham shouted, "Come on and support the pole!" Men from both sides ran towards the commotion, some with arms drawn. Wilson rushed into the center of the fray, where he brandished his pistol and ordered everyone to stop where they were. Most froze, but one man aimed his musket at Wilson, who managed to wrestle it away. Wilson again read the riot act, and the crowd, perhaps chastened by the fracas, retired to their homes.[27]

To deter Brady and his ilk, the pole-raisers organized an armed guard to stand watch around the pole at night. Bonham and others instructed the guard to violently resist anyone who attempted to cut down the pole. One man vowed to "blow [any assailant] through" with his gun. In guarding the pole, the group defended their claim to speak for the community. They also connected their pole's symbolic power with their ability to protect it—a pole toppled shortly after being raised did not signal a strong resistance movement. Their opponents, for the moment, seemed deterred. Some feared the guard would make good on their promise of violence. Others worried Bonham would use his authority as constable to persecute them. One man lamented to a friend that he had wanted to tear down the liberty pole, "But when the officers of Government take a decided part with the rioters, what can possibly be expected."[28]

Tensions continued to mount as pole-raisers ostracized those in town who opposed their actions. Joseph Priestley, an English scientist and theologian residing in Northumberland, complained to John Adams that his baker refused to sell him bread because he thought Priestley disliked the pole. "Such was the spirit of this place," he wrote, "or rather of the lower class of people." But Priestley's characterization was not quite correct. The leaders of both the pole-raisers and their opponents had comparable levels of above-average wealth. Bonham and Brady, for example, both owned about $300 worth of property, whereas the average Northumberland property holder was worth $171. Bonham's neighbors certainly would not have viewed him as "lower class." In addition to his post as constable, he owned two houses, a servant, and a carriage. However, owning little or no property did make a man more likely to support the liberty pole. Several poorer men appear in the historical record as pole-raisers, while none appear among the pole's opponents. Still, while some scholars argue that communities like Northumberland broke along economic lines, class constituted only one determinant of who would or would not become a regulator. For example, Joseph Haines, the man who supplied the wood for the second pole, was worth $400. Despite their relative wealth, such men despised the excise and the government that clung to it. They believed in their right to resist government overreach and rallied with their poorer neighbors to demonstrate their resolve.[29]

On October 2, county lieutenant Bernard Hubley, Jr. ordered the Northumberland militia to cut down the pole, but his men refused to comply. In a letter to the president, Hubley explained, "[The captain] really believed any Person that would Attempt to take it down, that they would loose their Lives thereby." But while local militiamen feared reprisals from their neighbors, outsiders from Wyoming in Luzerne County had no concern for the men of Northumberland. One week later, a troop of Luzerne volunteers cut down the Northumberland pole, expressing thereby their "abhor[rence] ... that in a [r]epublican government, the few should give laws to the many." Wilson and Hubley then wrote to the governor, requesting that the volunteers remain in Northumberland for a few extra days to quell the "disorderly and riotous spirit" that had awakened in the county due to the "baneful & poisonous heads" of the recent liberty poles raised by the "Northumberland anarchists."[30]

But even after the pole had fallen, its impact continued to haunt the town. Divisions over the pole disrupted the election for county sheriff that October. Robert Irwin, a Republican, received the majority of votes, but Federalist John Brady, brother of William Perry Brady, contested the results. Brady accused Irwin of spreading the rumor that he had opposed the liberty pole. Many in town had publicly refused to vote for Brady because of his brother's previous actions. Jonathan Walker, one of Bonham's critics, alleged that Daniel Montgomery confided that he and the other "pole people" were determined to "run Robert Irwin in their own defense ... [as] a number of them might be indicted for the pole business" and they "had nothing to expect from John Brady" by way of favors if he became sheriff.[31]

Several friends of Brady's, including Wilson, wrote to Governor Mifflin complaining that the slander against Brady had cost him the election. They reported that the men of their county "furnished daily proofs of a disposition inimical to the cause of Government, by erecting what they call liberty poles." Friends of Irwin rode through the area, warning voters that "if [Brady] was elected, he would summon juries friendly to the Government, and that they would all be hung." The note concluded by asking Mifflin to appoint Brady as sheriff, although he had received fewer votes, for Pennsylvania law allowed the governor to choose a county sheriff from the two leading candidates in an election—a measure adopted in the wake of the road closures and aimed at suppressing regulations. Mifflin decided to commission Brady, explaining that he had been convinced by "a complaint that irregularities had been committed at the said election by the friends of

Mr. Irwin." Mifflin's actions confirmed regulators' suspicions that representative government offered an insufficient check on power. Even when they tried to use their votes to influence change, as their critics demanded, officials conspired to circumvent their choices. Clearly, the new system had not obviated the need for popular, extra-institutional action.[32]

Further trouble ensued on November 15, when Bonham arrested Wilson for assault on a warrant issued by Montgomery. The justice of the peace had received complaints from two men who had been at the tavern on the night of the second pole-raising. The first man claimed that Wilson had pointed his pistol at him, and the second asserted that Wilson had seized him. Wilson, fuming, appeared in court before Montgomery. He insisted that he had drawn his weapon only to execute his duty to suppress the riot. Believing his actions justified, Wilson refused to pay bail, informing Montgomery that he would rather go to jail. In the end, Montgomery discharged him. But Wilson remained outraged by the whole affair, feeling persecuted by the Northumberland officials. "I consider Daniel Montgomery Esq. to be the principal in this business," he vented, "and William Bonham the executor of all his secret orders." He began plotting his vengeance.[33]

Meanwhile, Washington viewed the flurry of pole-raisings and the failure of the loyalty oaths with alarm. He ordered federal forces to march west on September 25. Pennsylvania congressman William Findley asked Washington to delay the advance of troops, explaining that "it required time for the well disposed people to know in whom they could confide" and to create an alliance strong enough to compel their neighbors to submit. But Washington denied his request, citing the spate of new liberty poles as evidence that "the flame ha[d] caught in Maryland, and symptoms of it [had] been discovered in some other places in Pennsylvania." He could not "delay the expedition till the spring, lest the flame should spread further." As the pole-raisers intended, and their opponents feared, a liberty pole marked an entire town as part of the resistance.[34]

As fifteen thousand troops from Virginia, Maryland, New Jersey, and Pennsylvania marched west, no rebel army materialized to oppose them. Instead, federal forces faced liberty poles that had sprung up anonymously overnight just before they rode through western towns—a final display of dissent and a message to invading troops that though overpowered, these communities still believed in their cause. The army arrested hundreds of regulators, including Bonham. Unable to muster sufficient evidence to enter a charge of treason, the U.S. Circuit Court settled for a misdemeanor. William Perry Brady served as a witness for the state. The prosecution described Bonham as "an evil-disposed, pernicious, and seditious person." By raising a liberty pole, he had attempted "to encourage and incite the citizens . . . to oppose and resist the laws and authority of the said United States and [wage] insurrection and war against the same United States." The jury viewed liberty poles not as legitimate, extra-institutional forms of political expression, but as inflammatory symbols that encouraged rebellion and threatened law and order—a powerful legal statement against the alleged continuities between colonial and republican forms of expression. They found Bonham guilty, but Washington pardoned him, as he did all other transgressors.[35]

Back in Northumberland, Wilson brought charges for a misdemeanor against Montgomery for failing in his duty as justice of the peace to suppress a riot. In January 1795, the Supreme Court of Pennsylvania heard arguments from both sides to determine whether the case should go to trial. The defense argued that since "the mere erection of a liberty pole was innocent in itself," Montgomery could not have predicted that events would degenerate into chaos that night. Rather, Montgomery had done his best to maintain the peace in his refusal to interfere, since he "perceive[d] the inutility as well as the danger of opposing" the pole-raisers. He had judged it better to let them raise their harmless pole than to create a disturbance by attempting to obstruct them, as Wilson had done. As for the warrants against Wilson, the defense stressed that Montgomery had simply performed his duty. Since he did not witness the altercation that night, Montgomery merely followed due process after two citizens swore complaints against Wilson. Finally, the defense cautioned the court not to accept Wilson's characterizations of the liberty pole as seditious. After all, "It [is] essential to the freedom of a republic, that people should speak their minds on laws and all public transactions." Liberty poles, the defense argued, constituted a legitimate mode of political expression.[36]

The prosecution refuted these claims, maintaining that no onlooker, let alone a justice of the peace, could fail to appreciate the seditious nature of the liberty pole. He reminded the court of the context of insurrection, well known to Montgomery, promoted by rebels who raised liberty poles to enrage their neighbors against the government. In such a climate, Montgomery could not have been "so unconscious of his duty" as to misunderstand the raising of a liberty pole as a peaceful exercise, for poles were "the avowed standards of rebellion." Montgomery's failure to interfere reflected a dereliction of duty and perhaps even sympathy with the pole-raisers. Montgomery's issuing of warrants against Wilson further cast suspicion on his allegiances. Such action "more probably arose from a desire to screen the rioters or himself, and deter prosecutions, than a sense of duty and the advancement of public justice."[37]

The case pivoted, as Wilson's had, on whether raising a liberty pole constituted a breach of the peace. The judges unanimously agreed with the prosecution: "The setting up of a pole at any time, in a tumultuous manner, with arms, is a riot," they ruled. The judges insisted that Montgomery should have arrested those unlawfully assembled. But the ruling went further, arguing that raising and defending liberty poles "could only be attributed to an avowed design of giving aid to the insurgents, and intimidating the executives of government." As such, Montgomery's failure to act implicated him in treason against the federal government. The Whiskey Rebellion "would have been quelled [in] the beginning," they declared, had justices of the peace acted more vigorously in the execution of their duties. The judges ruled that a trial should take place, and Montgomery paid a $500 recognizance. However, no record of a subsequent trial exists.[38]

The Northumberland liberty poles became flashpoints for conflict in the community over the practice of politics in a republic. The poles forced all in town to choose which vision of government by the people they wanted for their new nation: one that countenanced an active role for citizens that hearkened back to the colonial era, or a new, more limited role that focused on institutional channels of political expression. As tensions reached a boiling point, residents displayed their willingness to enforce their views through violence. This debate extended into the courtroom, as both Wilson and Montgomery defended their actions based on their clashing positions on the pole's legitimacy. And while the state court ultimately sided with Wilson, Brady's election controversy demonstrates that tensions persisted and seeped into local politics. For the people of Northumberland, as with their many counterparts elsewhere, the excise tax laid bare the fractures that had been lurking under their community's surface since the end of the war. Although everyone in town opposed the excise, they divided over how to express their dissent. The Whiskey Rebellion was about something more profound than a mere tax law: it sparked significant conflict between ordinary people over what it meant to be a citizen in a republic.

During the Whiskey Rebellion, all involved saw the promises of their Revolution endangered. Many viewed regulator activity as an attempted usurpation of representative government by an armed minority. The effort to extort concessions from the government by force jeopardized the premise of majority rule and threatened the complete unravelling of law and order. "How nearly do the opposite extremes of toryism and anarchy approach each other?" observed the *Baltimore Daily Intelligencer.* "Are they not twin brothers?" But to the regulators, the excise displayed an ignorance of local conditions that made it smack of taxation without representation. Recourse to traditional resistance methods was both legitimate and necessary.[39]

This disagreement boiled down to a fundamental difference in opinion over the promise of representative government. To some, it meant citizens voted in elections and in between deferred to their representatives the business of legislating. If unhappy with the actions of their representatives, they could await recourse on the next election day. Until then, they could voice their opposition through petitions and remonstrances. But citizens could not disobey a particular policy without opposing the entire system of republican government.[40]

However, the regulators lacked confidence in the institution of representative government. Congress's passage of the whiskey excise and disregard for subsequent petitions revealed its indifference to rural conditions. Faced with an unresponsive government and an unjust law, they used traditional methods of popular regulation to protect their communities and pressure authorities for repeal.[41]

But they did not succeed. Resistance crumbled as soon as the federal government exerted real pressure, and the excise tax remained on the books until 1802. In the rebellion's aftermath, Addison confidently asserted, "the danger of sedition has been set before the people of this country, which, I trust, they will never forget, and, I believe, will never need to be repeated." But he spoke too soon. Liberty poles sprang up anew in 1798 as partisan division rekindled debates over the limits of political expression.[42]

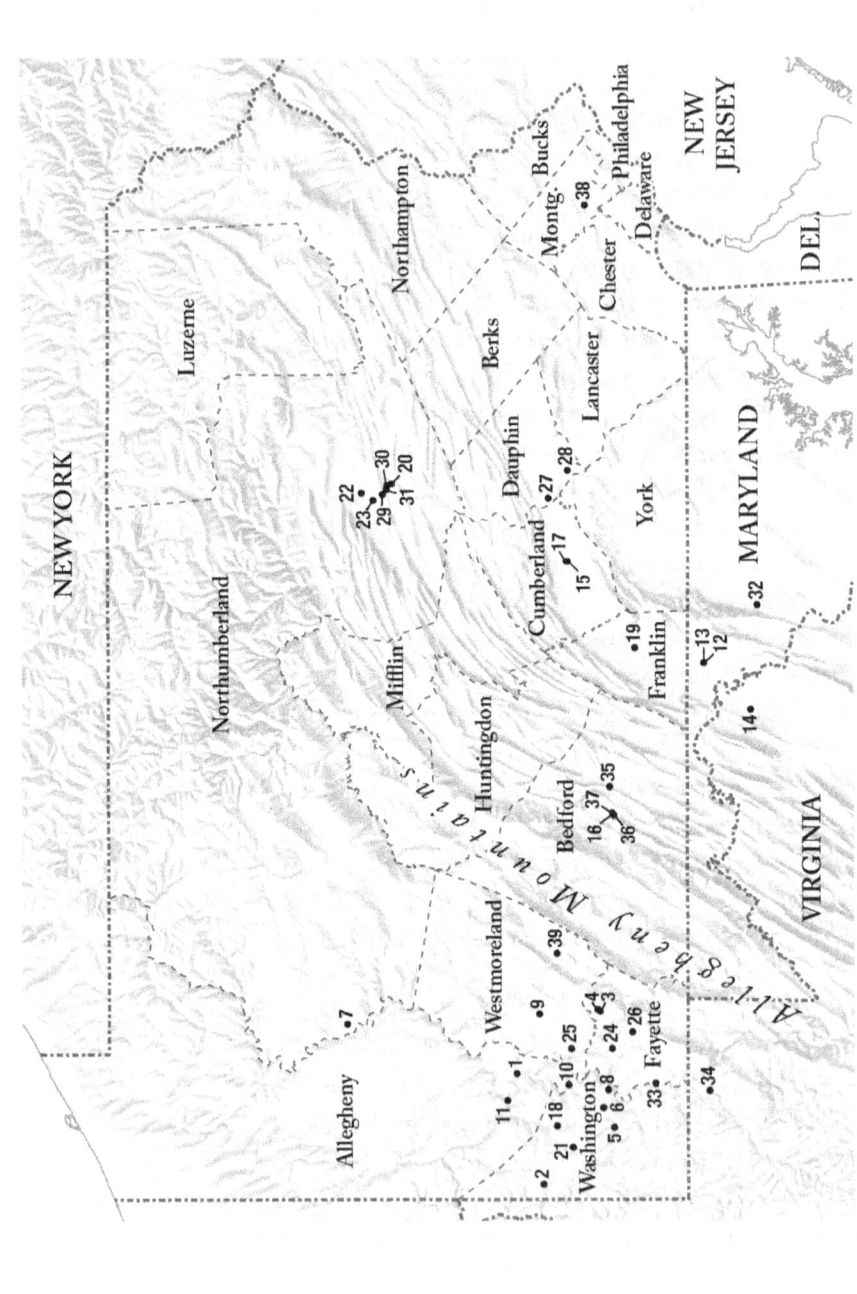

Liberty poles raised during the Whiskey Rebellion, 1794. (Nat Case)

1. August 1: Braddock's Field, Brownsville, Allegheny County
2. August 8: Washington County
3. August 10: Bullskin Township, Fayette County
4. August 11: Bullskin Township, Fayette County
5. August 13: Washington County
6. August 14: Washington County
7. August 14: Catfish, Madison Township, Lackawanna County
8. August 15: Washington County
9. August 15: Greensburg, Westmoreland County
10. August 15: Parkinson's Ferry, Washington County
11. August 18: Pittsburgh, Allegheny County
12. September 1: Hagerstown, Washington County (Maryland)
13. September 5*: Hagerstown, Washington County (Maryland)
14. September 8*: Martinsburg, Berkeley County (Virginia)
15. September 8: Carlisle, Cumberland County
16. September 10*: Bedford County
17. September 11: Carlisle, Cumberland County
18. September 11: Strabane Township, Washington County
19. September 16: Chambersburg, Franklin County
20. September 20: Northumberland County
21. September 25: Washington, Washington County
22. September 26: Milton, Northumberland County
23. September 30: Derrstown, Northumberland County
24. November 5*: Franklin Township, Chester County
25. No date: South Huntingdon Township, Westmoreland County
26. No date: Fayette County
27. No date: Harrisburg, Dauphin County
28. No date: Middletown, Dauphin County
29. No date: near Derrstown, Northumberland County
30. No date: near Wilson's Tavern, Northumberland County
31. No date: near Wilson's Tavern, Northumberland County
32. No date: Fredericktown, Cecil County (Maryland)
33. No date: Masontown, Fayette County
34. No date: Morgan's Town, Monangalia County (Virginia)
35. No date: Bloody Run, Bedford County
36. No date: Bedford County
37. No date: Bedford County
38. No date: Stony Creek, Montgomery County
39. No date: Fort Ligonier, Westmoreland County

Locations are approximations; * indicates an approximate date

❖ 4 ❖

# The Federalist Popular Politics of Assent

Nothing [is] more easy than to assert that liberty ha[s] always been destroyed by an excess of power in the Executives of Governments; but [I believe] it ha[s] more frequently been destroyed by democratic mobs, by the erection of whiskey poles and liberty poles.
—George Thatcher, Fifth Congress, Second Session

In the years following the Whiskey Rebellion, Americans continued to struggle with the issue of popular political participation. But the battle took on a new shape as partisanship fractured American politics. Although neither side constituted an institutionalized party by modern standards—lacking national infrastructures, nominating conventions, and official memberships—both groups had a recognized ideological coherence and identity. The Federalist Party supported the Washington and Adams administrations and believed that the republic required a strong government to avert a descent into chaos. Federalists viewed anarchy as the greatest threat to liberty and defended institutions as the best bulwark against it. By winning the War of Independence, Americans had secured representative government as the institutional apparatus to maintain order. Citizens threatened the republic if they opposed laws passed by the will of the majority or undermined respect for elected representatives. "The very idea of the power and the right of all the people to establish government presupposes the duty of every individual to obey the established government," Washington proclaimed in his Farewell Address.[1]

Their rivals, the Republican Party, emerged out of the growing opposition movement, which by 1795 had loosely coalesced under the leadership of elite politicians like Thomas Jefferson and James Madison. Republicans viewed tyranny, not anarchy, as American liberty's major threat and so were suspicious of concentrated political power. They believed that the Revolution had secured for citizens the ability to resist and regulate government to protect the people from officials who abused their power.

The Federalists' dread of anarchy and the Republicans' fear of tyranny led each side to develop contrasting forms of popular politics. Grassroots Republicans insisted on an active political role for citizens. They drew upon traditional popular political rites to criticize the Federalists and condemn their legislation as an assault on American liberty. Local Federalists responded by mobilizing in support of government. They initially practiced a popular politics of assent that endorsed government policies with mass meetings, resolutions, and celebrations. But after the Republicans revived the liberty pole in 1798, Federalists expanded their popular politics to include destructive rituals as a targeted assault on dissidents.[2]

While usually painted as conservative, the Federalists, in fact, advanced and enforced a radical new vision for American politics. They advocated a break with past precedent and the embrace of a novel system that abandoned traditional resistance methods. "To [promote] a jealousy of government," opined a New York Federalist, "is adopting a principle, which may be proper where the government is independent of the People, but which in our country can only be viewed as contemptible." Republican government had initiated a new era, rendering the political culture of the past obsolete. In the Federalist mind, it was the Republicans who embraced conservatism as they stubbornly held on to old approaches. But Republicans viewed popular action as the bedrock of American liberty and a critical safeguard against tyranny.[3]

Grassroots partisans enacted these differing interpretations in clashes throughout the mid-1790s. But the conflict entered a fresh phase in 1798 when the Federalists in Congress passed new taxes and the Alien and Sedition Laws, which tightened executive control over immigration and criminalized criticism of the government. Republicans raised seventy-one liberty poles as they mobilized to resist what was, in their view, an unconstitutional accumulation of federal power and an assault on political expression. Unlike in 1794, the federal government faced not a localized regulation, but an expanding opposition movement spread across numerous states and loosely organized under the Republican party banner. The question of popular dissent in a republic morphed into a raging partisan battle.

The nation's deteriorating relations with France gave Federalist concerns over Republican opposition particular urgency. Federalists worried that political division would make the United States appear fragile and so invite a French attack. Some even believed that the Republicans were secretly in league with France and aimed to purposefully weaken the United States from within. Republican pole-raisers' Francophilia, displayed in their messages of liberty and equality and use of the liberty cap, stoked these fears. Federalists hoped that their new legislation would purge American politics of the French menace and fatally weaken Republican popular organizing, thus creating the type of harmonious, acquiescent political culture they believed the survival of the republic required.

When the Republican liberty poles challenged this goal, local Federalists organized to tear them down. In their assaults on liberty poles and those who raised them, grassroots Federalists vigilantly defended representative government by attacking its critics. Like their milder demonstrations, these actions represented a contrasting vision for popular politics in which citizens mobilized to give sanction to government. This time, though, they went beyond rival meetings and resolutions and instead clashed intimately with their opponents as they battled for control over the public sphere. The resulting conflicts created a divisive spiral in which the politics of assent and dissent intensified each other and deepened partisan rifts. As they raised and destroyed liberty poles, grassroots Federalists and Republicans fought in person and in the press to claim popular backing, legitimize their actions, and weaken the other side.

By introducing the Federalists' popular politics of assent and charting its evolution, this chapter reveals a heretofore unstudied violent and confrontational element of Federalist organizing. In doing so, it explores the dialectical development of the First Party System on the ground. Grassroots Federalists used direct action and the press to diminish the appearance of Republican strength, neutralize the growing opposition movement, and solidify the installation of a new political system. By resisting these tactics, grassroots Republicans challenged Federalist control of politics, public space, ritual, and narrative, creating a dynamic and combative popular political culture that defies typical descriptions of the First Party System as elitist and deferential. Instead, it reveals this period as a moment of intense contestation in which Americans struggled to make meaning of their transition from subjects to citizens, with the Federalists advancing a new vision and Republicans clinging to the old.

Two shared assumptions shaped the First Party System's partisan conflict: the importance of foreign affairs and the dangers of political parties. Those in the early republic interpreted their domestic politics through an international lens, with a particular eye to developments in Europe. Although most Americans in 1789 had cheered the start of revolution in France, Federalists withdrew their support in late 1792 after the September Massacres of some fifteen hundred people. They were further horrified a few months later when radicals known as Jacobins executed King Louis XVI and thousands of civilian opponents. As the French Revolution spiraled out of control, Federalists worried about the spread of radicalism beyond France and into North America. "Our greatest danger is from a contagion of levelism," one Federalist observed to a friend, insisting that "a noisy set of discontented demagogues" in North America issued "wild rant[s]" advocating for "entire equality." Federalists particularly dreaded the combination of radical ideas with violent actions. "Hardly had the word *equality* been pronounced, when the whole [French] kingdom became a scene of anarchy and confusion," recounted a Federalist pamphlet detailing scenes from the Reign of Terror. These images of mass violence haunted Federalists who believed that the spread of French extremism would bring anarchy and death across the Atlantic. The successful uprising of enslaved people in the French colony of Saint-Domingue confirmed Federalists' worst fears.[4]

As French forces went to war in Europe and on the high seas, Federalists grew increasingly anxious that France would attempt an invasion of the United States. To deter hostilities, Federalists believed that the nation had to appear not only militarily strong, but also politically unified. "Unanimity amongst ourselves is now the only thing which can insure our safety," explained the *Spectator*. "If the French can get us divided, as they have other nations which they have conquered, we will fall an easy prey to them." Unfortunately, the growing Republican opposition movement drove an increasingly deep and obvious wedge in the American populace. Complaining of a liberty pole–raising in Newburgh, New York, the *Daily Advertiser* bemoaned

Republican divisiveness: "will any real friend of America suffer party or personal prejudice and passion to hurry him into any action calculated to sow divisions among the people, when it is obvious that *division now* would be our *utter ruin*?" Many Federalists even accused Republicans of secretly aligning with France and artificially inflaming domestic tensions to facilitate a French takeover.[5]

Republicans stoked these fears through their open sympathy with French revolutionaries and disdain for the Federalists' increasing British affinities. They denounced the Federalists as the "British party" and accused them of exaggerating the French threat to facilitate an American alliance with Britain. Such a development, argued a Republican newspaper, would "reduce us to our former condition of *British Vassals!* and undo all that France has done for us." Republicans worried that failure of the revolution in France would embolden the Federalists to promote monarchy in America. Jefferson explained to a French friend: "I hope [your revolution] will end in the establishment of some firm government, friendly to liberty, and capable of maintaining it. If it does, the world will inevitably become free. If it does not, I feel the zealous apostles of English demidespotism here will increase the number of its disciples." To Republicans, the Federalists' Francophobia and Anglophilia marked them as counter-revolutionaries who secretly longed to reunite with Britain and reverse the gains of the American Revolution.[6]

But the Federalists drew a firm line between the peaceful resolution of the American Revolution and the violence and chaos raging in France. "The cause of France is compared with that of America during its late revolution. Would to Heaven that the comparison were just," remarked Hamilton. "Would to heaven that we could discern in the Mirror of French affairs, the same humanity, the same decorum, the same gravity, the same order, the same dignity, the same solemnity, which distinguished the course of the American Revolution." Instead, the French had ushered in an era of "horrid and systematic massacres." The United States had escaped such domestic turmoil by avoiding the democratic excesses that had wrought havoc in France. The Federalists worried that the Republicans' embrace of extra-institutional politics and French ideals would initiate an American Reign of Terror.[7]

Concerns over foreign affairs meshed tightly with a widespread distrust of party politics. In the early republic, Americans rejected the concept of a loyal opposition and instead viewed political parties as evil. An opposing party did not represent a legitimate ideology and policy alternative, but rather constituted a fringe group that divided Americans to gain or hold power. Partisans claimed that only their side represented the broad consensus of the citizenry. Thus, early Americans did not understand party conflict as a competition in which each side vied for power in a series of elections. Rather, they viewed it as a short-term battle to vanquish their foes and eliminate factionalism from American politics.[8]

Partisans legitimized their political divisions by externalizing them through suspicions that their opponents were in league with a foreign power. The idea of a treasonous alliance supported the illusion of one party defending national harmony and security from outside influences. By "othering" political rivals as dangerous aliens, partisans claimed to speak for authentic American citizens. Each side maintained that the current internal discord was artificial, the product of foreign meddling facilitated by domestic puppets. This perspective encouraged Federalists and Republicans to collapse the distinctions between domestic political opponents and hostile foreign nations and thereby cast their own party as the key to the republic's survival.[9]

Within these contexts, Federalists viewed Republican resistance as not simply incompatible with a republican system of government, but a potentially fatal threat. Popular displays of opposition could either trigger a revolution from within or facilitate an invasion from without. As such, Federalists viewed liberty poles through the prism of these concerns. "Liberty poles have been erected in the United States by those who are unfriendly to the Federal Government, and are intended as beacons to invite faction, turbulence, insurrection and rebellion in our country," wrote the *Berkshire Gazette*. Federalists pointed to the poles of the Whiskey Rebellion, as well as the French liberty caps that often adorned Republican poles, as evidence that these emblems portended revolution. At minimum, they signaled disunity and a challenge to the government's authority, which would, according to one Federalist, "disarm" the United States and "inspire its enemies with confidence, and invite their aggression." The *Albany Gazette* concurred, lamenting that liberty poles would raise "the drooping spirits" of the French who would be "encouraged ... to view us a divided and discontented people." Holding on to an outdated mode of politics was not merely stubborn, it had immense costs.[10]

As the interrelated threats of France and the Republican party escalated between 1795 and 1799, the Federalists' popular politics of assent correspondingly intensified. Grassroots Federalists progressed from rituals of assent to counter-demonstrations to attacks on Republican liberty poles. As they moved through each stage, Federalists grew increasingly frustrated with Republicans' stubborn devotion to traditional resistance methods and became more and more vehement in their insistence that all Americans must adapt to the new system.

Republicans, for their part, expressed anger, frustration, and fear that the Federalists aimed to implement a new, more limited form of doing politics through controversial legislation and extra-institutional enforcement. They viewed Federalist attacks on their liberty poles as an attempt to shut down popular political activity and so insulate the government from the will of the people. The result, they feared, would be a reversion to monarchy. In their minds, Federalist actions only made the need for popular mobilization more necessary.

In the early years of Washington's presidency, Federalists limited their popular politics to endorsements of the new administration. Public celebrations of Washington during his tours and birthday, for instance, indicated popular assent to government. These displays strengthened the republic by showing that elected officials acted in accordance with the popular will and enjoyed the support of the citizenry. In 1793, when France declared war on Britain and Washington proclaimed American neutrality, local Federalists organized meetings and drafted resolutions to demonstrate their approval. For instance, the people of Charlestown, Massachusetts, affirmed their belief that every citizen had a duty "to give their firm support to the Supreme Executive of the United States, in his exertions to maintain peace, and avoid the calamities of war." Even in Richmond, Virginia, the heart of Jeffersonianism, Federalists met and passed resolutions in favor of the Neutrality Proclamation. Federalist papers in nearly every state spread news of the meeting.[11]

But these displays took on a more combative edge in the face of growing popular dissent. In the winter of 1794, word reached the United States that the British navy had seized 250 American ships sailing to and from the French West Indies. Washington sent Chief Justice John Jay to London to negotiate a settlement. The resulting treaty, signed on November 19, won a series of concessions from the British, including the evacuation of their outposts in the Northwest Territory and the granting of American trading privileges with the British West and East Indies. It did not, however, recognize American neutral shipping rights to trade with the French. Critics denounced the Jay Treaty for forging a closer, and so increasingly dependent, trade relationship with Britain and lamented the corresponding blow to Franco-American relations.[12]

Opponents of the treaty organized meetings and demonstrations to express their frustrations. On July 10, 1795, fifteen hundred Bostonians gathered in Faneuil Hall and roundly condemned the agreement. A second meeting the following Monday unanimously adopted a set of twenty anti-treaty resolutions. In Philadelphia, residents celebrated the Fourth of July by burning the treaty and Jay in effigy. Treaty opponents in Boston likewise carved Jay's face into a watermelon and paraded it through town, while the people of Portsmouth, New Hampshire, carted effigies of Jay and British foreign secretary Wyndham Grenville through the streets. A New York crowd famously stoned Hamilton after he tried to defend the treaty.[13]

In their actions against the Jay Treaty, opponents insisted upon their right as citizens to voice their opinions on federal policy and so, influence the political process. For example, the people of Camden, South Carolina, prefaced their resolutions against the treaty with their belief in the "duty" and the "right" of all citizens "to come forward and declare their sentiments with freedom and firmness, to the end that those who are entrusted with power, may be admonished to use that power only for the good of the people who have placed it in their hands, and beware to violate the sacred trust." The grandson of Benjamin Franklin, Benjamin Franklin Bache, eagerly reported on resistance activities in his Republican newspaper, the *Aurora General Advertiser.* He also distributed thousands of copies of the treaty to encourage further displays of opposition. "If the people make good use of the present moment of enthusiasm," he wrote his wife, "I think it yet in their power to prevent it finally becoming the Supreme law of the land, and this only by a vigorous expression of their Sentiments." Bache believed that popular organizing provided the best option for defeating the treaty. Like the whiskey excise opponents, Bache did not view elections as a sufficient check on government power. Representative government required traditional resistance methods to ensure it did not descend into tyranny.[14]

Federalists mobilized in response to counteract these displays of dissent. They held meetings as direct rebuttals, often in the same areas as anti-treaty demonstrations. In New York City, over seventy members of the Chamber of Commerce gathered and resolved in support of the Jay Treaty. Merchants and traders in Boston likewise passed pro-treaty resolutions and expressed their disapproval of the "attempts to excite an opposition to the Treaty in the minds of the people, and to detach their confidence from the government of the Union." These displays sought to demonstrate the widespread support for the government and treaty and so challenge the dissenters' claims to speak for the popular will.[15]

In their endorsements of the Jay Treaty, Federalists contradicted the idea that the people best protected their liberty by criticizing the actions of government. The Boston resolutions insisted that "in a free government like ours, a firm reliance of the people on the wisdom and integrity of those authorities which they have themselves constituted to manage their public concerns, and a chearful acquiescence in the decisions of rulers of their own appointment, are indispensable." Federalists repeatedly drew a sharp distinction between past and present. Americans now enjoyed a representative system of government, meaning that the people had to defer political decisions to their elected officials. Citizens could not use popular action to pressure politicians into changing course.[16]

Congress ratified the Jay Treaty that summer, and in response, the French Directory announced its intentions to seize any ships carrying British goods. In July 1797, John Adams sent envoys to France to negotiate for the recognition of American neutrality. But the French proved intransigent. Foreign Minister Talleyrand refused to meet with them, forcing the commissioners to deal with four unofficial agents, whom Adams subsequently nicknamed "W," "X," "Y," and "Z." These agents demanded a bribe of $250,000 and a sizeable loan to their government before the peace talks could begin. The Americans returned home without a deal. But as the prospect of a war with France grew, Congress began calling for the commissioners' communications to understand why the negotiations had failed. Adams delivered the "XYZ dispatches" to Congress, which the press quickly circulated across the country.[17]

The revelation of French obstinacy and corruption provoked a wave of anti-French feeling. About three hundred communities held local meetings where they passed resolutions in support of the Adams administration. The affair embarrassed the Republicans and emboldened the Federalists, delivering them majorities in both houses in the midterms. Congressional Federalists capitalized by passing a series of controversial measures aimed to put the nation on a war footing. They expanded the army and navy and suspended trade with France. To fund the enlarged military, Federalists introduced two new taxes: the Stamp Tax and the Direct Tax. Like its British predecessor, the Stamp Tax required the use of government-issued paper for official documents like wills, deeds, and bills of exchange. The Direct Tax was a progressive property tax that operated on a graduated scale. Assessors surveyed each freeholder's property, counting the windows, outhouses, and stories of each dwelling to determine its worth. The Direct Tax also applied to land and enslaved people, but at a fixed rate.[18]

In addition, Federalists passed the Alien and Sedition Laws in 1798 to clamp down on internal opponents. The Alien Law consisted of three pieces of legislation: the Naturalization Law lengthened residency requirements for citizenship from five to fourteen years; the Alien Friends Act allowed the president to detain and deport aliens he deemed dangerous; and the Alien Enemies Act enabled the automatic deportation of aliens from countries with which the United States was at war. These laws, Federalists hoped, would enable the federal government to control the flood of European immigrants who brought radical, disruptive ideas to the United States. Federalist Theodore Dwight explained the danger: "Escaping from their own country, embittered against its government . . . and holding the rights of man in one hand, and the seeds of Rebellion in the other, they harangue the mob, preach against the oppression of the laws, rail at all good men." These foreigners, he argued, were the "disturbers of Legislative decorum, and the authors of Whiskey-Insurrections." Federalists believed that firmer government control over immigration would help restore peace and consensus to American politics.[19]

The Sedition Law went even further in targeting popular resistance. The law made it a federal crime to organize with the intent of opposing the law, as well as to print or publicly make "false, scandalous, and malicious" statements against the government and its officials. Violators faced hefty fines and imprisonment. The Sedition Law reinforced Federalist denunciations of traditional modes of political participation by criminalizing all forms of popular resistance—citizens could not even legally meet to discuss their opposition to legislation and contemplate modes of redress. Federalists rejected any notion that such actions aligned with popular sovereignty or constituted a reflection of the popular will. On the House floor, one Federalist proclaimed, "if they oppose the law, they are insurgents and rebels; they are not the people." The Federalists used the Sedition Law to legislate into existence the type of political culture they believed the new system of republicanism required. And by curbing dissent, the Sedition Law fostered unity by "disarm[ing] France" and her allies "of that weapon, of which she could most effectually injure us, the power of spreading slander and sedition against the government."[20]

To Republicans, the Federalists' legislation of 1798 signaled a troubling consolidation of the federal government's power. "Our government is, and has been, in my opinion, long before the *Whiskey* business, endeavouring to place the executive in as strong and permanent a position as possible," warned *Greenleaf's New York Journal*, "and their late laws will, in my opinion, nearly compleat their object." Republicans feared that the new taxes formed part of a Federalist plot to enrich elites and impoverish the people. A witness to a pole-raising in eastern Pennsylvania reported hearing that soon "we should have a number of great Lords and the people would be slaves. And also that the President would make himself to be a king of the country." Indeed, the Stamp Tax seemed to attest that the Federalists had no reservations about emulating their British predecessors.[21]

Republicans voiced particular outrage at the Alien and Sedition Laws. They argued that the Alien Law granted too much power to the executive branch by enabling the president to deport any alien who opposed him. "He can thereby considerably diminish the influence of such political principles he dislikes," argued "Cato" for the *Stewart Kentucky Herald*, and so "do a great deal in this way towards securing his own election." Similarly, they denounced the Sedition Law's muzzling of political expression, which insulated those in power from popular redress. "Cato" observed, "If then the officers of our government are not responsible to, but entirely secured from the interference of the people, is not the government assimilated to that in which all power originates independently of the will of the people?" Republicans condemned the laws as unconstitutional and tyrannical and a clear assault on the people's political power. One Republican warned, "our liberty is in greater danger [now] than it was when we lifted arms against King George, in the year 1775." Anticipating a second war of independence, Republicans turned to a Revolutionary symbol.[22]

In 1798 and 1799, Republicans raised seventy-one liberty poles to protest the Federalists' new legislation. Most of the pole-raisings occurred in northeastern areas where Republicans challenged Federalist elites: Connecticut, New Jersey, New York, Massachusetts, Pennsylvania, Rhode Island, Vermont, and the District of Maine. Southern Republicans enjoyed robust majorities and so raised only three poles, one each in North Carolina, South Carolina, and Virginia. In addition to a stronger Republican presence in local government, southern states also lacked a tradition of erecting liberty poles, as few southern Patriots had raised them during the Imperial Crisis. Further, these slave societies had good reason to avoid a revolutionary emblem that symbolized liberty—a fear seemingly confirmed when African Americans in Albany, New York, allegedly raised a pole with a flag that read "FREEDOM TO AFRICANS." Interestingly, this story appeared in only one paper and was not repeated elsewhere, which is uncommon for the era—perhaps suggesting that the report was apocryphal or that editors feared the consequences of circulating news of such an event.[23]

These pole-raisings attracted big crowds who partook in celebratory toasts, parades, and, on one occasion, the burning of the Alien and Sedition Laws. Republicans decorated their poles with signs denouncing the Federalists' legislation and foreign policy. "1776. LIBERTY, JUSTICE. THE CONSTITUTION INVIOLATE. NO BRITISH ALLIANCE. NO SEDITION BILL," read a pole in Newburgh, New York. As they had during the Whiskey Rebellion, pole-raisers erected their liberty poles in public spaces, like the town square or outside the local tavern. By marking these shared spaces, pole-raisers claimed to speak for their communities, implied unanimous approval of their pole, and intimidated potential dissenters.[24]

In reviving the practice of raising liberty poles, Republicans aligned themselves with the regulators of 1794 and the Patriots of the Imperial Crisis. When Federalists denounced these pole-raisings as violations of the Sedition Law (causing some pole-raisers to face legal action), Republicans stressed the legitimacy of their displays by turning to previous precedents. As one witness explained, "They connected with this [direct tax] law, the stamp tax, and alien and sedition acts, and said they had fought against such laws once already, and were ready to do it again." Republicans positioned the liberty pole as part of the traditional catalog of popular action Americans could employ when government overreached. But now this defense carried a further message: it insinuated that the Sedition Law constituted an attack on American political traditions.[25]

Federalists countered this notion by claiming that liberty poles could be considered seditious only in a republican context. The *Middlesex Gazette* argued: "In a country like ours where the people choose their own rulers and consequently have the right to advise them, and even to change them by elections if they please, I say in such a country it is not strange that men of candour should view with astonishment an ensign of Sedition under the specious name of a Liberty-Pole." If pole-raisers actually wanted to express their opinions on policy, they would use "a petition presented to Congress," since behavior aligning "with the principles of our Constitution" would be "more likely to have effect on the National Government." Federalists viewed liberty poles not as methods of political critique, but as emblems of opposition to the popular will and attacks on representative government. Echoing the criticisms of 1794, they insisted that liberty poles had no place in a republic.[26]

To Federalists, the combined threats of internal and external enemies meant that they could not allow liberty poles to remain standing. Local Federalists organized and tore them down to destroy the visual symbols of sedition, diminish the appearance of Republican strength and political division, and inhibit their use as rallying points for further resistance activities. These actions, like Federalist organizing in defense of the Neutrality Proclamation and the Jay Treaty, endorsed a form of popular mobilization that defended the will of the majority. But this time, Federalists oriented their popular politics of assent around rituals of destruction that aimed to quash the opposition.

By tearing down Republican liberty poles, Federalists attempted to implement a new practice of politics through force. In this way, grassroots Federalists acted as an unofficial enforcement arm of the federal government and the physical manifestation of the Sedition Law's spirit. In Pownal, Vermont, one Federalist reported that he and his compatriots chopped down a liberty pole despite an armed Republican guard and a crowd of angry onlookers that they kept at bay "with [their] swords." In Ulster County, New York, a fracas between armed pole-raisers and destroyers led to a false rumor that the Federalists had killed several men of the opposing group. Federalists also threatened violence to force pole-raisers and their allies to either conduct or assist in the destruction of poles. For instance, in Wayne County, Pennsylvania, two Federalists accosted a man in his home in the dead of night, demanding that he provide an ax so that they could chop down the local liberty pole. When he refused, they "swore if he did not deliver the ax, they would plunder his house." Hence, in the wake of a new spate of liberty poles, Federalist popular politics evolved from rival gatherings to deliberate confrontations in which Federalists aimed to intimidate dissenters into silence and overawe onlookers with proof of their side's strength.[27]

While local Federalists did not coordinate with each other, their attacks on liberty poles contained certain patterns in how they organized, destroyed the poles, and justified their actions in print. They toppled liberty poles in armed, all-male groups, usually formed along institutional structures already in place. For example, militia units often attacked liberty poles. In other instances, militia captains assembled posses by asking for volunteers. A militia captain in Reading, Pennsylvania, circulated a sign-up list on the community's court day for those who wished "to go under [his] command and destroy the Sedition Poles at that time standing within the county of Berks." Sixteen men answered the call. Sometimes, civil officials headed the groups. This was the case in Queen's County, New York, when "great numbers" assembled under the leadership of a local judge, sheriff, justice of the peace, and district collector, in addition to several militia officers.[28]

The Federalists who tore down the poles were White men, which contrasts with the Republican pole-raisings.[29] White women did not erect liberty poles, but, since the pole-raisings were large, public events, they attended the celebrations and occasionally made the decorations. Federalists' militaristic destruction of the poles, however, made no room for women. But in their rhetoric, the reverse was true. That is, Federalists celebrated women in their speeches as Republican Mothers, whereas Republicans rarely acknowledged them. Unlike Republicans' emphasis on White male equality, the Federalists' belief in an unequal social order allowed them to countenance a degree of political inclusion for minorities without granting them equal rights. However, the Federalists' hierarchy required a deferential society in which citizens submitted to the laws passed by their representatives. Ironically, their enforcement of this vision relied on a practice of destroying liberty poles that was exclusively White and male.[30]

While attacking liberty poles, Federalists engaged in ritualized behavior that inverted Republican pole-raising celebrations. For example, on November 15, 1798, over one hundred people gathered in Vassalborough, in the District of Maine, and erected an eighty-five-foot-tall liberty pole. The pole-raisers made a series of toasts denouncing the Sedition Law and Federalist paranoia: "May the virtues of our rulers shine so conspicuously, that they need not pass any unconstitutional bills to ward off the darts of thunder." At the base of their pole, the Republicans burned copies of the Alien and Sedition Laws. The Federalists of Vassalborough and the surrounding areas criticized these actions as "an open insult to the Government and to the People." One week later, a party of men led by their militia captain destroyed the pole and drank their own celebratory toasts. "May the Jacobins throughout the Union either fall by the weapons of reason, like the Opposition Pole this day," they cried, "or become as insignificant as the junto of Jacobins [in] Vassalborough." Similarly, Federalists in Hackensack, New Jersey, carried out a mock funeral procession, eulogy, and burial for the liberty cap they tore off of their local pole.[31]

Such displays presented a "ritual alternative" to Republican popular politics. Federalists contested Republican control of the public sphere and offered a different form of political action for people to participate in and read about. Their popular politics of assent provided citizens with a form of political activity that aligned with the principles of republican government and defended its implementation. Furthermore, these spectacles downplayed the appearance of Republican strength and so minimized political division to both domestic and international onlookers. Federalists infiltrated the spaces where Republicans had raised poles and occupied them with their own ceremonies. They displayed their numerical force and emphasized the lack of effective Republican opposition to counter them. The Vassalborough Federalists underlined this point with their description of the local "junto of Jacobins" as "insignificant." Painting Republicans as a minor fringe movement had the dual benefit of weakening Republican claims to represent the popular will and diminishing the appearance that American society was deeply divided between two equally powerful political camps.[32]

Federalist destructive rituals also often included the elimination of all evidence of the liberty pole's existence. In Wallingford, Vermont, Federalists felled a pole, burned it, and "scattered the ashes to the wind." In the District of Maine, Federalists chopped a liberty pole into pieces "so that no more remembrance of so offensive an object might be seen." By burning, hacking, or burying the poles, Federalists removed any trace of Republican opposition from the landscape. These erasures further solidified Federalist control of public spaces in their communities and purged any signs of political division from the American countryside.[33]

The Federalist press amplified these local actions by disseminating accounts of them beyond their immediate communities. Federalist printers employed two rhetorical strategies that, like the destructive rituals, diminished the appearance of Republican strength. First, Federalist writers and editors emphasized that Republicans comprised only a tiny minority and that their liberty poles did not speak for their communities. A man of Butternuts, New York, insisted that the local liberty pole "was erected by very few individuals, and before the three quarters of the town could hear of that proceeding." Reporting on a liberty pole in western Pennsylvania, one man claimed that "a few sneaking, cowardly reptiles came creeping in from the country, and embraced the most silent hours of the night to accomplish their design." He stressed that town residents had played no part.[34]

In addition, Federalists maintained that the support Republicans did enjoy was artificial. Rather than expressions of genuine popular opposition, Federalists claimed that liberty poles provided "testimony of the surprising influence which a sly insidious man may have over the simple." Their accusations that pole-raisers had been duped enabled Federalists to attack the Republicans as dangerous without aggrandizing them. This narrative suggested that the Republicans were not a real power rival, but rather a minority who inflated their perceived influence through deception. "We believe that the raising of Liberty Poles, and the discontents against the Stamp Act, has been excited by misrepresentations, by private revenge or by a false zeal," proclaimed the Federalists of Butternuts. Elsewhere, Federalists claimed that pole-raisers were "dupes," "degraded and deluded characters," and "ignorant and misguided followers" of demagogues who stirred up hatred of the government. Once people awoke to the conspiracy, opposition would melt away and unanimity would be restored.[35]

Federalists used the idea of Republican "dupes" to further justify the Sedition Law. As one Federalist explained, the law combatted those demagogues who aimed "to misrepresent the character and conduct of the magistrates, to pervert the judgment of the people, and render it impossible for them to make a right choice." Rather than an attack on political expression, the law provided a necessary weapon in the defense of a functioning public sphere: "It forbids not diffusing information, but diffusing corruption, among the people; misleading their judgment, and seducing them from their duty." Together, the Sedition Law and the popular politics of assent would strengthen the republic by silencing those voices who stirred up discontent and undermined popular support of the government.[36]

In their actions and words, the Federalists sought to combat their opposition without acknowledging its power. By attacking dissidents while simultaneously emphasizing their insignificance, Federalists defended the federal government from criticism and diminished the appearance of division. They used legislation, political action, and press coverage in a multi-pronged attempt to install the political culture they envisioned. This strategy would have been more effective, though, had the Republicans acquiesced and remained silent.

Republicans expressed outrage at Federalist attacks on liberty poles and contested the idea that poles were illegitimate in a republic. "How changeable are the opinions of men!" observed the *Bee*. "Some twenty years ago a flag staff mounted with the American standard, was called a Liberty-Pole ... now they are called Sedition Poles." The Republican press repeatedly emphasised the poles' revolutionary symbolism and rejected that they constituted "an *offence* committed against the principles of republicanism" or were somehow "incompatible with the good order of society." The Federalist position indicated their betrayal of the Revolution and American political traditions. "Is there any thing in bare poles that is offensive to the gentlemen," asked the *Aurora*, "or is it the patriotic spirit of ''76' they are disgusted with?" Antipathy to an exercise of popular political expression is "only to be found in that class of beings who *maintain monarchy* to be the *ne plus ultra* of human excellence." Little wonder, then, that Federalists echoed the actions of the British redcoats by tearing down liberty poles.[37]

The Republican press drew this connection plainly and warned that, like the British, the Federalists aimed to rob Americans of their liberty and institute a reign of tyranny. "Is our condition in such circumstances better than when we were the degraded colonists of England?" asked the *Aurora*. "The only difference is that then our tyrants were *foreign*[,] here they are *domestic*." To Republicans, Federalist actions against liberty poles provided further corroboration of what their legislation had already made plain: Federalists aimed to magnify their own power by subjugating the people. The *Centinel of Freedom* warned, "Citizens beware! The men who will pilfer from you the *Emblem of your Freedom,* would were it in their power, rifle from you the SUBSTANCE." The Republican press also refuted Federalist claims that Republicans' use of the liberty cap proved their allegiance to the Jacobin mob. "The cap was the emblem of liberty long before the French Revolution," observed one newspaper. The Federalists promoted this false link to use anti-French sentiment as a cover for their "hatred of liberty."[38]

Republicans also took issue with Federalists' claims to speak for the majority. They maintained that those "who stile themselves federalists . . . are very inconsiderable in point of number and abilities." Because they were a minority, Federalists who attacked liberty poles often had to do so on the sly or with force. After Federalists cut down a liberty pole in Springfield, New Jersey, Republicans chided them for doing it "assassin like" at night to avoid an open confrontation. "Debased indeed must be the wretches, who at midnight will purloin from their neighbours the emblem of their freedom." Elsewhere, Republicans accused Federalists of arming themselves with "pistols, swords, and bludgeons" and "terrify[ing] women and children" to gain access to local liberty poles. These depictions contradicted Federalist accounts that emphasized their confident, celebratory, and uncontested campaigns.[39]

On the ground, Republicans mobilized to defend their liberty poles from assailants. Some areas formed armed guards. In Reading, Pennsylvania, a crowd assembled "firmly resolved to guard and prevent the destruction of the Pole" from Federalist militiamen who had toppled several others nearby. Their show of force persuaded the Federalists to abandon their plan, and as they rode away the crowd cheered and waved their caps. When unsuccessful in preventing the destruction of their poles, Republicans raised replacements. For instance, Republicans in Mendham, New Jersey, put up a pole "as like the former as possible and with the same kind of cap on top" after Federalists cut down their previous one. They printed a warning in the newspaper stating that anyone who made a move on the new pole "shall be made acquainted with every person concerned in the erection." With these actions, Republicans reclaimed their control of space and ritual in their communities. By reiterating their commitment to opposition, they challenged the messaging of the Federalists' popular politics that attempted to minimize their depth and strength. Republicans' defense of their liberty poles frustrated Federalists' implementation of a new system of politics that held no room for opposition and defied grassroots attempts to enforce it.[40]

At the elite level, Federalists likewise struggled to use the Alien and Sedition Laws to achieve their envisioned political culture. Led by Secretary of State Timothy Pickering, the Federalists indicted editors of the four major Republican newspapers, including Bache, as well as several outspoken Republicans under the Sedition Law. The Federalists won every trial but lost in the court of public opinion as imprisoned Republicans embraced martyrdom, writing plaintive accounts of their ordeals and raising money to pay their fines. In addition, the Alien Law turned out to be little more than an empty threat. President Adams kept a handful of aliens under surveillance, but he did not deport anyone during his tenure.[41]

The 1798 legislation proved even less successful in the long term. The new taxation produced widespread resistance in eastern Pennsylvania in which regulators harassed tax collectors and refused to have their properties assessed.[42] In addition, Republican newspapers boomed in the aftermath of the Sedition Law, with forty-four new papers founded in the two and a half years following the law's passage. Finally, the Federalists' popular politics of assent failed to adequately combat the Republican opposition and stifle the party's growth. Indeed, their attacks on liberty poles mobilized further Republican reaction, which had electoral consequences in 1799 and 1800.[43]

The events of the mid to late 1790s clarified the lines between the two parties. Put simply, Federalists stood for a strong central government, British relations, and a new vision for politics based on assent and acquiescence, whereas Republicans emphasized individual liberty, French ties, and the traditional modes of popular influence on government. But these differences derived from the shared assumption that the new nation was fragile. Both sides agreed that the American experiment in republicanism faced grave danger from threats both foreign and domestic. They clashed over what those threats were and how best to protect the republic from them. To each side, either the erection or destruction of liberty poles confirmed the danger that their opponents posed to the survival of the republic.

And thus, when the Federalists attempted to install their new system of government by eliminating popular resistance through legislation and popular mobilization, Republicans fought back. In doing so, Republicans denied their opponents the peaceful and consensual politics they desired. These conflicts produced a vibrant and decentralized political culture in which Federalists enacted their brand of popular politics and so encouraged a further articulation and defense by Republicans of their own. Their struggle marked the mid to late 1790s as a period of intense contestation. Partisan identities hardened as Americans fought over two competing visions of what politics in the United States would look like.

❖ 5 ❖

# "Wandering Apostles of Sedition"

### Itinerant Republican Activists

They have sent runners everywhere to blow the trumpet of sedition.
—Fisher Ames, December 18, 1798

On December 18, 1798, Fisher Ames wrote to his friend Christopher Gore in a fury over recent events in his hometown of Dedham, Massachusetts. "The struggle with our Jacobins is like the good Christian's with the evil one," he seethed. Ames recalled that Republican support had waned after the publication of the XYZ dispatches. But over the past year, "The alien and sedition bills, and the land tax, were chosen as affording topics of discontent, and, of course, a renewal of the popularity of the party." Amidst the Republican resurgence, a "vagabond ragged fellow" named David Brown had come to Dedham "telling everybody the sins and enormities of the government." Brown's agitating inspired residents to raise a liberty pole in protest of the Federalist administration. But Ames maintained that the danger was not confined to Dedham. "They have sent runners everywhere to blow the trumpet of sedition," he warned Gore.[1]

These "runners" were a cohort of grassroots Republican activists who traveled through the Northeast preaching opposition to the Federalists and inspiring liberty pole–raisings in local communities. They argued that economic and political inequality were mutually reinforcing. That is, the wealthy enjoyed disproportionate political influence and used it to secure legislation that enriched themselves and impoverished the masses. The activists specifically pointed to the Direct Tax and the Stamp Tax as evidence of this plot. By increasing economic inequality through burdensome taxes, the Federalists sought to weaken the people and keep them subject to elite power. The Federalists attacked popular political mobilization and insisted on a passive citizenry as part of this scheme. They cheered the promises of representative government and denounced resistance to trick the people into surrendering their best weapon against harmful policies.[2]

In addition to the action in Dedham, farmers in eastern Pennsylvania resisted the execution of the Direct Tax by refusing to have their properties assessed, intimidating tax collectors and assessors, and raising liberty poles in the fall of 1798. The regulators echoed the sentiments of Brown and local radicals, like German Calvinist preacher Jacob Eÿermann. They denounced the tax as an attempt to strip poor farmers of their land and independence. "If things should go on the way they had begun," one declared, "we should have a number of great Lords and the people would be slaves." The regulators insisted that the Direct Tax would put them at the mercy of wealthy elites who monopolized political and economic power.[3]

Grassroots radicals and the resistance they encouraged pressured elites in both parties to respond. The Federalists condemned Brown and Eÿermann as Republican rabble-rousers. In the courts of law and of public opinion, critics accused the activists of deceiving the people and drumming up opposition in otherwise peaceful areas. "Eÿermann created the disturbance" in his town, declared one witness. "[Without him] there would have been little or no opposition to the assessment." Federalists depicted these men as inflammatory agitators and partisan demagogues who relied on illegal displays of opposition, rather than serious thinkers with legitimate critiques employing time-tested resistance methods. In doing so, Federalists diminished the power of these crowd actions and dismissed the political arguments embedded within them by denying that they represented the popular will.[4]

Republican leaders welcomed the popular disapproval of Federalist policies, but they worried that grassroots opposition would go too far and discredit the movement. At the beginning of 1799, Jefferson explained their difficult position in a letter to Madison: "Opinion is manifestly veering [against the Federalists] . . . if so we shall be gainers on the whole." But, he cautioned, "the only question is whether [popular agitation] will not carry things beyond the reach of rectification" through "rash or threatening" actions. Radicals like Brown and Eÿermann, and the extra-institutional protests that they inspired, bolstered Federalist claims that Republicans were extremists who undermined law and order and destabilized the republic. As a result, the Republican establishment embraced the Federalists' strategy of scapegoating. Republican politicians and newspapers criticized extra-legal actions and blamed the activists for sparking them. In doing so, they worked to isolate the radicals from the party and avoid a backlash.[5]

This chapter explores a cohort of political thinkers who saw the Federalists' vision for representative government as an intertwined economic and political threat. Their stories reveal a class of Republican leadership that influenced people on the ground in ways both more intimate and radical than party elites. These activists fueled an undercurrent of popular resentment and encouraged a spate of pole-raisings that simultaneously opposed the Adams administration and challenged the Republican establishment. As such, Brown, Eÿermann, and others like them pressured leading politicians to reckon with grassroots politics and the place of community action within representative government.

The documentary record of this grassroots movement is sparse. Brown and Eÿermann both appeared in court, and so their words and actions survive in the depositions, court records, and press reports of their trials. Their stories must stand in for the bulk of these activists who did not leave behind any records. However, Massachusetts farmer William Manning's *The Key of Libberty*, the only surviving manifesto of Republican radicalism, provides the movement's foundational text. First penned in 1797 and subsequently revised several times, *The Key of Libberty* lays out Manning's plan for a new form of political organization that would restore power to the people.

Manning viewed society, and especially government, as a perpetual struggle between "the Few," meaning wealthy, influential men whose incomes far outstripped their labor, and "the Many," the farmers, artisans, and laborers who produced all property. Federalists claimed that the Few were best suited to the complicated work of governing, but Manning criticized this argument as an excuse for the Few to exploit the Many: "[They] are ever hankering and striving after monarchy or aristocracy, where the people have nothing to do in matters of government but to support the Few in luxury and idleness." Manning cited "the Excise Act, Stamp Act, land tax, the alien and sedition bills" as evidence of a Federalist plot to amass wealth and power in the hands of the Few.[6]

To facilitate a true republic governed by the Many, Manning proposed a national association, called the Labouring Society, that would instruct ordinary citizens about political matters through a monthly publication and local classes. The Labouring Society would mobilize the lower orders into a voting bloc that could wrest power from the Few. Currently, the Many lacked the necessary knowledge and organization, while the Federalists had both. "If the Many were one-quarter part so well organized as the order of Cincinnati and the other orders of the Few are, they would always carry their points in elections," Manning insisted. However, alarmed by Shays's Rebellion, he did not believe in extra-institutional regulation: "All laws made by [the people's] representatives must be obeyed, let them be ever so wrong or bad in their opinion . . . [T]here is no remedy for grievances but by petitioning and using their rights in elections." He hoped that the Labouring Society would provide dissatisfied citizens with an apparatus for translating their grievances into political change, thereby making regulations like Shays's Rebellion and the Whiskey Rebellion unnecessary.[7]

In *The Key of Libberty*, Manning depicted the Federalists as elitists who used their power to enrich themselves and keep the people submissive. He characterized the Direct Tax and Stamp Tax as key instruments in the Federalists' assault on liberty and popular sovereignty. As activists like Brown and Eÿermann traveled through the Northeast, they echoed these claims. But in their actions, these itinerants proved more radical than Manning. Rather than the formation of new institutions like the Labouring Society, they encouraged popular resistance, liberty poles, and regulation as the means to defend the Many from the Few.

Fisher Ames led the Federalist cause in his town of Dedham. He had first developed a taste for Bostonian high society and Federalist principles as a delegate to the state ratification convention in 1787 and representative to the General Court the following year. Ames defeated Samuel Adams for a House seat in the First Congress and was reelected for three consecutive terms until failing health forced his retirement. Ames detested the growing Republican opposition who aimed to "se[t] mobs above the law." "Shall I be called upon to offer my proofs?" he asked his fellow representatives on the House floor in 1796. "They are here, they are every where. No one has forgotten the proceedings of 1794." Ames believed firmly in the supremacy of majority rule and viewed popular resistance as an assault on representative government.[8]

But he worried that his party was losing the battle for public opinion. "The Jacobins in fact have possession of the ground, and they will not fail to fortify themselves in their acquisition," he wrote to Secretary of the Treasury Oliver Wolcott, Jr. Ames feared that "the Jacobins had the people so long" and had filled their "weak heads" with false arguments against the government. "Emissaries are sent to every class of men, and even to every individual man, that can be gained. Every threshing-floor, every husking, every party at work on a house-frame or raising a building, the very funerals are infected with bawlers or whisperers against government," he insisted. Although Ames's grumblings sound like one man's frustrations and, perhaps, paranoia, he was not alone in his concern.[9]

Federalists elsewhere also worried about grassroots Republican agitation. A pamphlet published in Worcester, Massachusetts, bemoaned the "number of itinerant declaimers [who] roam about the streets, like wolves in sheep's clothing," telling all who would listen "frightful stories of the plans laid by their rulers, to enslave them and their children." In western Massachusetts, Thomas Dwight reported seeing men "riding and running from place to place writing and preaching constantly against the government itself and more against the administration of it." Peter Van Schaack of New York similarly lamented the widespread "attempts to poison the Publick Mind by exciting jealousy and distrust [of government], in which taxes form a copious theme." These complaints reveal a group of itinerant activists who spread contempt for the Federalist regime throughout the Northeast.[10]

Federalists feared that these radicals undermined national security by stirring up opposition to the new taxes. As ever, the Federalists argued that majority rule formed the backbone of representative government and that resistance tactics were illegitimate. For the republic to function, the people had to submit to the will of the majority as expressed in Congress. The Quasi-War heightened these concerns, as popular unrest could hamper military preparations and embolden the French. The people must prove "that they are worthy of the government they at present enjoy" by "cheerfully submit[ting] to the expenses of maintaining it," explained future congressman Daniel Dewey. By stressing the necessity of the taxes, Dewey and other Federalists contested the radicals' arguments that the measures were part of a plot to funnel wealth to the elite.[11]

During the summer of 1798, Ames took matters into his own hands and organized a Fourth of July dinner and oration for sixty of his neighbors to promote the Federalist cause and denounce Republican resistance. He read an address to the president that excoriated the rebellious and anarchic tendencies of the opposition: "It is the duty of every Patriot, of every wise and candid man, to yield all constitutional obedience, to the constitutional laws of his country, and use his best endeavours, to allay the ferment of zeal and passion, and to promote harmony and order, rational due obedience." As the assemblage nodded and toasted in agreement, Ames condemned popular mobilization and regulation as the tools of traitors.[12]

But despite Ames's efforts, Dedham experienced a Republican resurgence a few months later when David Brown arrived spouting criticism of the Federalist elite. Brown was an itinerant political activist and Revolutionary War veteran from Bethlehem, Connecticut, who had preached opposition to the Federalists throughout Massachusetts for the past two years. Brown lectured to crowds from his manuscript entitled "Dissertations." He also met privately in residents' homes to discuss his political philosophy. In addition to inspiring opposition to the Federalists, Brown hoped to gain enough subscribers to have his manuscript published before the next election.[13]

In his teachings, Brown declared that the wealthy had amassed too much political power and used it to increase their own fortunes at the expense of the common people: "all our administration is as fast approaching to Lords and Commons as possible, that a few men should possess the whole country and the rest be tenant to the others." Republican government did not protect the interests of ordinary citizens because officials were the "representatives of speculators and not of the people." The new political system was a sham. Americans found themselves shackled with "the same chains of American tyrants that we once sported ourselves from under Britain." He compared "the land tax, stamp act, and treason-law" with "the exorbitant taxes Britain were about to fetch on us without representation." To Brown, claims of representation rang hollow. Economic inequality empowered a select few, creating a cursed cycle in which the Federalist elite amassed more and more wealth at the expense of others while claiming that their actions represented the will of the majority.[14]

Brown argued that the Federalists used their ideas of a passive citizenry to weaken the masses and consolidate their grip on power. Their version of representative government demanded the people's unthinking submission.

"Like the subjects of Julius Caesar," he lamented, "we must bow down and worship our Leaders as the Gods of Jupiter and Mars." Federalists cultivated an improper reverence for elected officials and condemned popular political resistance so that they could line their pockets with impunity. They wanted to limit the people's role in government not because representation worked, but because it did not. So if the people did not want "to be brought into abject slavery," they had to fight back.[15]

Brown advocated popular resistance and regulation to combat the Federalist threat. "All the petitions and remonstrances to Congress they take no notice of it," he complained. "And if [the people] do not get a redress of their grievances by petitioning for it, they will finally break out like the burning mountain of Etna, and will have an unconditional redress of their grievances." In his travels, Brown had seen such resistance in several Massachusetts counties where people refused to pay the Direct Tax. He hoped the Federalists would take notice. "I never knew a government supported long after the confidence of people was lost, for the people are the government," Brown warned. Now was the time, he told the residents of Dedham, to make their frustrations known.[16]

Although there is no evidence that Brown ever met William Manning, their writings share several striking similarities. Brown echoed Manning's construction of a conflict between the Few and the Many: "There [always] has been an eternal struggle between the laboring part of the community and those lazy rascals that invented every means that the Devil, has put into their heads, to destroy the laboring part of the community." They both believed that the Few used their authority to enrich themselves and impoverish the people, thereby maintaining their hold on power. In addition, Brown and Manning both insisted that the Federalists inflated the threat of France to raise taxes and create a standing army. "They wish for a standing army of slaves to execute their arbitrary measures," wrote Manning, and they "will catch hold of every little misunderstanding or uneasiness" as "a pretext to raise and keep a standing army." Likewise, Brown accused the Federalists of beating the drums of war to create a "pretext to enslave the farmers" and fund an army who will "hurl you into prison . . . if you will not submit." And they both estimated that the Federalists had the support of only one-eighth of the population. These echoes hint at a larger movement in which such ideas circulated and spread.[17]

In October, a few weeks after Brown had left for Andover, a group inspired by his teachings raised a liberty pole on Dedham's main road with a liberty cap on top and a sign that read "Liberty and Equality—No Stamp Act—No Sedition, or Alien Bills—No Land Tax—Downfall to the Tyrants of America—Peace and Retirement to the President—Long Live the Vice-President and the Minority—May Moral Virtue be the basis of Civil Government." The Dedham Republicans had heeded Brown's warnings and used their liberty pole to depict the Federalists' legislation as a tyrannical assault on the intertwined promises of their Revolution: liberty and equality.[18]

A week later, district judge John Lowell ordered federal marshal Samuel Bradford to "demolish" the "Symbol of Sedition." But the local Federalists cut it down before he arrived and saved the "libellous label" as evidence for the marshal. "The Government must display its power *in terrorem*," Ames fumed. "Though the liberty-pole is down ... the devil of sedition is immortal." Matching Ames's ire, the Federalist press denounced the liberty pole as "a rallying point for the enemies of a Free Government" and an emblem of "insurrection and civil war." In nearby Salem, a judge cited the Dedham pole as evidence of the need for the Sedition Law.[19]

Bradford issued arrest warrants for those involved in the pole-raising for violating the Sedition Law. In March 1799, officials apprehended Brown in Andover. The court set his bail at $4,000. Unable to pay, Brown awaited his June trial date in a Salem jail. But his imprisonment did not allay Federalist fears, for his fellow activists remained at large. "There is now on foot a plan of the Jacobins" to upend the Federalist regime, declared the *Salem Gazette*. "Already one, Brown, is now in our jail committed for seditious conduct to accomplish such purposes; and from most respectable authority I am assured the plan is assiduously pursu[ed] by the disorganizing agents in every county in the Commonwealth." Aided by a posse of Dedham Federalists, officials arrested Benjamin Fairbanks, a former town selectman and a member of one of Dedham's most prominent families, alleging that he had helped lead the pole-raising.[20]

In June, the U.S. Circuit Court in Boston indicted both Brown and Fairbanks, and they appeared before Samuel Chase, associate justice of the U.S. Supreme Court, for trial. Both men initially pleaded not guilty, but they reversed their pleas in recognition of the strength of the state's cases against them. At Fairbanks's sentencing Ames testified on his behalf, recommending leniency because Fairbanks had been duped by Brown and the Republicans: "unfortunately, the scene he lives in and the persons in whom he misplaced his confidence, has exposed him, and many others like him, *to delusion,* and in consequence *to guilt.*" Ames denounced Brown, in particular, as a "wandering apostle of sedition" who spread "bold falsehoods" and "artful and inflammatory sophistry." Ames conceded that Fairbanks had acted criminally on this occasion, but given the circumstances and Fairbanks's prior unblemished record, Ames assured the court of his confidence that the defendant would behave as a good citizen in the future.[21]

Fairbanks submitted a written statement to the court that also emphasized his ignorance. He admitted to attending the pole-raising, but insisted that he had not understood "how heinous an offense it was." "I am in my heart a friend to my country," he averred, and pledged to do his "duty as a good citizen, in support of the laws and government of the United States" in the future. Chase accepted Fairbanks's statement and "wished him and all who had been deluded" a return to confidence in their government. He sentenced Fairbanks to just six hours of imprisonment and imposed a token fine of $5 plus the costs of the proceeding ($10.50). The judge explained that Fairbanks had already demonstrated his "reformation." Rather than confront the criticisms of government or the political rifts in Dedham, the participants preferred to excuse Fairbanks as the victim of deceit. They would rather fault Brown, the outsider and rabble-rouser, for the unrest.[22]

As a result, Brown received neither supportive witnesses nor the court's sympathetic ear at his sentencing. Despite Brown's admission of guilt, Chase had the prosecution examine all seven of the state's witnesses to establish the degree of his culpability. One man testified that he had seen Brown reading from his manuscript to a crowd of people, telling them that the object of government "was to plunder and steal." The witness asserted that Brown "appeared to him to make impressions on several of the bystanders, unfavourable to the government." The court did not offer the defendant a chance to cross-examine. The prosecution also read excerpts from Brown's manuscript to demonstrate his hatred of the federal government.[23]

Instead of the leniency that he had shown Fairbanks, Chase scolded Brown for the "malignity and magnitude" of his crimes. He demanded that Brown reveal the names of his subscribers, but Brown refused, fearing he would "loose all my friends." Brown apologized to the court for his behavior and promised upright conduct in the future. Given his poverty, he asked the judge to limit his punishment to imprisonment, as he could not afford a fine. Unmoved, Chase handed down the most severe sentence issued under the

Sedition Law: a $400 fine, plus $80 in court costs, and eighteen months' imprisonment. Because of his inability to pay the fine, Brown served an additional six months.[24]

By scapegoating Brown, Chase insulated the Federalists and their vision for representative government from the popular opposition the Dedham pole-raisers displayed. Rather than take their criticisms seriously, the court dismissed them as the product of Brown's misrepresentations and falsehoods. In doing so, Chase facilitated an avoidance of Brown's critiques and their purchase in the Dedham community. This interpretation had the effect of dismissing Dedham's activism and Brown's arguments, and yet making Brown and others like him appear dangerous.

As a result, mainstream Republicans worried that the story of Brown and the Dedham liberty pole would paint the entire party as radical levelers and anarchists. In the wake of his trial, the Republican press distanced the party from Brown by demonizing him as a liar and trickster. The *Independent Chronicle* asserted, "All the means which a vicious ingenuity could suggest appear to have been used by [Brown] to create discontent and to excite among the people hatred and opposition to their Government." Several months later, the paper went further, reminding readers that the Dedham liberty pole was "raised by a shallow, deluded set whom artful rogues had set on and then left in the lurch." But the *Independent Chronicle* remained supportive of liberty poles and critical of the Federalists' destruction of them: "It is true in '75, the British Government destroyed the poles as the rallying posts of sedition and rebellion; but they were tyrants for so doing. And it is true in '98, the American Federal Government did the same; but they were not tyrants for doing it, because the Sedition Law forbids our calling them so." The *Aurora* similarly denounced the Federalists for prostrating the Dedham pole like "the mercenary hirelings of George the Third," but did not mention Brown.[25]

A few months later, word reached Dedham that farmers in eastern Pennsylvania refused to pay the Direct Tax, intimidated assessors with armed force, and raised liberty poles of their own. Ames wrote to the president of Yale, Timothy Dwight, with alarm. "Pennsylvania is revolutionized," he declared, "[and I fear that] a civil war will break out."[26]

The Pennsylvania resistance to the Direct Tax began in the fall of 1798 in Northampton and Bucks Counties, but shortly spread to Montgomery,

Berks, Dauphin, York, and Lancaster Counties. Rural German-speakers in these areas flooded Congress with petitions containing thousands of signatures. While they awaited legislative change, regulators prevented the execution of the tax by pledging noncompliance, refusing to have their properties assessed, violently threatening assessors and tax collectors, and raising liberty poles. Occasionally, women scared off assessors by dousing them with boiling water, leading some to refer to the tax resistance as the "Hot Water War." But these women's actions proved the exception. In all other instances, regulators only threatened violence.[27]

The people of eastern Pennsylvania opposed the Direct Tax because they feared that it would strain their already tight resources and set a precedent for further taxation. In the late 1790s, cash scarcity, debt, and foreclosure plagued the region's farmers. Although the average family owed less than six dollars under the Direct Tax, many worried that the federal government would use the assessments as the basis for further property taxes that they could ill afford. They believed, as one man put it, that if they "did not oppose the laws they would certainly loose their lands."[28]

They also objected to the tax because it constituted the latest in a series of policies that favored speculators over farmers. State law allowed speculators to hold huge tracts of land with only a small down payment. Beginning in the late 1780s, the state government prosecuted farmers for unpaid taxes, but granted extensions to speculators. The Direct Tax Law continued this trend by applying the land tax to the value, not the size, of the property. As a result, a farmer who cleared fields and built a house paid a higher tax than a speculator who owned unimproved land. And by taxing both houses and land, the law posed a double burden to small farmers. The people of Dauphin County emphasized the imbalance in their petition to Congress: "[It] is now well known, that the owners of Houses in Pennsylvania will pay much more in proportion to the value of their property than the holders of uncultivated land." One regulator warned that this skewed policy would enable speculators to buy up the land of destitute farmers and "lease it out again to the people for their life or perhaps two lives." While regulators in 1794 had begged for a land tax, those in 1799 found this iteration wanting.[29]

As their countrymen to the west had done, eastern Pennsylvanians turned to regulation to protect their communities. Local politicians and militia captains spearheaded the opposition. Jonas Hartzell, a Northampton brigadier general and Republican state assemblyman, stirred up the people of Millerstown in Macungie Township, warning them "that the Laws of Congress lately made [were] very dangerous to the liberties of the people ... and that the people should not be so still about it." Hartzell advocated regulation, not insurrection. He informed a friend that Congress had received numerous petitions against the Direct Tax and Stamp Tax, and so "the people should only keep the tax assessors back so that the rates should not be taken before the next Congress," when the laws would likely be repealed.[30]

In Hamilton Township, the Reformed preacher and political activist Jacob Eÿermann drummed up support for the regulation with a radical message similar to that of David Brown. Eÿermann had left Germany for Philadelphia in 1796. After arriving in the United States, he traveled through Pennsylvania as a Calvinist minister, temporarily settling in Hamilton Township at the start of 1798. Eÿermann campaigned vigorously against the Direct Tax as a Federalist ploy to strip the people of their property and enslave them. He warned that the Federalists were "cursed, damned villains and Robbers" who had "made such laws to rob the people." Eÿermann insisted on the need for resistance. "The people should oppose the law," he told Hamilton residents. Popular mobilization would force officials "to draw back, and then the people would be free, otherwise they would be bound, and tax after another would ensue. The people would have to pay tythes and every other species of taxation, and they would be slaves." Under such a regime, "they would be as bad off as they were in Europe." Like Brown, Eÿermann did not trust representative government to protect the people's liberty and instead saw in current policy the specter of absolutism.[31]

Eÿermann also claimed that the Direct Tax was illegitimate because it disproportionately burdened farmers over speculators and merchants. Several Hamilton residents recalled Eÿermann reading from a book that he pretended contained the Constitution and concluded that "the people were under no obligation to obey the laws" because Congress "had no right to pass such laws." Eÿermann encouraged the people of Hamilton to resist the execution of the Direct Tax and told would-be assessors to decline their posts. He warned the assessor for Hamilton Township that if he accepted his commission, he "might meet with some evil." For his part, Eÿermann vowed that he "would lay his black coat aside and fight for a whole week." To Eÿermann, like Brown, the answer to the failures of representative government lay in popular mobilization.[32]

Those across eastern Pennsylvania agreed. Regulators raised liberty poles and used them to launch their area's opposition. Led by militia captain and justice of the peace Henry Jarret, the people of Millerstown raised a liberty pole in late December 1798. Jarret's men paraded around the pole, removed their hats, huzzaed for liberty, and "swore they would rather die than submit to the Stamp Act or House Tax Law which was slavery and taking their liberty away." Shortly after, Jarret circulated a written association committing all who signed to oppose the execution of the Direct Tax Law. Similar events occurred in Weisenberg Township, where militia captain Conrad Spering led a liberty pole–raising and passed around a paper declaring that those who signed "would defend themselves against the Government." In other areas, regulators threatened to tie assessors to the local liberty pole if they attempted to measure their properties.[33]

From the start, eastern Pennsylvanians used liberty poles as the focal point of their movement. The poles not only signaled opposition, they also served as gathering areas to organize resistance and sites of public justice to intimidate collaborators. Liberty poles also placed the regulation in its wider context. In addition to referencing the Imperial Crisis and the Whiskey Rebellion, liberty poles linked the communities in eastern Pennsylvania with the scores of areas across the Northeast that had also raised poles over the past several months. Unlike in 1794, this regulation formed part of a larger partisan opposition movement—a fact that made it all the more threatening to the Federalists.[34]

That winter, the Adams administration grew alarmed at the "palpitation on the political pulse" and cracked down on the restive Pennsylvanians. Congress rejected the regulators' petitions, upholding their legislation as vital "to guard not only against the usual consequences of war, but also against the effects of unprecedented combinations to establish new principles of social action, and the subversion of religion, morality, law, and government"—in other words, to suppress popular political resistance. On February 20, federal district court judge Richard Peters issued seventeen arrest warrants for the ringleaders of the opposition. On March 6, federal marshal William Nichols's deputy arrested Eÿermann, interrupting his delivery of a funeral sermon. The marshal took Eÿermann and the other prisoners to the Sun Tavern in Bethlehem, Northampton County, pending transportation to Philadelphia for trial in the federal district court.[35]

The following morning, militia captain John Fries led four hundred men, including Jarret's troop, to the Sun Tavern to liberate the prisoners. When they arrived, Fries entered the tavern unarmed and assured Nichols that he and his men would not hurt any officials as long as Nichols did not remove the prisoners to Philadelphia. Fries offered to post bail for the detained if the marshal allowed them "to be tried in their own courts, and by their own people." But Nichols refused to surrender his charges unless forced by an armed challenge. After several hours, Fries gave in. He led a group of armed men into the tavern to demand the prisoners, but instructed them "not to fire first." Nichols acquiesced and released the prisoners. Neither side fired a shot. Fries "expressed a great solicitude for the safety of Eÿermann" and confirmed with Nichols that he had been released before departing, vowing that the party "would not march without him." The posse disbanded peaceably and returned home, while Eÿermann fled to New York state.[36]

Despite the lack of violence, Federalists decried the crowd action as an unlawful revolt, which they named the "Northampton Insurrection," and later "Fries's Rebellion." They viewed the lawlessness in Northampton as the beginning of a second Whiskey Rebellion. "ANOTHER INSURRECTION has broken out [in Pennsylvania]," declared the *Gazette of the United States*. "A most rebellious disposition pervades the whole county of Northampton, insomuch that no man dare avow his attachment to government." A contributor to the *Oracle of Dauphin* from Trenton, New Jersey, related that "the spirit of disaffection to the Federal government, on account of the tax act, is spreading itself into the northern part of this state, bordering on Northampton county." In their correspondence, Federalist elites discussed their suspicions that most eastern Pennsylvanians "would join the French, if they invaded the country." The Federalists saw no difference between popular resistance to legislation and revolution against the government. In their eyes, the regulation and prison rescue proved that the eastern Pennsylvanians were traitors bent on sabotaging the republic.[37]

The Federalists' reaction confirmed the fears of mainstream Republicans. Even before the rescue in Bethlehem, Jefferson had worried that the discontent in eastern Pennsylvania would lead to an outburst, which the Federalists could spin as rebellion. "[Insurrection] is the only thing we have to fear," he confided to a friend. "The appearance of an attack of force against the government would check" the popular progress toward Republicanism and instead "rally [the people] round the government." Despite having once advocated "a little rebellion now and then," Jefferson condemned the extra-legal tactics of the regulators in favor of "the constitutional means of election and petition." He feared that the regulation would strengthen Federalist claims that the Republican opposition was made up of radicals set on undermining representative government. Even the *Aurora* bemoaned the rescue: "No republican can justify the conduct of those people who resisted the marshal in the execution of his duty; it was highly reprehensible and ought to be punished." The leading Republican newspaper disliked the optics of the regulation and implied that party loyalists in other areas should not ally with the easterners.[38]

In the meantime, Nichols rode to Philadelphia and reported the prison break to Judge Peters, stressing the need for a strong force to restore law and order in Northampton. Peters wrote to Secretary of State Timothy Pickering of the "treasonable opposition" and the necessity of "military force." On March 12, Adams issued a proclamation declaring the direct action in Bethlehem treasonous and ordering all tax resisters in eastern Pennsylvania to cease their opposition by March 18. On the morning of the eighteenth, two hundred men from Bucks and Northampton Counties met under the leadership of Fries and Jarret to declare their intention to obey the president's proclamation and submit to the law. The Republican press eagerly spread word of the "tranquility and submission" in Northampton. "The terrible *hot water* insurrection in Northampton county is cooled down to an ordinary process at law, to which all the parties have voluntarily submitted," reported the *Aurora*. The regulation had ended.[39]

But the Adams administration had already begun military preparations to suppress the supposed revolt. Days before the rescue, Congress passed the Eventual Army Act, authorizing the president to mobilize state militias to augment the army in case of emergency, including domestic insurrection. To the Adams administration, the regulators' prison break provided such a crisis. On March 11, the day before he issued his proclamation, Adams invoked the Eventual Army Act and placed Brigadier General William MacPherson in command of a force to put down the rebellion. He added militia units from Pennsylvania, Maryland, New Jersey, New York, and Vermont to MacPherson's 600 regulars, for a total of 2,920 men. Writing to Secretary of War James McHenry, MacPherson's aide-de-camp Robert Goodloe Harper stressed the need for the government to demonstrate its power to enforce the law and "overawe the rebels." Failure to do so would "appear to them as proof of weakness on the part of the government, which must encrease their audacity!" Accordingly, Adams ordered the troops to assist the local authorities in taking the assessments and arresting those active in the tax resistance and rescue.[40]

Despite the reports of submission, the army marched for Northampton on April 4. "Government should not cringe," declared one Federalist on the eve of the mission. Ahead of their arrival, MacPherson distributed a pamphlet he had written that explained why the regulation constituted such a serious threat to the republic: "Congress must decide when, and in what manner, [the power to tax] ought to be exercised, and this decision must be declared by a majority. When declared, it must be obeyed; otherwise the Constitution must be destroyed, with it all government, law and order must perish, and disunion, civil war, and anarchy must ensue." His forces aimed to restore respect for the law and demonstrate that a disgruntled minority could not employ extra-legal tactics to counter the will of the majority.[41]

After receiving intelligence that "the people were in very great disturbance, and were everywhere raising Liberty-Poles," MacPherson instructed Major Mahlon Ford, commander of a detachment of artillerists, to destroy any poles he encountered. "With respect to the Liberty, or more properly speaking Sedition Poles, should any appear on your route, it's my wish they should be cut down as they can be considered in no other light than as rallying points for the disaffected." The men complied, which angered Republicans throughout Pennsylvania.[42] The *Aurora* reported that the troops destroyed multiple liberty poles as part of their "system of terror," which also included entering homes in the middle of the night, requisitioning supplies from civilians without compensation, and abusing their prisoners.[43]

Within two weeks, MacPherson's forces arrested thirty-one men and received bail from ninety-two others. At no point did they encounter any armed opposition. In May, Pickering received word that Eÿermann had made his way to New York, and the secretary of state instructed New York district court judge John Sloss Hobart to arrest the radical refugee. "This Eyerman has been in America but two years and a half; and wears a clerical garb to cloak his licentiousness in morals as well as politics," seethed Pickering. "I earnestly hope the miscreant may be arrested and secured." The following month, New York officials apprehended Eÿermann and transported him to Philadelphia for trial.[44]

The U.S. Circuit Court indicted Eÿermann for violating the Sedition Law, as well as participating in a prison break and conspiring to oppose the Direct Tax Law. On October 16, he appeared in court before Judges Bushrod Washington and Richard Peters and pleaded not guilty. District Attorney William Rawle told the court that Eÿermann had spent his time in the United States "recommend[ing], both by his advice and example, an opposition to those laws by which the whole community were bound." Rawle called a number of witnesses who confirmed that Eÿermann had preached opposition to the people of Hamilton "in a violent manner," instructing them "not [to] let the assessors take down their taxation." In addition, Nichols testified that "Eÿermann's deliverance was a particular object" of Fries and his posse's, a fact that illustrated Eÿermann's centrality to the rebellion.[45]

As in Fairbanks's sentencing, the prosecution blamed the defendant for the community's opposition. Rawle asked several witnesses whether the people of Hamilton would have resisted the execution of the Direct Tax had it not been for Eÿermann. In every instance, they testified that Eÿermann had caused the regulation. "If this minister had not come into [our] neighborhood," claimed one resident, "there would have been no disturbance there." "I knew of no other person there who went about to advise the people to opposition," stated another. Unable to afford an attorney, Eÿermann did not mount a defense. He merely stated that any wrongdoing had been unintentional and asked the court for leniency.[46]

In his charge to the jury, Judge Washington upheld Rawle's contention that Eÿermann had caused the regulation in Hamilton Township. He asserted that citizens oppose the government only when someone "more knowing, and more wicked than the general mass of society, endeavors to advise and mislead the ignorant and unwary." As for the prosecution's case, Washington affirmed that "the proof is as clear against him as any thing can possibly be." The jury deliberated for only fifteen minutes, returning with a verdict of guilty on all three counts. Washington sentenced Eÿermann to one year's imprisonment and a $50 fine.[47]

The courts convicted thirty-one others of conspiracy, unlawful assembly, and prison break. Jarret received the harshest sentence: a $1,000 fine and two years' imprisonment. Fries and two others were found guilty of treason and sentenced to death. Eÿermann, Jarret, Fries, and thirteen others petitioned Adams for clemency, promising to never attempt another regulation. "We reflect with abbhorrance on our past Conduct," wrote Eÿermann, "and make the sacred Promise as before God, that in future through his Grace we will demean ourselves not only on our own part as peaceable and obedient

Citizens but use all our Endeavours to encourage amongst our Neighbours the same spirit of true Citizenship." Despite his cabinet's advice to the contrary, Adams issued a general pardon to all of the insurgents on May 21, 1800, just two days before Fries was scheduled to hang. He later explained his reasoning: "What good? What Example would have been exhibited to the Nation by the Execution of three or four obscure miserable Germans, as ignorant of our Language, as they were of our Laws and the nature and definition of Treason?" Adams stripped the regulation of its political meanings and widespread appeal. His words diminished the movement to a mere blunder by lowly foreigners who did not know better.[48]

Since the beginning of the tax resistance, Adams and his colleagues had described the Pennsylvania regulators as too ill-informed to understand their actions. During the regulation, leading Federalists called the participants "ignorant & mulish," "strongly prejudiced," "deluded," and "silly." They believed that a handful of rabble-rousers like Eÿermann and Fries had stirred a credulous population to rebel. Most were too simple to understand their accusations against the government, nor could they comprehend the seriousness of their crimes. "The stupid Spirit of Insurrection which so blindly led the ignorant people of Northampton, was soon quelld, by the appearance of some troops," explained Abigail Adams.[49]

Eager to downplay the events in Northampton, the Republican press latched on to the idea that the regulators acted out of ignorance. "The people are a plain people—they have but a limited knowledge of the world," explained the *Bee*. The paper also observed that the regulators' "weapons" were merely "*ridicule* and *hot water*," and so the Adams administration need not have sent in federal troops. Similarly, the *Aurora* emphasized that the Pennsylvanians' "opposition was directed against a tax, of which they mistook the nature," and that local authorities could have dealt with the conflict. Like the Adams administration, the Republican press minimized the regulators' critiques. They portrayed the regulation as a misunderstanding to which the Federalists characteristically overreacted.[50]

Itinerant radicals like Brown and Eÿermann warned all who would listen that the Federalists' economic policies constituted an attack on the people's political power. They provided a piercing critique of the Federalists' vision of representative government—one that linked Federalist notions of deference and majority rule with economic and political subjugation. This narrative clarified and intensified the threat that the Federalists posed, which encouraged resistance in Dedham and regulation in Hamilton.[51]

But neither party took these ideas seriously. Mainstream Republicans distanced themselves from the radicals and downplayed the unrest that they caused. Party leaders and editors indicated their unease with the popular politics of their supporters, fearful that these tactics would turn public opinion against them. Eager to save face, they disavowed Brown and the Pennsylvania regulation. In doing so, Republican elites moved away from the radical wing of their party and toward their opponents' vision for political culture.

The Federalists denounced all opposition to their legislation as traitorous. As the Republican leadership feared, the Federalists cited the radicals as examples of Republican firebrands who misled the people to rebellion with their inflammatory and deceitful rhetoric. "The main object of [Brown's] writings," raged an Andover man in the *Columbian Centinel*, "is to alarm the Farmers, Mechanicks, and Labourers, with an apprehension, that the preservation of their liberty and property depends on a thorough Revolution."[52]

Indeed, the radicals did help to enact a revolution, albeit a peaceful one. By promoting a popular reaction to the Federalists' legislation, grassroots activists assisted the Republican leadership in provoking a revolt at the polls at the close of the decade. But although the radicals helped ensure Republican victories in 1799 and 1800, those they elected held different views on the place of the people in politics.

❖ III ❖

# Transformations

Absolute acquiescence in the decisions of the majority [constitutes] the vital principle of republics.
  —Thomas Jefferson, March 4, 1801

❖ 6 ❖

# From Poles to Polls

*The Elections of 1799 and 1800*

Let that party set up a broomstick, and call it a true son of Liberty, a Democrat, or give it any other epithet that will suit their purpose, and it will command their votes in toto!
—George Washington, July 21, 1799

In the winter of 1799, the residents of Small Lotts, New Jersey, raised a liberty pole with a liberty cap and a flag that read "WE WILL DEFEND OUR RIGHTS." The *Centinel of Freedom* praised this political display: "[The pole], although the neighborhood is small where it was erected, is evincive of the patriotic spirit that actuates them, and augurs much good at the next election." The paper cheered the Small Lotts pole and those elsewhere as signs of a Republican wave soon to crash over the Federalists and wash them out of office. Grassroots mobilization, the editor believed, would translate into a strong turnout on election day and so, a formidable Republican voting bloc. The era of Federalist dominance seemed to be drawing to a close.[1]

Meanwhile, local Federalists intensified their attacks on liberty poles and pole-raisers. The most widely publicized incident occurred that April when Federalist militiamen waged a two-day campaign against liberty poles in Reading, Pennsylvania. The action sparked a partisan firestorm in the press and led to the beatings of two newspaper editors. In Pennsylvania, the Republican press highlighted these events during the state's gubernatorial contest to turn popular opinion against the Federalists. The Republican party repeated this tactic in the 1800 presidential campaign, emphasizing the Adams administration's repressive legislation, violent troops, and assaults on popular political expression.

The Pennsylvania governor's race of 1799 and the presidential election of 1800 formed a referendum on the power of the citizenry in a republican government. Unhappy with the Federalists' muzzling of grassroots dissent, Republicans fought back electorally. Ironically, they used their votes to counter their rivals' claim that citizens had a political role only through elections. But these Republican victories contained a further irony: with the "friends of the people" in office, grassroots Republicans abandoned the extra-institutional regulatory tradition and the Federalists, once in opposition, refused to revive it. By the end of the First Party System, Americans raised liberty poles to celebrate the government's achievements and demonstrate support for elected officials, not resist legislation and organize regulations.

Federalist attacks on Republican popular politics triggered a backlash that helped secure two major Republican electoral victories at the end of the decade. However, rather than guaranteeing the place of grassroots dissent in American political culture, the Republican ascendancy initiated a new threat. Republicans increasingly trusted electoral politics and mobilized in support of officials. At the same time, Federalists proved hesitant to engage in significant popular action to resist or regulate the government. As the age of Federalism came to an end, the traditions of popular political expression hovered on the verge of extinction.

During the 1799 regulation, eastern Pennsylvanians erected nineteen liberty poles as part of their resistance to the Direct Tax, Stamp Tax, and Alien and Sedition Laws.[2] Communities gathered to construct their poles, adorn them with political messages, and toast their cause. For instance, Henry and Peggy Lynn Hembolt hosted a pole-raising at their home in Montgomery County on the evening of December 22, 1798. The Hembolts and their friends passed around whiskey and cider while they made their decorations: a liberty cap and a board that read "The Constitution Sacred, No Gagg laws, Liberty or Death." Their pole condemned the Sedition Law as unconstitutional and linked their display with the Revolutionary struggle.[3]

The soldiers and militiamen sent to put down Fries's Rebellion resented the poles, especially Captain William Montgomery's Lancaster Troop of Horse. Montgomery and his troop were prominent Federalist leaders in their community. Montgomery and nine of his men served on a committee of correspondence supporting James Ross, the Federalist candidate for governor in 1799. Indeed, Ross had been second lieutenant of the Lancaster Troop earlier in the decade. Several men of the troop represented Lancaster in the state legislature, and two of them, Thomas Boude and Robert Jenkins, sat as Federalists in Congress from 1801 to 1803 and 1807 to 1811, respectively. The troop despised the Republican opposition movement and signed a circular denouncing them as being "opposed to the whole administration of the Federal Government; and under the pretense of supporting the Constitution, are assailing it with all the Arts that malice can invent." Including, of course, liberty poles.[4]

As the Lancaster Troop set out in the spring of 1799, their orders were to rendezvous with several other troops in Reading, Berks County, before riding on to Northampton. When the troop arrived in Reading, they were infuriated to discover that four residents had raised liberty poles on their properties. Viewing the poles as an insult to government and a troubling display of Republican audacity, the Lancaster Troop made their way to the offenders' homes.[5]

On the morning of April 3, fifteen members of the Lancaster Troop arrived at the house of Jacob Gossin, a blacksmith. They seized Gossin's workmen, pointed their pistols and swords at him, and demanded that he destroy the liberty pole in his yard or they would pull down his house. "Like highwaymen," Gossin described, "with a pistol in one hand and a sword in the other, they approached me, threatening to dispatch me instantly, if I uttered one word." As Gossin hesitated, one of the men allegedly kicked his child and threatened his wife. When he still refused to fell his pole, the militiamen seized Gossin's ax and downed it themselves. They then rode on, carrying away the ax.[6]

The troop went next to the home of John Strohecker, a mason, arriving at noon. As Strohecker and his family were eating lunch, the Lancaster Troop entered the house. Inside, they found a small wooden pole with a rag on top, a pretend liberty pole that Strohecker's children had made. The men took the pole outside and cut it to pieces, "to the great terror of the children." They reentered the house, according to Strohecker, "with their swords drawn, cursing and swearing most profanely and violently." The troopers stole several of Strohecker's rudders, as well as the rag that had adorned the children's pole.[7]

The militiamen next visited Rudolph Sample. As he exited his house, they surrounded him and ordered that he cut down the liberty pole that stood a few yards from his front door. Sample refused. The men then pointed their swords at him, insisting, Sample claimed, "that in case I made the smallest hesitation, they would beat me in a manner that would make me repent my non-compliance." Sample acquiesced and felled his liberty pole under the watchful eyes of the troopers, who next rode to Isaac Feather's house.[8]

Feather, an innkeeper, came outside to investigate when he heard the front window of his house shatter. He found the men of the Lancaster Troop standing in his yard. The militiamen seized Feather and demanded that he cut down the "damned liberty pole" that stood in front of his house. The men warned Feather that should he hesitate or resist, "they would run their swords through [his] body." Once Feather downed the pole, the men departed.[9]

Word of the Lancaster Troop's campaign circulated through Reading that evening. The following morning, Jacob Epler and his neighbors stood guard at the liberty pole near his house. The Lancaster Troop approached Epler's property, but stopped about eighty yards away upon seeing the armed defenders. After a brief parlay between the two parties, the men of the troop admitted that they had no formal orders to cut down the liberty pole. They rode away for Northampton, allowing Epler's pole to remain standing and eliciting cheers from his supporters.[10]

On April 9, the local Republican newspaper, the *Reading Adler*, printed an article by the pseudonymous "A Friend to Truth," who condemned the troopers' harassment of the people of Reading. The author detailed their trip through the area and alleged that this "party of banditti" terrorized women and children in their crusade against "the Ensign of true Liberty." "A Friend to Truth" also claimed that the militiamen had flogged a young boy who begged them not to throw pieces of a torn-down liberty pole into the Schuylkill River. The author denounced the violence as suited only to "a country where despotism prevails." To the Lancaster Troop, these were fighting words.[11]

Eleven days after the *Reading Adler* ran the condemnatory article, the Lancaster Troop rode back to Reading to await their discharge from MacPherson. Robert Goodloe Harper, a Federalist from South Carolina who was serving as MacPherson's aide-de-camp, accompanied them. As a congressman, Harper had helped to formulate the Alien and Sedition Acts and campaigned vigorously for their passage. He firmly believed that only a strong federal government and a large standing army could protect Americans from the French menace. Any attempt to challenge that authority posed a national security risk. Accordingly, after the *Reading Adler* criticized the federal force, Harper led the Lancaster Troop to the newspaper's door.[12]

Harper and the troopers barged into the printing office and accosted the editor, Jacob Schneider. They demanded to know the identity of "A Friend to Truth," but Schneider refused. "Like banditti of robbers and assassins," he reported, they "with violence forced me out of my office . . . damning themselves if I did not proceed instantly without the smallest resistance, they would with their swords split my scull, cut off my head, &c." The men marched Schneider to a nearby inn where Captain Montgomery lodged. He interrogated Schneider, who still withheld the name of the author. Infuriated, Montgomery promised that the tight-lipped editor would "feel the effects of our displeasure for six months at least." The captain ordered his men to take Schneider to the Market House and give him twenty-five lashes. Forced to strip at gunpoint, Schneider felt six cracks of the Lancaster trumpeter's cowhide whip before Captain Thomas Leiper's Fourth Troop of Philadelphia City Cavalry, a Republican unit, intervened to stop the violence.[13]

After his whipping, Schneider applied to the local magistrate for warrants to arrest his attackers, but Montgomery blocked those arrests. Montgomery marched his troop out of Reading the next evening. Republicans denounced the Lancaster Troop's violence and evasion of justice as a dangerous precedent. The *Aurora* challenged its readers, "After the outrages which were committed . . . in Reading, which of you will say, that it may not be his turn next, to be assaulted in his house and treated with barbarian fury?" The Federalist threat to political expression was not abstract—the incidents in Reading demonstrated that Federalist militia units could invade private property and violently assault those who dared to criticize them with impunity.[14]

In contrast, the Federalists described the events in Reading as an essential defense of law and order. Gottlob Jungmann's *Weekly Advertiser of Reading*, a Federalist rival to the *Reading Adler*, claimed that Captain Montgomery and his troop had, in fact, met no opposition in their quest to rid Reading "of those Nuisances which have so long reared their audacious heads and waved their flags as a signal for sedition and defiance to the Laws." Omitting the vigorous defense of Epler's pole, Jungmann maintained that the troop felled the poles without any complaint or interference from the community. As for the whipping, he contended that the *Reading Adler*'s charges were so outrageous and unwarranted that they entitled the Lancaster Troop to seek satisfaction. While Jungmann clarified that he did not condone extra-legal violence, he emphasized that Schneider must have foreseen the possibility that "*his* hide would pay" when he decided to publish the article.[15]

Other Federalists on the Northampton expedition also came to the Lancaster Troop's defense. On May 10, Harper and Jonathan Williams, another of MacPherson's aides-de-camp, wrote to the *Aurora* to vindicate Montgomery and his troopers. Like Jungmann, they denounced the "sedition poles" as an attempt to undermine representative government and the laws of the nation. Harper and Williams contested the accusations of misconduct during the expedition, writing that the militiamen "confined themselves, entirely to cutting down the Sedition-poles" and did so with "the utmost propriety towards the inhabitants." They claimed that the Lancaster Troop had met no opposition as they passed through the area and so required no coercive methods. This narrative of events stripped the liberty poles of their symbolic power to stand for the popular will and signal Republican strength, and enabled Harper and Williams to imply that the troop fulfilled the majority's wishes by destroying them. They conceded that the troop did confront Schneider at his printing office after hearing of the *Reading Adler*'s spurious charges against them. However, in their version of events, Schneider confessed that he had written the condemnatory article. The trumpeter administered six lashes not for withholding the identity of "A Friend to Truth," as Republican reports had claimed, but for admitting that he was the author.[16]

The Federalist press rallied to Harper's and Williams's version of events. The *Philadelphia Gazette* extolled the two men's "candor and politeness," stating, "we could not desire a more clear or dispassionate refutation of the various slanderous imputations which have recently issued from the Aurora." *Porcupine's Gazette* insisted that their letter provided "an ample refutation of the infamous falsehoods, promulgated through the channel (or rather the *gutter*) of the [*Aurora*]." Federalists saw cutting down liberty poles and punishing a libelous editor as appropriate forms of popular action. Montgomery and his men had acted like responsible citizens by restoring obedience to an elected government among a rebellious minority. Moreover, given the troop's directive to assist in putting down Fries's Rebellion, their actions clearly aligned with their overall mission and authority while in the area.[17]

In response to Harper's and Williams's account, the *Aurora* printed a letter to the editor by "Marcellus," who reminded his readers that "*Sedition poles* are what were called in 1776, '*liberty poles.*'" He asserted that the Lancaster Troop had committed illegal acts of trespass and violent intimidation, for which the *Aurora* had provided "full and decisive evidence." "Marcellus" cited the admission of Schneider's whipping as proof that the troop did not "confin[e] themselves to cutting down Sedition poles," as the Federalists had claimed. "And yet," he concluded, "Mr. Harper sets up for a lover of law and order and an enemy to Jacobins—and he expects the public to give credit to what he says!" The Reading incident revealed the Federalists as hypocrites who professed to hate unlawful violence and disruption and yet committed such acts against those with whom they disagreed.[18]

Republican fury intensified after General MacPherson and President Adams commended Montgomery and his men for their "orderly and soldier-like conduct" in suppressing Fries's Rebellion. To Pennsylvania Republicans, this high-ranking approval demonstrated the administration's complicity in the violence. The *Herald of Liberty* criticized the president's "audacity" in thanking militiamen who acted more like "the cruel master of a Turkish Galley, than men who were sent by the President to enforce Law & Good Order." The *Aurora* similarly denounced MacPherson, who "said much about the fitness of obedience to the laws; but whether he performed his promises, and whether he manifested *his* respect and reverence for the laws, let the case of SCHYNDER [sic] declare, which happened under his nose."[19]

Republicans and Federalists used their press coverage of the incident to advance their own ideas of the role of citizens in a republic. Federalists commended the Lancaster Troop for practicing a popular politics of assent that reinforced government authority and the will of the majority. Indeed, the troop had acted within its mandate to compel obedience to the law. But to Republicans, the Lancaster Troop's campaign against the people of Reading offered further proof of Federalist misrule. The troop's assault on political expression would, according to "A Friend to Truth," "be more apt to excite the people to insurrection and raise them against their government, than to enforce obedience and peaceable quietness." They regarded the Federalists as posing the greatest threat to national stability because of their intolerance of popular political participation.[20]

The *Aurora*'s coverage of the Northampton expedition led to another confrontation at a Republican printing office. Leiper and his men submitted letters to the *Aurora* detailing the misconduct by Federalist troops. The Republican militiamen described troops breaking into houses in the middle of the night, requisitioning supplies and billeting in civilian homes without compensation, cutting down liberty poles, and burdening prisoners with heavy chains and long marches. "Had I conceived that some things which I have witnessed here, could have taken place, I should never have given my assent to march a mile on the expedition," wrote one disgusted correspondent. Leiper's men stressed that the guilty parties in Northampton surrendered voluntarily and displayed no violent sentiment. They contended that a force of such size imposed an unnecessary burden on the local population and constituted a foolish flexing of federal muscle.[21]

On May 15, John Morrell, captain of the Third Troop of Philadelphia City Cavalry, and his lieutenant, Pieter Miercken, entered the *Aurora*'s printing office and demanded to know who had written the letters. The editor, William Duane, refused to name the authors. The men left, but returned two hours later with thirty reinforcements. The group descended upon Duane, hitting him several times and dragging him out of his office by the throat. Once outside, the men continued to rain down blows, eventually also using a cowskin. The assailants left Duane unconscious in the street.[22]

In the attack's aftermath, Duane linked his assault to the precedent set by the Lancaster Troop in Reading. After authorities ignored such a blatant contravention of justice, Duane maintained, "it was hardly to be expected that any *republican* printer or editor should be exempt from similar violence." In fact, Duane contended that his attackers whipped him "in imitation of *Captain Montgomery*" and his men. Frustrated by the authorities' inaction and fearful of further assaults, Pennsylvania Republicans pinned their hopes for change on the upcoming gubernatorial election.[23]

With incumbent Thomas Mifflin not running, the 1799 race for the governor's chair pitted Republican Thomas McKean against Federalist James Ross. McKean served as chief justice of the Pennsylvania Supreme Court, and Republicans celebrated his credentials as a signatory to the Declaration of Independence and veteran of the Revolutionary War. In contrast, Ross had avoided military service and, as a senator, had helped to write the Sedition Bill. Republicans underscored these political sins by linking Ross to the events in Reading. They contended that, if elected, Ross would complete the Federalists' mission of silencing dissenting voices. He was, as one article insisted, "the candidate of *the Lancaster county* troop."²⁴

Republican writers adopted the idea of the partisan "dupe" pioneered by the Federalists and hoped that the Federalists' recent violence would open the people's eyes to the deceit. "Numbers have been induced to join their party, not from an evil design, but merely from thinking them the real friends to the country," observed Philip Morin Freneau, a Republican writer and newspaper editor. But the Federalists have "thrown off the mask," for "Captain *Montgomery's* new method of *preserving the laws inviolate*, [has] clearly exhibited the cloven foot." The Republican press insisted that the recent attacks proved that the Federalists were tyrants who must be vigilantly opposed: "The conduct of the Lancaster troop ought to awaken [the citizenry] to a sense of danger. If such is *federalism*, it is highly time they understand it and guard against it." With Ross as governor, any Republican who attempted to express dissent "will be served, according to the examples you have seen in Reading and Philadelphia." The election offered the chance to protect popular political expression and so preserve the people's ability to combat government tyranny.²⁵

The Federalists, on the other hand, warned that a Republican governor would exacerbate instability. By electing a Federalist, citizens could "suppress the spirit of anarchy and insurrection; [and] retain the true republican characteristics—equality of rights and subjection to the constitution and laws established by the will of the whole society." Federalists alluded to both the Whiskey Rebellion and Fries's Rebellion as evidence that Pennsylvania Republicans were anarchic rabble-rousers who could not be entrusted with power. Several members of the Lancaster Troop served on committees of correspondence in support of Ross, believing that only his election would ensure the "happiness and tranquility of the state."²⁶

But the Republican press flipped their opponents' accusations of disorder and claimed instead that the Federalist troops' lawlessness proved that Ross and his ilk posed the real threat of anarchy. "Let the people look to the case of SCHYDER [sic]," declared the *Aurora*. "No man can say, that his turn may not come to be tied up to a post and whipped at the discretion of a banditti—If the laws are no longer to protect the citizen, let it be publicly announced, that each citizen may arm himself and prepare for his defense." The *Herald of Liberty* concurred, arguing that "the extreme indifference" with which the administration viewed such "a flagrant breach of the law by a military force" demonstrated that "our Liberty is only the phantom of a skeleton, & our Constitution truly, a bundle of miserable shifts and expedients." It was the Federalists, not Republicans, who would doom the republic.[27]

By August, Pennsylvania Republicans felt confident that the events in Reading had increased anti-Federalist sentiment among voters. Elijah Griffiths, a doctor at the Philadelphia almshouse, wrote to Jefferson that "the whipping business which follow'd the Northampton expedition" had soured many in Pennsylvania against the Federalists. He had "no doubt of Mr. McKean's being Elected to the Governor's chair by a very respectable majority." Washington, too, saw a connection between liberty poles and Republican electoral prospects. In a letter to Jonathan Trumbull, he lamented, "Let that party set up a broomstick, and call it a true son of Liberty, a Democrat, or give it any other epithet that will suit their purpose, and it will command their votes in toto!" He added, "As an analysis of that position, look to the pending Election of Governor, in Pennsylvania."[28]

As the Republican press had hoped, and Griffiths and Washington had prophesized, McKean won with 53 percent of the popular vote that November. With the memory of the Lancaster Troop's treatment fresh in their minds, Reading Republicans turned out in record numbers on election day. In the congressional and presidential elections of 1796, Reading's Berks County had voted only 43 percent and 55 percent Republican respectively. In the 1798 congressional election, however, that number rose to 69 percent. In the 1799 gubernatorial election, the county voted 84 percent Republican. In the borough of Reading, voters delivered 86 percent for McKean. Statewide voter turnout for the previous three gubernatorial contests had hovered around 30 percent. For the election of 1799, this figure jumped to 57 percent. In Berks County, 80 percent of all registered men voted in the election. The 1799 election found the people of Reading more politically engaged and anti-Federalist than ever before.[29]

Still, McKean was an unlikely champion for liberty pole–raisers and their allies. Only five years earlier, pole-raisers had burned McKean in effigy for his criticism of Pennsylvanians who violently opposed the whiskey excise tax. While he became a staunch Republican over the next few years, he never publicly changed his position against extra-legal political action. Nevertheless, in 1799, the vast majority of Reading men cast their vote for him. Their recent tangle with Federalist troops helped explain McKean's overwhelming success in Reading.[30]

The 1799 gubernatorial election in Pennsylvania offered a rehearsal for the presidential election of 1800. Republicans had seen the success of emphasizing Federalist misconduct. They positioned a vote for Jefferson as the best, and perhaps last, step to defend American liberty and the right of the people to engage in popular politics. But as in Pennsylvania, Republicans rallied behind a candidate who ultimately did not share their views on grassroots resistance and regulation.

The Republicans celebrated McKean's victory as the beginning of a positive shift in the party's political fortunes. After the election, James Monroe wrote to the new governor to congratulate him and augur his victory as a sign of things to come. "I considered [your election] as the happy commenc[e]ment of a change in our political system," he wrote. "I trust we are daily gaining ground, and that the election which is to take place this fall will secure for us—those liberties we acquired by revolution." McKean also believed that the tide of public opinion had turned against the Federalists. "I can assure you there is now a strong counter-current," he told Samuel Adams, "and our old fashioned republican principles are once more become fashionable." It seemed as though the Federalists' grip on power was coming to an end.[31]

As the Republican elite celebrated, their supporters similarly cheered the dawning of a new era. "May the example of Pennsylvania be followed by the Union," cried the citizens of Potts Grove in Montgomery County as they toasted McKean's triumph. "Rarely has so great a cha[n]ge taken place in the minds of any people, as the State of Pennsylvania," declared the *Herald of Liberty*. Confident in their ability to replicate McKean's victory, Republicans anticipated the 1800 presidential contest with excitement and expectation.[32]

Echoing the McKean campaign, the Republican press reminded its readers of the objectionable legislation of 1798 and argued that another Federalist electoral victory would guarantee a further assault on popular political activity. Charles Pinckney, cousin of the Federalist Charles Cotesworth Pinckney, explained that voters had to use the election as an opportunity to demonstrate "a marked disapprobation of this [sedition] law, by a change of men." Voting Republican would, he argued, "enable your members fully to know what are your opinions, how far you will go, and how much you are content to bear." In this way, Republicans positioned the 1800 election as a referendum on the Adams administration's controversial legislation and an opportunity to avoid further obnoxious laws.[33]

Republican newspapers also reported on intensifying liberty pole conflicts as the election neared. On July 4, 1798, in Hackensack, New Jersey, local Federalists had vandalized the town's liberty pole by stealing and burying the liberty cap that had stood atop it. The *Centinel of Freedom* warned the pole's assailants that their actions "had the good effect to awaken the people of this country from a lethargy into which they appeared to have been falling . . . and roused them to farther exertions of the same nature." Undeterred, the Federalists chopped down the pole in the winter of 1800—an action, the *Centinel of Freedom* claimed, that demonstrated "that the Anglo-Federalists of that place, begin to be *panic struck* as to the event of the ensuing election, knowing that the people of that County are beginning to arouse from their former state of lethargy and supineness." Federalist direct action offered additional evidence of their weak position and further reason to vote against them in the fall.[34]

Republican politicians and editors hoped that the Federalists' objectionable legislation and their draconian methods of enforcement would rouse the citizenry to the danger that the party posed. Republicans adopted the Federalists' language of dupery and claimed that the Federalists' misrule would reveal their elitism and corruption. One Republican paper declared, "the people at large will not be duped any longer by those *exclusive federalists*, the mist is fast dispelling from before their eyes." The Republican leadership also subscribed to this theory. In a letter to Edmund Pendleton in January 1799, Jefferson predicted that the Alien and Sedition Laws, the Stamp Tax, the Direct Tax, and the expansion of the military would ensure that "the understanding of the people could be rallied to the truth . . . by exposing the dupery practised on them." The liberty pole in Small Lotts, observed one newspaper, demonstrated that "the people" had begun to "enquire" as to the cause of their persecution and learned "how they have been duped by a certain class of men in the county, and the genuine republican cause thereby strengthened." Finally, the people were ready to strike back.[35]

Once the citizenry awoke to the Federalist danger, Republicans maintained that they would win the election handily. Like their opponents, Republicans bought into the concept of an imagined American consensus disrupted by a fringe partisan movement. The *Centinel of Freedom* asserted that "there is a large majority of republicans in the aggregate of the United States" and that the Federalists' "evil machinations and villainous intrigues" had obscured this reality. One Republican estimated that only "*one tenth* of society" were true Federalists and that the remainder of their followers had been "secured by favors, or deluded, by their enchantments." He warned his listeners against confusing "the *deceiving few*" with "the *deceived many.*" Most Americans would align with the Republicans once they realized their mistake.³⁶

The Federalists, on the other hand, greeted McKean's election with apprehension. Like their opponents, they saw in their Pennsylvania defeat the probability of more losses. Pennsylvania congressman Samuel Sitgreaves wrote to a colleague in Massachusetts of his "despondency" over "the recent triumph of Jacobinism in Pennsylvania, at the Election of Governor, the general interest which that occasion had excited throughout the Union, and the possible influence of the event on the many." Another Federalist declared that the Republican victory marked a "gloomy aspect" on the "political horizon." "I shall not be surprised ere long we see a *McKean* at the head of every public department," he lamented. Federalist printer William Cobbett predicted that the Republican capture of "undeniably the most influential State in the Union" had unleashed "a struggle, which will terminate in the complete triumph of Democracy." They could not afford a repeat in 1800.³⁷

The Federalists feared that the Republicans had embraced their prescriptions for political action through elections, not just crowd action. "Here [at the polls] at last the jacobins have taken their post, and here they have intrenched themselves to assail our sober and orderly liberty," warned Fisher Ames. Federalists worried that the critics of government had channeled their talent for mobilizing extra-institutional action into turning out Republican voters. A Federalist circular in New Jersey explained their tactics: "On the expiration of his [Mifflin's] office, the present governor was [brought] in on the same principles, which now serve the advocates of Mr. Jefferson: The same *means* were employed in boasting of *republicanism* and crying out, against *government* and *taxes."* Ames similarly warned that "the Jacobins have been everywhere in movement, preparing every engine of power and influence" to win the presidency.³⁸

Amid these concerns, Federalists took solace in their conviction that radical Republicans had duped most of their supporters. In a sermon to congregants in Concord that summer, a Federalist minister asserted that "by far the greater part of those who have appeared in opposition to government, have been influenced and misled by false information." He assured his listeners that once properly informed, the administration's critics would reverse their positions. Writing to his brother from Monongalia County, Virginia, Peregrine Foster explained that although his neighbors possessed "prejudices against the measures of Government," it took only "twenty minutes" of reasoned explanation to "remov[e] the veil which misrepresentation and prejudice had placed over their political eyes" and turn them into "firm Federalists." Foster believed such a feat could be repeated across the nation.[39]

Fearing that Republican efforts outpaced their own, Federalists exhorted each other to combat the Republicans' misinformation campaign and emphasize the threat that Jefferson's election posed. One writer compared the exigencies of the ensuing election to those of the Revolution. "It is high time therefore, for us to awake from our lethargy, and attend to the means of our safety," he warned. New York minister Claudius Herrick, too, stressed the importance of the election and the growing strength of the Republicans. "And will Federalists still slumber? . . . Let them wake to their duty—defend our social institutions—support men of integrity, and tried virtue, and vindicate our constitution and government against the machinations, and calumnies of Jacobins," he declared. "The infernal *spirit of Jacobinism* never sleeps," warned the *Columbian Centinel*.[40]

In particular, Federalists filled their publications with accusations that Jefferson was an atheist and would usher in an age of godlessness and disorder. One pamphlet explained, "if there be no God, there is no law." Hence, any vote for Jefferson would be a vote "to destroy religion, introduce immorality, and loosen all the bonds of society." Federalists argued that Jefferson's alleged atheism proved his affinity for Jacobinism and that his election would unleash an American version of the French Terror. "Convulsions, tumults, insurrections, terror and destruction are but the natural fruit of having such ambitious, unprincipled and atheistical characters in office," insisted Noah Worcester of Concord. Federalists needed only to remind themselves of the disturbances of the past decade to confirm that Republicans were hostile to all hierarchy, order, and authority.[41]

But the Federalists fell short. That fall, Jefferson won nearly 62 percent of the popular vote and eight more electoral college votes than Adams (although tying with his running mate, Aaron Burr, and eventually elected by the House of Representatives). Of the counties that had hosted liberty pole conflicts in the preceding years for which election data is available, 89 percent voted Republican. As historian Alfred F. Young succinctly put it, "The 'people-out-of-doors' had come indoors to vote." Republicans invoked the Federalists' legislation and attacks on dissenters to deny Adams a second term. But Jefferson's election was not a victory for the tradition of community mobilization and resistance that grassroots Republicans championed. As president, he proved intolerant of popular displays of opposition and eschewed the radical strand within the Republican coalition that had helped propel him into office.[42]

On March 4, the day of Jefferson's inauguration, Republicans across the country took to the streets in celebration. They paraded through their towns, played music, raised liberty poles, and toasted to the "completion of the revolution of 1776, and the commencement of the era of true liberty." A Rhode Island paper declared that "The FOURTH OF MARCH, 1801, will become as celebrated in history as the 4th of July, 1776. . . . The election of a Republican President is a new Declaration of Independence." But in office, Jefferson proved cool to any form of a politically radicalized and active citizenry.[43]

Jefferson first indicated his position in his inaugural address. He emphasized that "absolute acquiescence in the decisions of the majority" constituted "the vital principle of republics" and the bedrock on which the American experiment stood. Although he clarified that "the minority possess their equal rights," his majoritarian stance left no room for the citizenry to regulate the government. Rather, Jefferson left it to institutional politics to defend minority rights: "equal law must protect [them], and to violate would be oppression." Jefferson hoped that the federal government could rule by consensus and avoid the development of an opposition. Now that the people had elected representatives who would govern for the public good, partisanship could give way to harmony. "We are all republicans, we are all federalists," he proclaimed.[44]

To help achieve this consensus, Jefferson and his fellow Republican elites shunned the more radical elements of their coalition. Although Duane and other radical Republican editors had provided the backbone of the Republican opposition and Jefferson's campaign, the new president snubbed them in his distribution of most government printing contracts. "I think Duane's zeal merits tenderness and satisfaction," Jefferson explained to Madison, "while his precipitancy makes him improper to be considered as speaking the sense of the government." Instead, the more moderate Samuel Harrison

Smith of the *National Intelligencer, & Washington Advertiser* received the lucrative printing contract of the House of Representatives. Jefferson even awarded contracts to some moderate Federalists, including the *Connecticut Journal*'s Thomas Green, the *Rutland Herald*'s Samuel Williams, and the *North Carolina Journal*'s Abraham Hodge. The Federalist press returned the favor by distinguishing Republicans, "the well informed, well disposed citizens, who opposed the federal party," from Jacobins, "the *rubbish* of our community." According to this distinction, true Republicans spurned the radical notion of an active, participatory citizenry as Jacobin nonsense.[45]

Having dissociated himself from his embarrassing left flank, Jefferson then cracked down on his right. In a letter to McKean after the governor's reelection in 1802, the president complained of the "tory presses" who by "licentiousness" and "lying" had "deprive[d] [newspapers] of all credit" with the public. As a cure, he advocated for the states to prosecute a few of "the most eminent offenders." Connecticut, New York, and Pennsylvania officials obeyed and charged a number of Federalist editors with seditious libel against the president. "The Tories in Pennsylvania are not only humbled but subdued," McKean reported to Jefferson. The Republican leadership proved as equally intolerant of popular criticism as their predecessors.[46]

The Republican ascendancy ensnared the Federalists in a bind: they now formed the opposition party, the legitimacy of which they had long denied. Unsure of how to proceed, leading Federalists expressed a range of opinions. Some maintained that the only "remedy for our national decline" was "a total change of our rulers" by election. Others advised that disenchanted Federalists utilize the methods of opposition "designated in our constitution and laws," like petitions and remonstrances, but stop well short of "open opposition to the laws." In a letter to his constituents, Harper affirmed that the Federalist party would not "resor[t] to those factious and profligate arts which have been employed against themselves." Federalists would scrutinize the conduct of the government, but present their criticism based on "truth and fair argument, not by slander, misrepresentation and falsehood." And some, seeing no way forward, abandoned public life. "I renounce the wrangling world of politics," Ames wrote in 1803. "I will not be a Tom Paine for the federal side."[47]

Grassroots Federalists proved less hesitant to express their opposition, although their methods lacked the radicalism of the Republicans. The Napoleonic Wars had strained American relations with Great Britain and France as both nations denied American ships neutral trading rights, seizing their goods as contraband and impressing their sailors into service. To pressure the European belligerents without entering a costly war, Jefferson placed an embargo on all American maritime commerce. But the Embargo Act of 1807 fell heavily on seaport cities where unemployment soared, as well as on farmers who saw their prices plummet due to the contraction of market demand. Federalist newspapers denounced the embargo as a Republican plot to weaken New England commerce. In response, sailors organized, marched, and rioted to show their displeasure. Federalists in New England and New York organized local meetings and flooded Congress with petitions demanding repeal. Many marked the anniversary of the embargo in 1808 as a day of mourning. Citizens lowered flags to half mast, rang church bells and fired cannons, and marched solemnly through the streets.[48]

Still, these Federalist displays lacked the extra-legal violence and resistance of earlier Republican movements. Although smuggling did occur, communities did not organize to break the law, nor did they coordinate with other disaffected areas or enforce unanimity through regular violence and intimidation. Likewise, the Federalist press encouraged acquiescence and the confinement of dissent to institutional channels. "The duty of every loyal citizen [is] to *obey* all its provisions," affirmed the *Columbian Centinel*, advocating that Federalists restrict their opposition to "point[ing] out the impolicy of the measure" and "at the ensuing elections withdraw all confidence from [pro-embargo officials]." The *Boston Gazette* similarly advised its readers to "assemble and express their sentiments upon the measures of the Government in a firm, dignified and constitutional manner!" Federalists should not engage in popular resistance or regulation.[49]

Despite this moderation, Jefferson proved no more willing to countenance political opposition than had his Federalist predecessors. He instructed Secretary of the Treasury Albert Gallatin "to crush every example of forcible opposition to the law." Echoing the words of his adversaries a decade earlier, the president denounced expressions of dissent as "amount[ing] almost to rebellion & treason." On January 17, 1809, Jefferson issued a circular letter empowering all state governors to use the militia, if required, to enforce the embargo.[50]

Meanwhile, grassroots Republicans demonstrated their approval of Jefferson and his policies by raising liberty poles. On July 1, 1802, the residents of Ludlow and Granby, Massachusetts, celebrated abolition of the Whiskey

Excise Tax by raising a liberty pole with the American flag "for the purpose of expressing their hearty approbation of the present administration, and their joy at the repeal of the Internal Taxes." They then toasted Jefferson, Burr, and Congress. On the second anniversary of Jefferson's inauguration, the people of Paterson, New Jersey, gathered by their liberty pole "in commemoration of the day whereon political delusion took its flight, and gave us Jefferson." In 1808, the people of Murfreesborough, North Carolina, erected a ninety-five-foot liberty pole in support of the embargo. "May the Embargo continue until European Despots respect our rights," proclaimed the pole's sign. Rather than an icon of resistance, Republicans now raised poles to affirm their support of government.[51]

British attacks on American shipping continued, as did British arming of their Indigenous allies in North America, leading Jefferson's successor, James Madison, to declare war against the empire in June 1812. As news of the declaration spread, Republicans across the country raised liberty poles as "emblem[s] of their patriotism." But Federalists opposed the war, denouncing it as a mistake driven by partisan and anti-British hysteria. Federalists petitioned Congress, declaring the war "the worst of all possible evils," and held local antiwar rallies. Republicans, in turn, condemned these displays of opposition as treasonous. "A barrel of tar to each state South of the Patomac will keep all in order," Jefferson wrote to Madison. As for the North, he called for the "rougher drastics" of "hemp and confiscation."[52]

The war provoked clashes between grassroots partisans as distrust and suspicion mounted. Republican crowds trashed Federalist printing offices and the homes of suspected pro-British free Blacks. These conflicts occasionally turned bloody, as was the case in Baltimore, where Federalists gunned down Republican assailants that June. Republicans then broke into the city jail and attacked those responsible, killing one and injuring several others. A convention of New York Federalists condemned the violence, arguing that Republican attempts to silence Federalist dissent would create a government "republican in its forms; [but] in spirit and practise, arbitrary and despotic." Perhaps unknowingly, they echoed earlier Republican condemnations of Federalist attacks to the letter.[53]

In the winter of 1814, twenty-six New England Federalists met in Hartford, Connecticut, to protest the war. They issued resolutions that criticized the past decade and a half of Republican governance and called for a series of constitutional amendments to check the South's disproportionate federal power. The delegates sought to revoke the three-fifths clause in the Constitution and to remove the requirement of a two-thirds majority in Congress for declarations of war, embargoes, and admitting new states to the Union. They also proposed limiting the presidency to one term and requiring that the president come from a different state than his predecessor. The Republicans declared the convention treasonous for its challenge to government during wartime. "Such is the character and lot of all opposition," reflected one delegate. "While it struggles, it is faction; when it triumphs, it is the people." Still, the Hartford Convention constituted a far cry from the popular protests of the 1790s. While accused of advocating disunion, the Federalist delegates merely recommended a set of institutional changes to the already existing governing structure. They were not regulators, and they raised no liberty poles.[54]

The First Party System concluded with a series of twists. The Federalists' attempts to secure their vision for the republic by destroying liberty poles and silencing their opponents proved their ultimate undoing. The Republicans won by adhering to the Federalist prescription for political change, shifting from poles to polls. And once in power, Republicans cracked down on Federalist displays of dissent.

But these twists do not amount to a simple role reversal. Grassroots Federalists' popular politics were tamer than those of their Republican counterparts. They organized, petitioned, and demonstrated, but they did not raise liberty poles, nor did they attempt to regulate the government. Likewise, Federalist elites expressed uncertainty over how to act as the opposition party. The Federalists' unease likely softened their dissent. While critical and distrustful of the Republicans in power, they proved hesitant to employ the extra-institutional methods of the colonial era that Republicans had fought to keep alive over the previous decade.

The Republican beat the Federalists at their own game, but their victory came on their own terms. Jefferson's attacks on Federalist expressions of opposition aligned with his earlier reaction to the Republican popular politics of the late 1790s. He was the apprehensive beneficiary, not the catalyst or champion, of the Republican popular movement. But for grassroots Republicans, who distrusted the federal government's centralization of power, the election of officials who would govern according to the popular will was critical. Under Republican rule, grassroots actors transformed the liberty pole from a symbol of dissent that referenced revolution to one that expressed popular approval of the Jefferson and Madison administrations and celebrated the people's triumph over the Federalists. As a result, far from assuring the place of popular political resistance and regulation in American politics, the Republican ascendancy threatened it as never before. [55]

❖ 7 ❖

# Partisan Politics and Poles in the Nineteenth Century

The Whigs of Wheeling, Va. have raised a Liberty Pole *two hundred and thirty feet high*. We hope they will not forget that the essential thing is, to raise their majority.

—The *Log Cabin*, August 8, 1840

The liberty pole's evolution to a partisan symbol, begun under Jefferson, reached its completion with Andrew Jackson's second presidential campaign and first victory. In 1828, Jackson's devotees raised scores of hickory poles—a reference to the nickname "Old Hickory," which the general had earned for his strong performance during the War of 1812. These were purely partisan poles—they represented allegiance to Jackson without expressing a position on current government policy. Democrats raised them to signal their enthusiasm and commitment to Jackson's campaign for president, not to enact resistance or regulation.[1]

This practice outlasted Jackson and spread beyond just his supporters. Throughout the antebellum era, both Whigs and Democrats raised liberty poles for their candidates. There is no better illustration than the 157-foot-tall liberty pole that New York City Whigs raised in celebration of William H. Seward's 1838 gubernatorial victory. The pole-raisers placed a marble slab at the base of the pole that read "Erected by the Whigs and Conservatives, To commemorate their glorious triumph in 1838, Wm. H. Seward, Governor elect, 10421 Majority, New York, Dec. 20th, 1838." Those assembled burned no effigies, circulated no pledges, and stationed no guards—they merely placed election returns at the foot of the pole. Rather than an emblem of popular resistance to government, this liberty pole served as a memorial to the Whigs' electoral triumph.[2]

The Second Party System finished the transformations to American political culture begun at the close of the First. Having witnessed several peaceful rotations of power, antebellum Americans had more trust in institutional politics than their predecessors. Most people accepted the notion of a loyal opposition and heralded partisanship as a boon to democracy. Even Jefferson admitted to a friend in 1811 that political parties "are perhaps essential to preserve the purity of the government, by the censorship which these parties habitually exercise over each other." Competition between political parties reassured many Americans that institutional politics checked the powerful, represented minority views, and invigorated public debate. As a result, they felt comfortable channeling dissatisfaction with government into voting for a preferred party. In other words, they now believed that American institutions could accurately represent the popular will. As a result, critics could focus less on the institutions themselves and more on the people in charge of them.[3]

This emphasis on party competition led more White men to demand and exercise their right to vote. Whereas three-quarters of the states had suffrage property requirements in 1790, only one-quarter did by 1840. By 1860, all states had eliminated property requirements for White male citizens and only six states required tax-paying to vote. The expansion of the suffrage accompanied other political reforms, including secret ballots, party nominating conventions, increased polling places, and the selection of presidential electors by popular vote in every state except South Carolina. Antebellum party leaders also employed more spectacle in their campaigns than before. They vied to mobilize voters with barbeques, bonfires, parades, hot-air balloon rides, and pole-raisings. Due in part to these developments, the Second Party System witnessed the highest voter turnout in American history, peaking at 78 percent in 1840.[4]

But this focus on institutional politics came at a cost—it sacrificed the more decentralized politics of the 1790s pole-raisers and pole-destroyers. Whereas political actors had previously mobilized and articulated beliefs independently of elite politicians and election cycles, they now relied much more so on the mechanisms of representative government. The consolidation of the two-party system, the expansion of White male suffrage, and the confidence in political institutions led most antebellum Americans to seek political change through institutional channels, especially voting. In this new context, regulations waned and the liberty pole became a mere adjunct to electoral purposes—a tame partisan emblem.[5]

By limiting legitimate political activity to institutional politics, antebellum political culture isolated traditional extra-institutional resistance outside of the mainstream, rendering such actions the desperate resort of those on the fringe of the "real" political community. Those who sought change by "proper" means, like moral reformers, used elections, petitions, and resolutions. Even regulators focused their efforts on pressuring politicians and forming voting blocs. Antebellum Americans denounced extra-institutional actors as mobs, rioters, and criminals. Rather than engaging in collective action on behalf of the broader community, these individuals were outsiders who disrupted good order and social peace. These developments pushed the disenfranchised further to the margins and rendered traditional resistance methods illegitimate. So, although ostensibly defeated in 1800, the Federalist vision for politics prevailed as representation largely replaced resistance.

While the liberty pole had undergone significant transformations in the first fifty years of its life, the next fifty proved remarkably stable. Its meaning as a domesticated partisan symbol endured with only two exceptions: the Nullification Crisis and the Civil War. In both instances, clashing ideas of government power and the federal union eclipsed partisan concerns, and so marked a temporary reversion to the type of pole conflicts that dominated the 1790s. But for most of this period, party politics reigned supreme and served as the primary avenue for those seeking political change. And so, antebellum Americans used liberty poles to signal party allegiance, assess supporters' strength and resolve, and mobilize voter turnout. When partisans tore down their rivals' poles, they did so because their opponents challenged their preferred electoral outcomes, not because their foes threatened the survival of republican government.

In the decades after the War of 1812, debates over the citizen's role in American politics continued as some fought to enact a vision of political expression beyond voting and others decried extra-institutional politics as tyranny of the minority. Moral reform provided the major avenue for White middle-class men and women to practice popular politics. For the most part, these movements engaged in institutional advocacy, relying primarily on meetings, petitions, and resolutions to influence legislative change on a particular issue. For instance, by 1831, Sabbatarians, who sought official observance of the Christian Sabbath, sent over nine hundred petitions to Congress demanding an end to Sunday mail service. Likewise, temperance advocates gained tens of thousands of signatures for their petitions denouncing the evils of alcohol. White and Black abolitionists formed associations and petitioned against the institution of slavery, while also attempting to grow their movement through print material and lecture circuits. For those excluded from the franchise, especially White women and people of color, these methods offered avenues for political expression that their status otherwise precluded.[6]

Moral reformers faced opposition from those who denounced them as a threat to majority rule. In his 1829 report on Sabbatarianism, Kentucky congressman and future vice president Richard M. Johnson warned of the "catastrophe" that would befall the United States if it allowed "combination and influence" to dictate policy. Likewise, newspapers criticized the temperance movement for its attempt to "subjec[t] masses of men to their control." William Ellery Channing, a Unitarian preacher, worded his condemnation in even starker terms, drawing a connection among all reformers: "We fear that in this country, an influence is growing up through widely spread Societies, altogether at war with the spirit of our institutions. . . . They are a kind of irregular government created within our Constitutional government." To their critics, reform movements constituted a rival voice to "the people's," one that sought disproportionate attention for minority views by lobbying for legislative change. After all, such organizing would be unnecessary if the majority of Americans supported these causes.[7]

Like the Federalists, critics coupled their arguments with violent crowd action to silence those who challenged the will of the majority. Communities burned prohibitionists in effigy and vandalized their property. Temperance advocates retaliated by breaking into private dwellings and destroying any alcohol inside. Abolitionists received the harshest backlash, suffering arson and brutal violence. In 1835 alone, abolitionists faced over sixty popular uprisings against them in which seventy-one people died.[8]

Debates about dissent, majority rule, and how to seek political change persisted into the antebellum era. But important shifts were underway. Activists proved more willing to employ institutional methods, indicating a greater trust in the political process than in the 1790s. Even regulations shared this trend. The rural, popular movements that arose during the antebellum era to challenge economic inequality bore the marks of a changing political culture in which extra-institutional action appeared increasingly illegitimate.[9]

Rural Kentuckians responded to an economic downturn in 1819, which plunged thousands into debt, by turning to the ballot box. In 1820, over two-thirds of voters elected representatives to the state legislature who were committed to debt relief, but the Kentucky Court of Appeals declared their legislation unconstitutional. In 1824, voters returned a progressive majority to the legislature, which attempted an impeachment of anti-relief judges and, when that failed, created a new court. The so-called "Kentucky Relief Wars" ended in 1826 after the relief side sustained a series of electoral losses.[10]

The New York Anti-Rent Wars more strongly echoed eighteenth-century regulations. In 1839, landlords in eastern New York increased rent rates and tenants organized committees to negotiate with the landlords. Landlords refused to meet with these organizations and retaliated by suing for back rents. But tenants blockaded roads, violently threatened the sheriffs who attempted to serve papers, and disrupted foreclosure sales. As Anti-Rent sentiment spread, regulators returned to the colonial tradition of "playing Indian" by disguising themselves in Indigenous garb. These roving bands assaulted rent-payers, landlords' supporters, and officials who attempted to enforce payment. One participant affirmed the legitimacy of their actions: "Law and order ceases to become binding when the main feature of all law, equality, and the rights of the people to govern themselves is broken down in a manner that would disgrace many a nabob of older countries." Hence, regulation was an appropriate response to unjust laws.[11]

Beginning in 1844, Anti-Renters institutionalized their movement, creating nominating conventions and electoral committees for local and state elected offices. At the same time, the party establishments of both the Whigs and the Democrats began making overtures to Anti-Renters, hoping an alliance with the agrarian movement would give them an electoral edge. In doing so, party men advised the Anti-Renters to cease their extra-legal activities and rely instead on institutional politics. At first regulators resisted, but a display of force by the state militia in the summer of 1845 overawed them and most Anti-Renters turned instead to electoral politics. In 1846, John Young, a Whig, won the governorship, coasting to victory by an eleven-thousand-vote majority, almost all of which came from Anti-Rent areas. After that, the Anti-Rent movement fizzled out.[12]

When dissenters did employ extra-institutional methods, such as rescuing enslaved fugitives, striking, or rioting, the public denounced them as outsiders engaged in illegitimate behavior. Hence, these actors could no longer claim to represent their communities or the popular will. Scholars point to the rise of the professional police force and their crackdowns on crowd action during the antebellum era as evidence of this shift. After all, the police could not suppress legitimate political behavior. "Only if the police could plausibly claim that mob action was itself a *nonpolitical* act would its suppression of that activity also look like a nonpolitical act," explains political scientist Kimberly K. Smith. In the antebellum era, many Americans viewed extra-institutional crowd action not as a method of politics, but rather as a disruption caused by deviants. Often, critics cited the participation of African Americans and immigrants to prove that such activities existed only on the margins.[13]

The transition from the First to the Second Party System transformed American political culture. In the 1790s, many people believed that popular resistance and regulation provided a necessary mechanism for defending liberty from government tyranny. But as the nation gained more experience with democratic politics, Americans' confidence in their institutions increased and they demonstrated a greater willingness to work within them to seek change. As a result, most focused less on the power of the federal government and more on those who held power within it. They dismissed those who sought political change through extra-institutional methods. In this climate, the liberty pole shifted from a protest to a partisan symbol as parties and elections emerged as the seemingly most legitimate and effective means of influencing politics.

The first poles of the era appeared during the 1828 presidential election, which pitted war hero Andrew Jackson against incumbent John Quincy Adams. These poles made from hickory wood evoked Jackson's reputation as a tough, unyielding frontiersman ready to defeat the soft, would-be aristocrat of New England. The hickory poles also drew on the earlier pole-raising protest tradition to reinforce Jackson's image as a political outsider.

They symbolized Jackson's promise to subvert the status quo, challenge political corruption and elitism, and empower ordinary White men. The Jackson campaign emphasized this message by hammering Adams for his alleged "corrupt bargain" with Henry Clay in the presidential election of 1824. Despite winning the most electoral votes, Jackson had fallen short of a majority, forcing the presidential contest into the House of Representatives, where Adams eventually triumphed. President Adams made Clay his secretary of state, leading to widespread accusations that the two men had brokered a "corrupt bargain" behind closed doors.[14]

Adams's supporters denounced the hickory poles as idolatrous and representative of Jackson's blasphemous and anarchic tendencies. "We discover a great similarity between the worshippers of hickory poles, and those who worshipped the golden cal[f] under the Mosaic dispensation," declared the *Delaware Journal*. "The worshippers of Jackson and *hickory poles*, wish to lead this happy people back to barbarism." But the promises of Jacksonianism proved irresistible to most voters, for he won with 56 percent of the popular vote and 68 percent of the electoral college, confining the younger Adams, like his father, to one term.[15]

The liberty pole temporarily reverted to its more radical origins during the Nullification Crisis. In 1828, Congress passed a high protective tariff to stimulate domestic manufacturing. Southerners decried the "tariff of abominations" as a plot to enrich the industrializing Northeast at the expense of the agricultural South, which would pay more for manufactured goods while selling their exported crops on unprotected international markets. John C. Calhoun, Jackson's South Carolinian vice president, led the opposition. Calhoun advanced a doctrine of nullification, which held that a state could deem a federal law unconstitutional and so declare it null and void within its territory. Nullification provided an institutionalized form of regulation—one in which a state government could shelter its citizens from a burdensome federal law. In November 1832, South Carolina convened a Nullification Convention that declared the enforcement of the tariff within the state illegal and threatened secession should the federal government intervene.[16]

Although no lover of tariffs, Jackson could not countenance this assault on majority rule. That December, he issued a proclamation denouncing nullification as unconstitutional and "incompatible with the existence of the Union." Congress passed legislation that gradually reduced the tariff over the next eight years but authorized the president to use military force to compel payment in every state. South Carolina wisely retracted its nullification ordinance.[17]

The nullification controversy temporarily revived debates over regulation's legitimacy, and with them, regulatory liberty poles. In July 1831, fifteen hundred Charleston nullifiers raised a liberty pole with a model ship on top that said "Hurrah for Free Trade." In Greenville, a Unionist stronghold, residents decorated their liberty pole with the American flag to demonstrate their opposition to nullification. Unlike the Democratic hickory poles, these emblems displayed resolve for a cause, not a candidate, and so signaled a brief return to the 1790s brand of pole-raising. By 1833, South Carolina remained the only state without a two-party tradition, which helps explain why the sole exception to the antebellum partisan poles occurred within its borders.[18]

Elsewhere, partisan poles abounded, and not just among Democrats. In 1840, the Whigs eagerly adopted liberty poles as part of William Henry Harrison's Log Cabin Campaign—their retort to a Democratic newspaper's editorial that mocked Harrison's age with the infamous quip, "Give him a barrel of hard cider, and settle a pension of two thousand a year on him, and my word for it, he will sit out the remainder of his days in his log cabin." The Whig press turned the insult into an asset. They celebrated Harrison as a man of the people and painted the Democrats as elitists who turned up their noses at ordinary Americans. Whigs across the nation built log cabins and held mass rallies complete with raucous singing, fiery speeches, and lots of hard cider.[19]

Whigs raised scores of liberty poles alongside their log cabins. Reminiscent of the 1828 hickory poles, the Whig poles positioned Harrison as a non-establishment candidate who would represent the common man. After the Whigs of Providence, Rhode Island, erected their log cabin, they planted next to it a ninety-foot-tall liberty pole—"deep and firm, in token of the depth and firmness of our unified determination"—to support Harrison for president. In Winchester, Virginia, Whigs decorated their log cabin with banners bearing the names Harrison and Tyler. On their accompanying pole, they raised a flag that read "Union of the Whigs for the sake of the Union." In Washington, D.C., the Tippecanoe Club of Washington raised a white flag on their liberty pole for every state that voted Whig in 1840.[20]

The Whigs used the traditional moniker of "liberty pole" to evoke the earlier poles and distance their symbols from the Democratic displays. Whigs emphasized that their liberty poles symbolized "a return to first and correct principles," rather than the hero worship and "hickory pole patriotism" of the Democrats. Occasionally, they even placed liberty caps on top of their poles to demonstrate "the defence of their assailed rights." Despite recalling revolution, the Whigs remained committed to seeking change through institutional means. "From the top of this splendid Pole, on the evening of the 4th of November next, we will wave the stripes and stars, over one of the greatest political victories ever achieved in this or any other country," affirmed the *Hudson River Chronicle*. Their poles, like their opponents', served only to excite and mobilize the electorate to vote—not to resist particular laws. After Harrison succumbed to pneumonia just a few weeks after his inauguration, his supporters flew mourning flags from their liberty poles.[21]

As the antebellum period wore on, partisan poles grew further entrenched in American political culture as raisers linked their poles closely with their candidates. In 1844, the Whigs renamed theirs "Clay poles" and "Ash poles," a reference to Henry Clay's Ashland estate in Kentucky. Likewise, the Democrats referred to their hickory poles as "Polk Stalks," after their nominee, James K. Polk. As the Second Party System gave way to the Third, liberty poles achieved a new uniformity. By the elections of 1852 and 1856, virtually all pole-raisers adorned their poles with flags bearing the two names at the top of their tickets. Liberty poles flying "Scott and Graham," "Pierce and King," "Fremont and Dayton," and "Buchanan and Breckenridge" functioned, like modern-day lawn signs, as markers of the surrounding area's partisan allegiance and a promise to vote the party ticket.[22]

The liberty pole's transformation into a purely partisan symbol allowed antebellum newspaper editors to use pole-raisings to track party feeling across the country and anticipate election results. In 1834, the *Baltimore Patriot* reported that a resident of Southwark, Pennsylvania, cut down the local hickory pole, which had "once [been] surrounded by thousands." No one re-erected it. Instead, a nearby community raised a liberty pole, a sign of growing anti-Jacksonian sentiment. Editors also used the state of a local pole as an indication of the surrounding community's political leanings. For instance, the *North American and Daily Advertiser* described a hickory pole in Bucks County as "shabby and decayed." "Shall we pursue the simile, and reflect how the hickory pole and the hickory party topple down together?" the paper asked. A neglected pole signaled a decline in party loyalty and enthusiasm. By the mid-1840s, the Jacksonian-era hickory poles in eastern Pennsylvania appeared "twisted and shattered," and the flags bearing Democratic messages "ha[d] been torn to ribbons"—a sign, claimed the *North American* of Philadelphia, that the area had switched allegiance to the Whigs.[23]

But editors hailed a strong pole and an enthusiastic raising as a good omen for future party fortunes. In 1844, the *Ohio Statesman* heralded a report of a hickory pole in Bellefontaine, Ohio, with the headline "THE DEMOCRACY AWAKE IN BELLEFONTAINE." In their coverage of pole-raisings, editors cheered the crowds of people present—sometimes numbering in the thousands—as an indication of future voting strength. Editors often bragged that the size of the pole signaled the potency of the pole-raisers' commitment to the cause. "The signs of the times indicate that the head of *James K. Polk* of Tennessee, will culminate in November, as high above that of Henry Clay, as our Polk Stalk does above the Clay Pole on Oglethorpe Street," declared the *Macon Weekly Telegraph*. But commentators also regularly insisted on the importance of translating the excitement of pole-raisings into voter turnout. In 1840, a New York paper reminded Whigs that in addition to raising liberty poles, they must "not forget that the essential thing is, to raise their majority" that fall.[24]

Although the antebellum poles no longer signified popular resistance to government, they remained meaningful and, as a result, contentious. Whig and Democratic papers smeared each other with stories of assaults on partisan poles, each claiming that the other "can't bear the emblem of liberty." But partisan competition for votes, not opposing visions for citizenship, animated these conflicts. Partisans assailed each other's poles to vent frustration, cause mischief, or challenge their rival's dominance in a community.[25]

When partisans re-erected their poles, they did so not to reaffirm their right of political expression, but to demonstrate their undeterred energy to elect their candidate. In 1844, after a handful of Whigs in Columbus tore down a hickory pole bearing the flag "The Democracy of Ohio," Democrats re-erected it and restored their flag. A local newspaper compared the Whig attack to the "corrupt bargain" of 1824. "The righting of the pole, the raising aloft of the flag, reminds us of the times of 1828 and '32," declared the paper, "when that foul bargain was rebuked, and its authors sent into a political retiracy [sic], as eternal as will be the infamy of the transaction." In other words, the Whig attack would inspire a strong Democratic response at the polls in defense of their principles, as voters had done when they elected and reelected Jackson.²⁶

Occasionally, these conflicts turned violent. During the 1834 mid-term elections, a clash between the partisans of Moyamensing, a township near Philadelphia, made national news. The area seemed primed for trouble, as the Whig headquarters, a tavern, stood across the street from the Democrats' tent. The Whigs erected a liberty pole outside of the tavern and surrounded it with ten feet of iron, while the Democrats raised a hickory pole. After the polls closed, rumors of an unexpected Whig upset circulated and several frustrated Democrats attacked their opponents' headquarters. Whigs poured into the street and confronted their assailants. During the melee, the Whigs tore down the hickory pole and, according to a Democratic newspaper, set fire to a wooden bust of Jackson. In response, the Jacksonians attacked the Whig liberty pole, while others threw bricks and stones at the tavern, prompting those inside to respond with gunfire. The Jacksonians charged the building and dragged several people and pieces of furniture outside. They piled the latter against the liberty pole and set it on fire. The tavern quickly began to burn, and the flames spread to several surrounding buildings. According to a Whig newspaper, the Jacksonians refused to let anyone intervene to suppress the flames. "Many were openly threatened that if they put a drop of water on the fire they would be beaten," claimed the *Baltimore Patriot*. Several papers estimated a total of $5,000 in damages, eighteen wounded, and one fatality.²⁷

A similar event occurred in 1840 when the Whigs of northern Baltimore celebrated Harrison's victory by cutting the local hickory pole to pieces. Armed with axes and clubs, the Democrats rushed to defend their pole. The resulting riot left a number of broken windows and several injured, including a police officer and a former mayor. "Political excitement" caused the conflict, explained the Baltimore *Sun*. "In the name of liberty, patriotism, and honor, we beg that more forbearance will be used in these electioneering contests."²⁸

Like their predecessors during the 1790s, partisan papers of the antebellum era smeared liberty pole assailants as monarchists and tyrants. The *Vermont Patriot* lambasted local Whigs as a "tory-whig gang" for their assault on a Democratic hickory pole "in imitation of their tory ancestors of the Revolution." The Whigs similarly painted the Democrats as enemies of 1776. One newspaper claimed that after a group of Philadelphia Democrats had ridiculed the raising of a Whig liberty pole, they "express[ed] their anti-American and monarchical feelings" by raising a hickory pole and adorning it with a flag that said "TORY POLE." Likely apocryphal, this anecdote nevertheless indicates the durability of the liberty pole's Revolutionary symbolism.[29]

More often, editors drew comparisons with the 1790s poles. "A Whig" issued a call for his party men to raise liberty poles throughout the nation in the *United States' Telegraph*. Referring to the Jeffersonians as "democratic Whigs," he positioned the current Whig party as the true heirs to the liberty pole tradition: "It is the legitimate insignia of Whig principles, consecrated by the patriotism and blood of the Revolution, and hallowed and rendered clear by its association with true democracy in the contest of 1800." This association implied that the Democrats inherited the Federalist traditions, which explained their propensity to attack Whig liberty poles.[30]

Democrats, however, cast the Whigs as neo-Federalists continuing the Hamiltonian policy of federal interference in economic development. In contrast, Democrats defended the Jeffersonian celebration of agriculture, individual liberty, and states' rights. Democrats used Whig attacks on liberty poles to reinforce these claims. "Democrats never assail any emblems of liberty," affirmed a Connecticut editorial, just as "Democratic Republicans never attack[ed] liberty poles!" But "not so with the federalists," who destroyed poles regularly, just like the "tory whigs" of the present day. Both sides used their opponents' attacks on poles to paint them as the Federalists reborn.[31]

During the 1840 campaign, the *Ohio Statesman* printed the *Aurora General Advertiser*'s coverage of the Reading liberty pole conflict of 1799 to warn voters against electing Harrison. The editor explained, "By these recollections we wish to impress upon our thinking republican fellow-citizens the fact, that the present party which is organized under the name of '*Whig*,' is *in body and soul* the same, which heretofore was known as the Federal party, and was guilty of such monstrous crimes." While the Federalists had used violence to subjugate American citizens, the Whigs now aimed to accomplish the same result through "pecuniary distress." The paper repeated the same points in three issues that August by reprinting accounts from Schneider and the other victims of Federalist suppression in Reading. The paper concluded the series with a firm warning: "And what reason have we to believe that the same aristocracy under the title of whigs, will behave in a manner less OVERBEARING and TYRANICAL, if they should get the same power into their hands, through the election of a federal President?" The *Ohio Statesman* echoed the McKean campaign, equating Harrison with James Ross and his Lancaster Country Troop of Horse. The paper declared that just as the pole-raisers of 1799 had defeated those Federalists, the "Federalists of the present day" would suffer the same fate.[32]

Although both parties emulated the Republicans in practice, their liberty poles differed in meaning from their predecessors of the 1790s. The newer poles reflected the major transformations in American political culture of the nineteenth century. Unlike the earlier anxieties over partisanship and representation, antebellum Americans embraced electoral politics as an effective vehicle for influence and agitation. Their acceptance of partisanship allowed Americans to differentiate between an individual administration and government as a whole. Hence, most dissatisfied Americans sought redress through a change in officeholders, not popular resistance and regulation. They trusted in the electoral process to defend their liberty and, in between, relied on institutional methods like petitions to influence their representatives. As a result, Whigs and Democrats used their poles to ensure their candidate's election, rather than to resist legislation.[33]

But these developments came at a cost. Partisanship's entrenchment made elections the key to political success, and so elevated voting as the ultimate form of political participation. As ordinary Americans looked forward to election day, their investment in a more regular, extra-institutional form of politics weakened. Electoral politics stripped the liberty pole of its original, more radical meanings as it became a mere campaign symbol. The antebellum era marked the narrowing of political activity originally championed by the Federalists, but ultimately claimed by the Republicans and inherited by both the Whigs and Democrats. They all agreed that popular sovereignty became manifest through representation in national politics, rather than direct and regular participation and regulation. That system held until 1860, when the results of the presidential election proved unacceptable to most in the South. Only then did the liberty pole return to its radical roots.[34]

The election of 1860 pitted Republican Abraham Lincoln against a fractured Democratic field. Illinois senator Stephen Douglas had the backing of northern Democrats, while Vice President John C. Breckenridge claimed southern support. Tennessee senator John Bell led the new Constitutional Union Party. Lincoln, Douglas, and Breckenridge followers all used poles to rally support during the campaign. In Milwaukee, Wisconsin, Republicans described their pole as "a symbol of the straight forward Republican principles" that would encourage citizens to support the party ticket. Elsewhere, editors used pole-raisings to emphasize party strength. For instance, a hickory pole raised by Douglas Democrats in Whitewater, Wisconsin, reassured those who worried that the area "was so steeped in Black Republicanism that not enough Democrats could be found in that vicinity to form a respectable school meeting." Clearly, the Democrats had enough supporters in Whitewater to raise and defend a pole.[35]

Tensions ran high in Occaquan, Virginia, where partisans clashed violently over a Republican pole raised on the Fourth of July with the flag "Lincoln and Hamlin." Many in the area abhorred the pole, believing it a symbol of "Black Republicanism" that threatened to end slavery, amalgamate the races, and subordinate the South. The residents of neighboring Brentsville met and resolved that "the flag was an insult to the people of Virginia, and incendiary in the object it was raised to promote, and should be torn down." Two weeks later, over forty armed men surrounded the pole and hacked it to pieces. Several skirmishes followed, including the beating of the man who owned the property where the pole had stood.[36]

Lincoln won the electoral college with 40 percent of the popular vote and a virtual northern sweep. The South Carolina legislature immediately called for a secession convention. Thousands of Charleston residents greeted the news by flooding the streets and raising a secession pole bearing the state flag. The pole, a Charleston paper reported, offered "evidence of their love and devotion to South Carolina, and their lively sympathies in the great Southern movement of resistance to fanaticism, and the establishment of an independent government." The *Philadelphia Inquirer* maintained that the pole-raisers pressured state officials: "The people have taken the matter of secession almost entirely out of the hands of politicians, and have determined upon prompt action." But the convention delegates agreed with the pole-raisers and unanimously voted for secession on December 20.[37]

Other Deep South states followed suit, and more secession poles sprang up as popular endorsements of the conventions' decisions. Texans in Galveston, Gonzales, and Houston raised poles bearing the lone-star flag. The residents of Mobile erected their pole and fired 101 guns to celebrate the secession of Alabama and 15 for their "sister State of Florida." By February 1861, all seven states in the Deep South had seceded from the Union and formed a new nation, the Confederate States of America.[38]

As Upper South state officials contemplated secession, ordinary citizens erected and destroyed poles to express their views. After residents of Petersburg, Virginia, raised a one-hundred-foot-tall secession pole on the main street, a group of Unionists secretly cut it down just before dawn. Fearing more violence, the mayor ordered a rival Union pole taken down. He then "interdicted by proclamation the erection of poles in the public streets." Similarly, in Knoxville, Tennessee, a gathering of Unionists toppled a secession pole and pledged to "fight against disunion in each and every form, as traitorous and damnable—even if Tennessee seceded." In the wake of Fort Sumter, residents defied local Unionists and greeted their states' secession ordinances with poles bearing the Confederate flag.[39]

Likewise, northerners deployed liberty poles to demonstrate their commitment to the Union and their intention to defend it by force. In Southington, Connecticut, Unionists raised a liberty pole and resolved "that our national government, constitution and liberty must be maintained at whatever cost of treasure and blood." In Winterport and Frankfort, Maine, residents erected a pole bearing the national flag and pledged "to support the Government in the defence of its undoubted constitutional rights." Northern newspapers eagerly reported on the nonpartisan nature of these pole-raisings, stressing that citizens joined together "without distinction of party" to raise a "Union pole." In Aledo, Illinois, Republicans and Democrats took bipartisanship even further by chopping down their two partisan poles, cutting them in half, and joining the pieces together to form a single Union pole. Although the electoral cycle and party competition persisted in the northern states during the war, only a handful of partisan poles appeared.[40]

By erecting poles, both Confederates and Unionists claimed the legacy of the American Patriots. Confederates described secession as an assertion of independence from a tyrannical North. "We recur to the principles upon which our Government was founded," declared Jefferson Davis in his farewell address to the Senate after Mississippi seceded. "We but tread in the paths of our fathers when we proclaim our independence." But Unionists saw the restoration of the Union as a defense of the Revolution's major achievement: a democratic republic protected by the Constitution. They believed that the permanent fracture of the Union would destroy the cause of self-government. "In this great struggle, this form of Government and every form of human right is endangered if our enemies succeed," Lincoln warned an Ohio regiment.[41]

As the war stretched on, poles attracted conflict. In the North, Unionists accused Copperheads—northern Democrats who favored a peace settlement with the Confederacy—of cutting down Union poles. "Miscreants who do such dastardly work are not deserving of the blessings of free government and would look better to emigrate South," declared a Vermont paper after four poles mysteriously toppled overnight. In addition, occupying troops used poles to wage symbolic warfare on the local populace. When Union forces won control of an area, they destroyed secession poles and substituted their own bearing the national flag. Likewise, Confederate troops tore down Union poles and Republican liberty poles whenever possible. Soldiers also used poles to hang effigies of their foes.[42]

Secession and war represented a rejection of institutional and partisan politics in the South. The Confederate States lacked confidence in the Democratic Party's ability to counter the power of a Republican president who had no obligation to southern voters. To them, the election of a sectional president constituted a failure of representative government. Like nullification, this challenge to federal power structures initiated a return to the more radical pole-raisings of the 1790s in which participants erected and destroyed poles to express their political ideas and intimidate their opponents without citing candidates or upcoming elections. Civil War pole-raisers dispensed with references to political parties and instead pledged allegiance to their own interpretations of their Revolutionary inheritance.[43]

After the war, both parties resumed raising poles bearing their candidates' names at election time. But partisan pole-raisings gradually waned as they seemed increasingly old-fashioned. "[The hickory pole is] emblematical, perhaps, of the fact that a great many Democrats are still innocently voting for Jackson, and that the whole party is digging in the dead past for the issues of 1868," scoffed the *Daily Cleveland Herald*. To many embroiled in the complex politics of Reconstruction, raising liberty poles felt out of date—a practice embedded in nostalgia, not political strategy.[44]

The Revolution's Centennial in 1876 offered further reminders of the liberty pole's age, and so, its growing irrelevance. Newspapers relived the redcoats' assaults on Patriot liberty poles, and communities raised "Centennial liberty poles" bearing the stars and stripes as they sang songs, gave historic addresses, and read the Declaration of Independence. These poles stood for the shared past that united citizens of different parties and sections. They communicated benign messages of patriotism and tradition. No one tore them down.[45]

The arc of the liberty pole reveals important transformations in American political culture. As politics became institutionalized in rival parties, Americans accepted a newer and narrower interpretation of popular sovereignty in which political parties limited local dissent by channeling it into national partisan competition. Antebellum Americans largely abandoned the traditions of community resistance and regulation and instead voiced their opinions through institutional methods. They dismissed those who did not as outsiders desperate to attack law and order through illegitimate means. As a result, political participation became more episodic, exclusionary, and controlled by elites.[46]

Of course, the triumph of the Federalist vision had its benefits. After all, traditional popular political methods were not without several flaws, including and especially a reliance on crowd violence. The transformations of the early nineteenth century created a stable system that showed the world that a republic could survive and maintain the confidence and support of the public. But no political system is perfect, and the cracks in this one have widened into the chasms of our present. Modern American politics continues to marginalize calls for institutional reform and instead center two-party competition. The resulting partisan pendulum hampers substantive change and locks the nation into an endless cycle of electoral contests in which all hope for a government that will serve the public good is boiled down to electing the right people to office. And so, political conflict largely plays out among an elite conducting partisan institutions and vying for election, rather than between ordinary citizens around a liberty pole.

❖ EPILOGUE ❖

# "Forgetting While Remembering"

Who can remember what a Liberty Pole is? Have any of us actually seen one and know what it stood for?
—Roy D. Goold, 1983

During the fall of 1919, the New York Sons of the American Revolution met with representatives from the New York Historical Society at Fraunces Tavern to discuss the creation of a liberty pole monument in City Hall Park. They hoped to erect a metal pole on the site where the Sons of Liberty had first raised their poles during the Imperial Crisis. But the men had both the American Revolution and the recently concluded First World War on their minds. Their resolution described the pole as "a memorial of the staunch and unflinching patriotism of the New York Troops and their valor and unparalleled success on the Battle Fields of Europe." In 1921, the group erected their monument. The plaque at its base declared it a commemoration of the "five liberty poles" of colonial New York City and a tribute "in grateful remembrance of all lovers of our country who have died that the liberty won on these shores might be the heritage of the world."[1]

Over sixty years later, the New York Sons of the American Revolution regretted that the monument had not done enough. Member Roy D. Goold penned an article for the organization's magazine that lamented the lost history of pole-raising. "Who can remember what a Liberty Pole is? Have any of us actually seen one and know what it stood for?" he asked. Goold

*Raising the liberty pole, 1776*, engraving by John C. McRae after F. A. Chapman, c. 1875. (Library Company of Philadelphia)

recalled the battles over the New York City liberty poles and the spread of the symbol across the colonies. But few Americans knew this part of their past. "Is it not time to re-erect and protect the Liberty Pole, to restore the forgotten symbol of our Nation, to re-unite it with the Flag?" he wrote.[2]

But the Revolutionary liberty poles have not been entirely forgotten. They live on not only in the New York City monument, but also in late nineteenth- and early twentieth-century art, northeastern street names, and community celebrations. For instance, every April the residents of Bedford, Massachusetts, hold a pole-capping ceremony in which Patriot reenactors raise a liberty pole and place a liberty cap atop it while Loyalist reenactors attempt to interfere. One participant commented, "There are these issues of authority and liberty, and I think it really is important that people understand their history." The annual reenactment deliberately centers the liberty pole as a key part of the American Revolution's story.[3]

Even protestors still rely on liberty poles. In April 2015, advocates for marijuana legalization and D.C. statehood raised a forty-two-foot liberty pole on the National Mall and chained themselves to it. One of the leaders

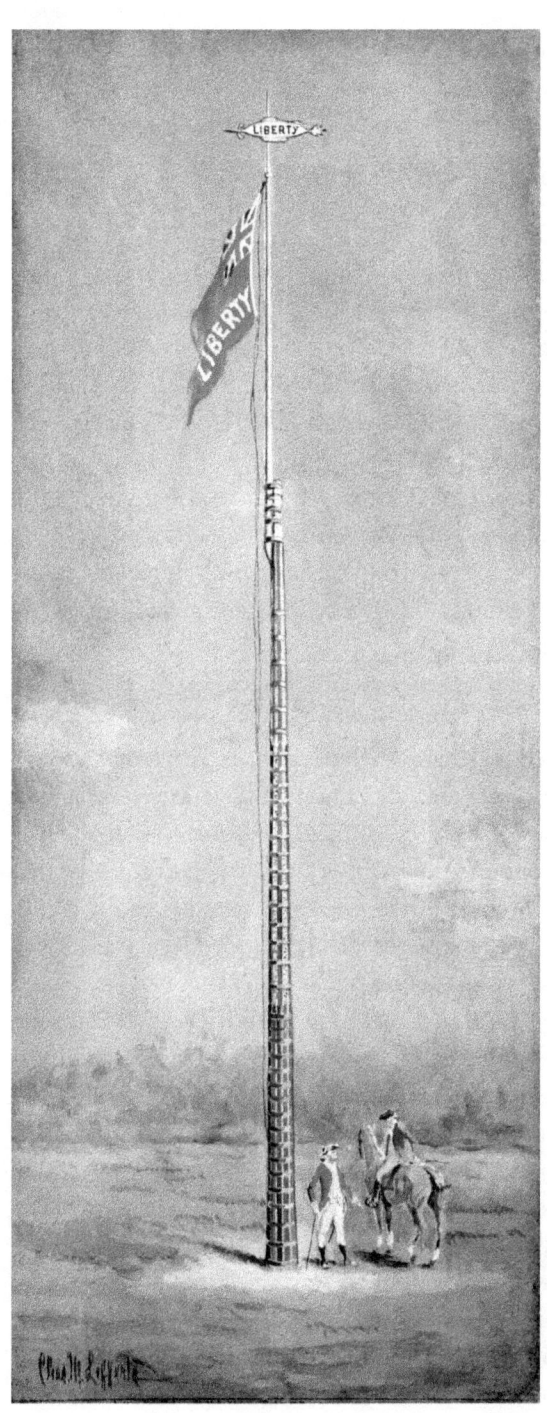

*Scenes from the American Revolution: Fifth Liberty Pole on the New York Commons*, Charles MacKubin Lefferts, c. 1910. (New York Historical Society; gift of Charles MacKubin Lefferts, 1920.130)

explained that their demonstration sought to highlight the federal government's undemocratic control of the District: "We see a lot of similarities between how the English treated the colonists and how Congress treats D.C. residents."[4]

In all of these ways, Americans continue to use the liberty pole to evoke the Patriot struggle and interpret its legacy. For the New York Sons of the American Revolution, the liberty pole calls to mind the Revolution's promise of freedom for all people, in the United States and around the world. For the residents of Bedford, their annual celebration provides a commentary on the balance between government power and individual liberty that the Revolution failed to perfect. For the D.C. activists, the Revolution's promise of self-government remains unfulfilled.

While far from ubiquitous, these efforts have sustained the place of the 1760s and 1770s liberty poles in American popular memory. The 1790s liberty poles, however, remain forgotten. There are no monuments, paintings, or celebrations of these poles. The only recent commemorative pole-raisings occurred as promotions for Liberty Pole Spirits, a whiskey distillery in Washington, Pennsylvania, that aimed to capitalize on the local Whiskey Rebellion history.[5]

Americans' preference for the earlier poles speaks to the broader ways in which popular memory centers the Revolution and overlooks the subsequent contests over its legacy. This "forgetting while remembering," as historian Alfred F. Young put it, offers Americans a simplified narrative defined by British malevolence and American resilience. This story is peopled by a handful of White men who bequeathed an uncomplicated legacy of liberty and prosperity to Americans in their founding documents. A mythic history defined by genius and consensus is comforting to those who look to the glory of the past to heal the wounds of the present. Moreover, phenomena like constitutional originalism and "Founders Chic," the hagiographies that dominate sales of books on early America, both demand and reinforce a cohesive founding vision.[6]

Americans have forgotten the early republic's poles because they represent division. They remind that neither the Revolution nor the federal Constitution yielded singular definitions of citizenship, popular sovereignty, or political expression. There is no pure concept of self-government handed down from the founding generation, nor is there a handbook for how American democracy should operate in practice. The liberty poles of the 1790s reveal the battles of the early republic as a reckoning with the instability of concepts at the heart of American politics. They show how early Americans struggled to define what it meant to live under a government of their own making. They challenge the whiggish view that political power unfolded slowly but inevitably to more and more Americans as they gained the right to vote and hold office. And most importantly, they demonstrate that so many of the features of American political culture that we now take for granted were once new and contested.

Liberty poles are not the panacea for what ails American democracy, but they can remind us that other ways are possible. For a brief period, pole-raisers envisioned a political system in which ordinary people played a more regular and immediate role. But that window closed as Americans increasingly turned to institutional politics as the best and most legitimate form of political participation. This shift was not inevitable—it was the product of choices. Understanding American political culture in this way means that we can imagine alternatives; people can make different choices if they want different results. In other words, there is nothing natural or inherently righteous about the way American politics currently operates. It is the result of paths taken at specific moments in time. There are, as there always have been, other paths to choose.[7]

# APPENDIX:
# RECORDED LIBERTY POLES RAISED, 1766–1799

This information is amassed from a diverse array of available primary and secondary sources. It is likely incomplete. Dates with asterisks are estimates. Some years also are estimates.

1. May 21, 1766: New York City, NY
2. August 11, 1766: New York City, NY
3. September 24, 1766*: New York City, NY
4. March 19, 1767: New York City, NY
5. July 22, 1768: Dedham, MA
6. December 14, 1769*: [unknown], GA
7. No date, 1769: Newport, RI
8. February 6, 1770: New York City, NY
9. May 19, 1774: Farmington, CT
10. September 1, 1774*: New Haven, CT
11. September 5, 1774: Shutesbury, MA
12. October 1, 1774*: Bridgewater, MA
13. October 29, 1774: South Kingston, RI
14. November 1, 1774*: Hanover, MA
15. November 7, 1774*: Sandwich, MA
16. December 17, 1774: Greenland, NH
17. December 30, 1774: Westmoreland, CT
18. No date, 1774: East Hartford, CT
19. No date, 1774: Farmingdale, CT
20. No date, 1774: Northford, CT
21. No date, 1774: Norwich, CT
22. No date, 1774: Barnstable, MA

23. No date, 1774: Braintree, MA
24. No date, 1774: Concord, MA
25. No date, 1774: Deerfield, MA
26. No date, 1774: Granville, MA
27. No date, 1774: Hadley, MA
28. No date, 1774: Machias, MA
29. No date, 1774: Middleborough, MA
30. No date, 1774: Milton, MA
31. No date, 1774: Nantucket, MA
32. No date, 1774: Petersham, MA
33. No date, 1774: Plymouth, MA
34. No date, 1774: Taunton, MA
35. No date, 1774: Vineyard Haven, MA
36. No date, 1774: Williamsburg, MA
37. No date, 1774: Worcester, MA
38. No date, 1774: Hagerstown, MD
39. No date, 1774: Kingston, NH
40. No date, 1774: Portsmouth, NH
41. No date, 1774: Westmoreland, NH
42. No date, 1774: Bergen, NJ
43. No date, 1774: Englewood, NJ
44. No date, 1774: Montclair, NJ
45. No date, 1774: Morristown, NJ
46. No date, 1774: Brooklyn, NY
47. No date, 1774: Easthampton, NY
48. No date, 1774: Hampton, NY
49. No date, 1774: Hempstead, NY
50. No date, 1774: Tappan Zee, NY
51. No date, 1774: Westchester, NY
52. No date, 1774: Carlisle, PA
53. No date, 1774: Providence, RI
54. No date, 1774: Bennington, VT
55. No date, 1774: Springfield, VT
56. No date, 1774: Wheelock, VT
57. March 1, 1775*: Elizabethtown, NY
58. March 1, 1775*: Shawangunk, NY
59. April 1, 1775*: Poughkeepsie, NY

60. June 1, 1775*: Savannah, GA
61. No date, 1775: Berkley, CT
62. No date, 1775: Pitt, NC
63. No date, 1775: Haddonfield, NJ
64. No date, 1775: Pequannock, NJ
65. No date, 1775: German Flatts, NY
66. No date, 1775: Charlestown, SC
67. No date, 1775: Williamsburg, VA
68. July 22, 1776: Huntington, NY
69. August 14, 1776: Boston, MA
70. December 6, 1783: Flat Bush, NY
71. December 13, 1783*: Jamaica, NY
72. No date, 1783: New Utrecht, NY
73. September 4, 1786: Bristol, NY
74. October 22, 1790: Camden, NC
75. December 27, 1792: New York City, NY
76. January 24, 1793: Boston, MA
77. February 6, 1793: Philadelphia, PA
78. July 4, 1794: Sussex, NJ
79. July 9, 1794: Lancaster, PA
80. August 1, 1794: Brownsville, PA
81. August 8, 1794: Washington, PA
82. August 10, 1794: Bullskin, PA
83. August 11, 1794: Bullskin, PA
84. August 13, 1794: Washington, PA
85. August 14, 1794: Madison, PA
86. August 14, 1794: Washington, PA
87. August 15, 1794: Greensburg, PA
88. August 15, 1794: Parkinson's Ferry, PA
89. August 15, 1794: Washington, PA
90. August 18, 1794: Pittsburgh, PA
91. September 1, 1794: Hagerstown, MD
92. September 5, 1794*: Hagerstown, MD
93. September 8, 1794: Carlisle, PA
94. September 8, 1794*: Martinsburg, VA
95. September 10, 1794*: Bedford, PA
96. September 11, 1794: Carlisle, PA

97. September 11, 1794: Strabane, PA
98. September 16, 1794: Chambersburg, PA
99. September 20, 1794: Northumberland, PA
100. September 25, 1794: Washington, PA
101. September 26, 1794: Milton, PA
102. September 30, 1794: Derrstown, PA
103. November 5, 1794: Franklin, PA
104. No date, 1794: Fredericktown, MD
105. No date, 1794: Bedford, PA
106. No date, 1794: Bedford, PA
107. No date, 1794: Bloody Run, PA
108. No date, 1794: near Derrstown, PA
109. No date, 1794: Fayette, PA
110. No date, 1794: Fort Ligonier, PA
111. No date, 1794: Harrisburg, PA
112. No date, 1794: Masontown, PA
113. No date, 1794: Middletown, PA
114. No date, 1794: Northumberland, PA
115. No date, 1794: Northumberland, PA
116. No date, 1794: South Huntingdon, PA
117. No date, 1794: Stony Creek, PA
118. No date, 1794: Morgan's Town, VA
119. January 1, 1798: Wallingford, VT
120. February 24, 1798: Skeensborough, NY
121. March 1, 1798*: Newport, RI
122. April 1, 1798: Huntington, NY
123. April 16, 1798: Salem, NY
124. April 17, 1798: Newark, NJ
125. April 25, 1798: Butternuts, NY
126. May 1, 1798: Paterson, NJ
127. May 7, 1798*: Washington, PA
128. July 4, 1798*: Hackensack, NJ
129. July 4, 1798: Morristown, NJ
130. July 7, 1798: Bloomingrove, NY
131. July 18, 1798: Fishkill, NY
132. July 18, 1798*: Goshen, NY
133. July 18, 1798*: Montgomery, NY

APPENDIX 153

134. July 18, 1798*: Newburgh, NY
135. August 10, 1798*: Herkimer, NY
136. August 13, 1798*: Ulster, NY
137. August 15, 1798: New Cornwall, NY
138. August 15, 1798: New Windsor, NY
139. August 16, 1798: Pownal, VT
140. August 17, 1798: New Hurley, NY
141. August 18, 1798: Florida, NY
142. August 27, 1798: Pleasant Valley, NY
143. September 1, 1798*: Newburgh, NY
144. September 15, 1798: Shaftsbury, VT
145. September 22, 1798: Grenville, SC
146. November 1, 1798: Dedham, MA
147. November 3, 1798*: Springfield, NJ
148. November 5, 1798: Albany, NY
149. November 15, 1798: Vassalborough, ME
150. November 28, 1798: Brownsburgh, VA
151. December 5, 1798: Bushwick, NY
152. December 12, 1798*: Bridgehampton, NY
153. December 12, 1798: Southampton, NY
154. December 30, 1798*: Millerstown, PA
155. No date, 1798: Lower Merion, PA
156. No date, 1798: Williams, PA
157. January 6, 1799*: Lebanon, PA
158. January 6, 1799*: Myerstown, PA
159. January 14, 1799*: Long Island, NY
160. January 23, 1799: Jones Town, PA
161. February 1, 1799: Roxbury, PA
162. February 6, 1799*: Reading, PA
163. February 6, 1799*: Reading, PA
164. February 8, 1799: Southampton, NY
165. February 16, 1799*: Blockley, PA
166. February 22, 1799: Middletown, CT
167. February 22, 1799: New Hanover, PA
168. February 25, 1799*: Jericho, NY
169. February 25, 1799: Greensburg, PA
170. March 6, 1799: New York City, NY

171. March 12, 1799: Hackensack, NJ
172. March 12, 1799: Small Lotts, NJ
173. March 16, 1799: Slauterdam, NJ
174. March 20, 1799: Wallingsford, VT
175. April 1, 1799*: Reading, PA
176. April 1, 1799*: Reading, PA
177. April 1, 1799*: Reading, PA
178. April 1, 1799*: Reading, PA
179. May 6, 1799: Washington, PA
180. May 27, 1799*: Wayne, PA
181. July 4, 1799: Jefferson's Village, NJ
182. July 4, 1799: North Farms, NJ
183. July 4, 1799: Bennington, VT
184. No date, 1799: Newbern, NC
185. No date, 1799: Greenwich, PA
186. No date, 1799: Milford, PA
187. No date, 1799: Millerstown, PA
188. No date, 1799: Penn Township, PA
189. No date, 1799: Weisenberg, PA

❖ NOTES ❖

### Introduction

1. Deposition of Francis W. Gibson, October 11, 1794, Deposition of Anthony Fearer, September 29, 1794, Rawle Family Papers (Historical Society of Pennsylvania); Ridner, *A Town In-Between*, 39–41.
2. Deposition of Francis W. Gibson, October 11, 1794, Rawle Family Papers.
3. Deposition of Francis W. Gibson, October 11, 1794, Deposition of Anthony Fearer, September 29, 1794, Rawle Family Papers; *Dunlap and Claypoole's American Advertiser*, September 20, 1794; Deposition of James Dill, September 28, 1794, Rawle Family Papers.
4. Ridner, *A Town In-Between*, 193.
5. *Carlisle Gazette*, September 17, 1794.
6. *Herald*, July 14, 1794.
7. For Madison's explanation of the difference between a pure democracy and a republic, see Federalist 10.
8. Morgan, *Inventing the People*, 13–14; Frank, *Constituent Moments*, 3–8; Morone, *The Democratic Wish*, 6–7, 44; for more on the idea of crowds as representative, see Smith, *The Dominion of Voice*, 27–28; for an argument that the notion of the popular will forms the foundation of the growth of American government despite an anti-statist political culture, see Morone, *The Democratic Wish*.
9. Rush, "Address to the People of the United States," *American Museum*, January 1787; Frank, *Constituent Moments*, 24.
10. Johnston, *The Correspondence of John Jay*, 3: 319; for recent work on this concept, see Fitz, *Our Sister Republics*.
11. Some books that have particularly influenced my thinking on the broad definition of politics include Freeman, *Affairs of Honor*; Waldstreicher, *In the Midst of Perpetual Fetes*; Camp, *Closer to Freedom*; Zagarri, *Revolutionary*

*Backlash*; Pasley, "*The Tyranny of Printers*"; Ben-Atar and Oberg, *Federalists Reconsidered*; Pasley et al., *Beyond the Founders*.

12. Some important examples include Newman, *Parades and the Politics of the Street*; Bouton, *Taming Democracy*; Slaughter, *The Whiskey Rebellion*; Newman, *Fries's Rebellion*; Travers, *Celebrating the Fourth*; Owen, *Political Community in Revolutionary Pennsylvania*.
13. Deposition of Peter Faulkner, December 10, 1794, Rawle Family Papers.
14. *Centinel of Freedom*, March 12, 1799.
15. Bellion, "Mast Trees, Liberty Poles, and the Politics of Scale in Late Colonial New York," in Roberts, *Scale*, 233; Young, *Liberty Tree*, 365; for a discussion of public space's illusion of neutrality and freedom, see Davis, *Parades and Power*, 13–14.
16. While the 1790s pole-raisings mainly occurred in rural, predominantly White areas, several during the Revolution took place in port cities where people of color likely participated. In the nineteenth century, liberty pole–raisings occurred in cities much more frequently than during the early republic.
17. For more on regulation, see Bouton, *Taming Democracy*; Newman, *Fries's Rebellion*; Frank, *Constituent Moments*.
18. Some prominent examples include Berkin, *A Sovereign People*; Bradburn, *The Citizenship Revolution*; Sharp, *American Politics in the Early Republic*; Bouton, *Taming Democracy*; Slaughter, *The Whiskey Rebellion*; Newman, *Fries's Rebellion*.
19. Some examples include Waldstreicher, *In the Midst of Perpetual Fetes*; Waldstreicher, "Federalism, the Style of Politics, and the Politics of Style," in Ben-Atar and Oberg, *Federalists Reconsidered*, 99–117; Newman, *Parades and the Politics of the Street*; Estes, *The Jay Treaty Debate*; Pasley, *The First Presidential Contest*; Owen, *Political Community in Revolutionary Pennsylvania*; for an argument that a younger generation of Federalists was more accepting of popular politics after 1801, see Fischer, *The Revolution of American Conservatism*.
20. *Pennsylvania Telegraph*, May 30, 1832.

## 1. The New York City Liberty Poles

1. *New York Gazette, or Weekly Post Boy*, February 5, 1770.
2. Smith, *The Freedoms We Lost*.
3. Maier, *From Resistance to Revolution*, 4; Gilje, *The Road to Mobocracy*, 23–25; Countryman, "'Out of the Bounds of the Law,'" in Young, *The American Revolution*, 37–69; Thompson, "The Moral Economy of the English Crowd

in the Eighteenth Century," 76–136; Young, *Liberty Tree*, 110–13; Smith, *The Dominion of Voice*, 25–28; for crowd action as "ritualized refusals of deference," see Smith, *The Dominion of Voice*, 23; for the importance of the Seven Years' War in creating a more unified popular political culture, see Newman, *Parades and the Politics of the Street*, 11–43; Deloria, *Playing Indian*, 10–26; for more examples, see Pauline Maier, *From Resistance to Revolution*, 6–9.

4. Young, "English Plebeian Culture," in Jacob and Jacob, *The Origins of Anglo-American Radicalism*, 189–92; Gilje, *The Road to Mobocracy*, 18, 20–21; Davis, *Parades and Power*, 97; for more on colonial rituals of rough music, see the essays in Pencak et al., *Riot and Revelry in Early America*; for rituals of public justice's transmission and transformation from Europe to North America, see Young, *Liberty Tree*, 144–79; Palmer, "Discordant Music," 5–62; for the difference between elite, organized spectacle and popular festivity, see Davis, *Parades and Power*, 156; Robertson, "Voting Rites and Voting Acts," in Pasley et al., *Beyond the Founders*, 61.

5. Gilje, *The Road to Mobocracy*, 17, 19, 25–30; Travers, *Celebrating the Fourth*, 17; Newman, *Parades and the Politics of the Street*, 11–22; for an argument that Pope's Day was not a plebian holiday, see McConville, "Pope's Day Revisited"; for the evolution of festive culture into the nineteenth century, see Davis, *Parades and Power*.

6. Young, *Liberty Tree*, 110–13; Smith, *The Dominion of Voice*, 25–28.

7. Gilje, *The Road to Mobocracy*, 42–47, 65–67; Irvin, "Tar, Feathers, and the Enemies of American Liberties," 197–238; Young, "English Plebeian Culture," 189–94; Young, "Ebenezer Mackintosh," in Young, *Revolutionary Founders*, 15–32; Molly Perry argues that colonists relied on traditional cultural rituals to "build a sympathetic transatlantic coalition" with those in Britain as part of their bid to win repeal, see Perry, "Buried Liberties and Hanging Effigies," in Hutchins, *Community Without Consent*, 36–66.

8. Maier, *From Resistance to Revolution*, 53–61; Maier, *American Scripture*, 99–107; Deloria, *Playing Indian*, 32–37; Perry, "Buried Liberties and Hanging Effigies," 56–57. For the precedent of crowds pulling down officials' homes, see Countryman, "'Out of the Bounds of the Law'"; Irvin, *Clothed in Robes of Sovereignty*, 140–41; Maier, *American Scripture*, 157–59; Hoock, *Empires of Imagination*, 52; Gilje, *The Road to Mobocracy*, 67; Waldstreicher, *In the Midst of Perpetual Fetes*, 30–32; Peter Shaw has evocatively described these events as "an orgy of symbolic destruction." See Shaw, *American Patriots and the Rituals of Revolution*, 15.

9. *New York Gazette, and Weekly Mercury*, February 12, 1770 (New York Historical Society); *The New-York Gazette*, May 26, 1766 (David Library of the American Revolution); Lurie, "Liberty Poles and the Fight for Popular

Politics in the Early Republic," 676–77; Montresor, *The Montresor Journals*, 367–68, 370 (David Library of the American Revolution); for the news of the Stamp Act's repeal, see *New-York Gazette*, May 21, 1766 (David Library of the American Revolution).

10. Fischer, *Liberty and Freedom*, 39–40; Young, *Liberty Tree*, 351.
11. *New York Gazette, and Weekly Mercury*, February 12, 1770 (New York Historical Society); Thomas Gage to Henry Seymour Conway, May 28, 1766, *The Correspondence of General Thomas Gage* 1: 92 (Small Special Collections Library at the University of Virginia); *New-York Gazette*, May 26, 1766 (David Library of the American Revolution); Montresor, *The Montresor Journals*, 367–68, 370 (David Library of the American Revolution); for a description of the king's birthday celebrations, see *New-York Gazette*, June 9, 1766; a flag displaying "King, Pitt, and Liberty" was paraded by Boston boys around the Liberty Tree in August 1765, see Fischer, *Liberty and Freedom*, 21.
12. Harden, "Liberty Caps and Liberty Trees," 74–80; Fischer, *Liberty and Freedom*, 41, 49; Young, *Liberty Tree*, 361–62; Bellion, "Mast Trees," in Roberts, *Scale*, 234; in 1790, Benjamin Franklin gave George Washington his walking stick with a gold liberty cap on top, see Young, *Liberty Tree*, 362.
13. Underdown, *Revel, Riot, and Rebellion*, 88, 177; Hole, *British Folk Customs*, 136–38; Harden, "Liberty Caps and Liberty Trees," 70; Newman, *Parades and the Politics of the Street*, 130; Young, *Liberty Tree*, 359, 367; Deloria, *Playing Indian*, 13, 16–18.
14. Young, *Liberty Tree*, 327–31, 336–37, 347; Fischer, *Liberty and Freedom*, 23–24, 26–27; Schlesinger, "Liberty Tree: A Genealogy," 437–46; Newman, *Parades and the Politics of the Street*, 24; Boston's Liberty Tree was allegedly planted in 1646, see Young, *Liberty Tree*, 363; for the tree as a political space for White women and boys, see Young, *Liberty Tree*, 345.
15. Fischer, *Liberty and Freedom*, 38, 42–43; Bellion, "Mast Trees," 233; Harden, "Liberty Caps and Liberty Trees," 76; Newman, *Parades and the Politics of the Street*, 25.
16. Bellion, "Mast Trees," 224–25, 228; Maier, *From Resistance to Revolution*, 6.
17. Taylor, *American Revolutions*, 47–53; Conway, *War, State, and Society in Mid-Eighteenth Century Britain and Ireland*, 236–47; Colley, *Britons*, 101–47.
18. McDougall, "To the Betrayed Inhabitants," quoted in Boyer, "Lobster Backs," 286; Boyer, "Lobster Backs," 351, see also Brutus, "To the Public," January 15, 1770, New York City (Library Company of Philadelphia); Cadwallader Colden to the Earl of Hillsborough, February 21, 1770, *The Colden Letter Books*, 2: 211.
19. Boyer, "Lobster Backs," 284–85; Young, *Liberty Tree*, 349.

20. Fischer, *Liberty and Freedom*, 44.
21. *New York Gazette, or Weekly Post Boy*, August 14, 1766; *New York Gazette, and Weekly Mercury*, February 12, 1770; Lurie, "Liberty Poles and the Fight for Popular Politics," 677; Fischer, *Liberty and Freedom*, 44; for a theoretical discussion of iconoclasm, see Bellion, "Mast Trees," 220–21.
22. *New York Gazette, or Weekly Post Boy*, August 14, 1766; Montresor, *The Montresor Journals*, 382–83; *New York Mercury*, August 25, 1766; Fischer, *Liberty and Freedom* 44; Thomas Gage to Duke of Richmond, August 26, 1766, *The Correspondence of General Thomas Gage*, 103–4; shortly after, Major Brown received two writs for £5,000 in damages, see Montresor, *The Montresor Journals*, 384.
23. *New York Gazette, or Weekly Post Boy*, September 25, 1766, March 26, 1767.
24. *New York Gazette, or Weekly Post Boy*, March 26, 1767; see also supplement to *New York Gazette, or Weekly Post Boy*, March 26, 1767, quoted in "The Liberty Pole on the Commons," 112–14; Fischer, *Liberty and Freedom*, 44–45.
25. Gage to Lt. Col. William Dalrymple, January 8, 1770, *Gage Papers*, quoted in Fischer, *Liberty and Freedom*, 45; Shy, *Toward Lexington*, 382; for more on tensions between colonists and troops, see *New York Journal*, October 23, 1766, November 6, 1766 (David Library of the American Revolution).
26. Brutus, "To the Public," January 15, 1770; *New York Gazette, or Weekly Post Boy*, January 15, 1770, February 5, 1770; Boyer, "Lobster Backs," 289–92; Fischer, *Liberty and Freedom*, 45–46; Colden wrote of the broadside: "Numerous Papers were dispersed about the Town exciting the People to sedition and to exasperate them against the soldiers then quarter'd in the Place." *The Colden Letter Books*, 2: 217.
27. *New York Gazette, or Weekly Post Boy*, January 22, 1770, February 5, 1770; Boyer, "Lobster Backs," 292–94; Fischer, *Liberty and Freedom*, 46.
28. 16th Regiment of Foot, "God and a Soldier all Men doth adore . . . ," New York City, January 19, 1770, *Early American Imprints, Series I: Evans, 1639–1800*, https://www.readex.com/products/early-american-imprints-series-i-evans-1639-1800.
29. *New York Gazette, or Weekly Post Boy*, February 5, 1770; Boyer, "Lobster Backs," 295–300; Lurie, "Liberty Poles and the Fight for Popular Politics," 677.
30. *New York Gazette, or Weekly Post Boy*, February 5, 1770, April 2, 1770; Boyer, "Lobster Backs," 295–300; Lurie, "Liberty Poles and the Fight for Popular Politics," 677; Gage downplayed the clash in a letter to Hillsborough: "Endeavours were not only used to Set the People against the Bill for quartering, but also against the Soldiers, and provoked them to a Quarrell. The Minds of the Soldiers were at length so sowered [sic], as to become alarming, and to require uncommon Care to restrain them from Excess.

But thro' the Diligence of the Civil and Military Powers, Harmony and good Order was soon restored." *The Correspondence of General Thomas Gage*, 248; Colden also stressed that the Sons of Liberty had inflamed the public: "An ill humour had been artfully worked up between the Towns People & Soldiers, which produced several affrays, and daily, by means of wicked Incendiaries, became more serious." *The Colden Letter Books*, 2: 210.

31. "To the Sons of Liberty in this City," February 3, 1770, New York City (New York Historical Society); *Pennsylvania Chronicle*, February 5, 1770; *New York Gazette, or Weekly Post Boy*, February 5, 1770; *New York Gazette, and Weekly Mercury*, February 12, 1770; *Minutes of the Common Council of the City of New York*, vol. 7, 203–24, 46–47; Boyer, "Lobster Backs," 304; some of the 16th Regiment vowed to take pieces of the liberty pole with them, but the Sons of Liberty set up a nocturnal guard to defend the pole to foil the soldiers, see *Pennsylvania Chronicle*, March 26, 1770.
32. William Tryon to Lord George Germain, November 26, 1776, quoted in "The Liberty Pole on the Commons," 126; Young, *Liberty Tree*, 351; Schlesinger, "Liberty Tree," 451.
33. Lurie, "Liberty Poles and the Fight for Popular Politics," 678; Young, *Liberty Tree*, 347; Fischer, *Liberty and Freedom*, 47–49; Schlesinger, "Liberty Tree," 445–52; Newman, *Parades and the Politics of the Street*, 24–26.
34. *Massachusetts Spy*, November 3, 1774, June 2, 1774; when war broke out, Patriot units from New York carried flags with liberty poles on them, see Fischer, *Liberty and Freedom*, 49; the residents of Plymouth decided to raise a liberty pole on top of their famous rock. But in their attempt to move Plymouth Rock to the center of town, they accidentally split the rock in two. They left half by the water and moved the other half into town, where it served as the foundation of their liberty pole until the rock was reformed in 1881, see Fischer, *Liberty and Freedom*, 48.
35. *New York Gazette, and Weekly Mercury*, April 23, 1770; Fischer, *Liberty and Freedom*, 47–49; Schlesinger, "Liberty Tree," 445–52.

## 2. Regulation, Ratification, and the Right to Resist

1. Frank, *Constituent Moments*, 68–69, 96.
2. Petition of Pasquotank Inhabitants, November 20, 1766, quoted in Kars, *Breaking Loose Together*, 67; Kars, *Breaking Loose Together*, 5–6, 65–68, 111–12; Chandler, "'Unawed by the Laws of their Country,'" 120–26; Taylor, *American Revolutions*, 70; Kay, "The North Carolina Regulation," in Young, *The American Revolution*, 76, 85.

3. The word "regulator" is capitalized when protestors referred to themselves with the term.
4. "The Governor's Answer, June 21, 1768," in *Historical Sketches of North Carolina*, 13; Kars, *Breaking Loose Together*, 2, 112, 138; Chandler, "'Unawed by the Laws,'" 126.
5. Edmund Fanning to John Gray, April 13, 1768, quoted in Kars, *Breaking Loose Together*, 139; William Tryon, Proclamation of Governor William Tryon, April 27, 1768, State Archives of North Carolina, quoted in Chandler, "'Unawed by the Laws,'" 128; Kars, *Breaking Loose Together*, 138–40, 144; Chandler, "'Unawed by the Laws,'" 126–29.
6. Council Minutes, June 20, 1768, quoted in Kars, *Breaking Loose Together*, 149; Kars, *Breaking Loose Together*, 148–49, 170–75, 179–85; Chandler, "'Unawed by the Laws,'" 129–41; Taylor, *American Revolutions*, 70–71.
7. Bill for preventing tumultuous & riotous Assemblies, etc., December 15, 1770, North Carolina General Assembly Session Records, State Archives of North Carolina, quoted in Chandler, "'Unawed by the Laws,'" 141; Kars, *Breaking Loose Together*, 186–87, 196–206; Chandler, "'Unawed by the Laws,'" 141–43; Taylor, *American Revolutions*, 71.
8. Ethan Allen, *A Brief Narrative of the Proceedings of the Government of New York . . .* (Hartford, 1774), 136, quoted in Shapiro, "Ethan Allen: Philosopher-Theologian," 242–43; Taylor, *American Revolutions*, 71–72; Shapiro, "Ethan Allen," 240–45; Greene, "Ethan Allen and Daniel Shays," 129–30. For the connection between the Green Mountain Boys and other land rioters in the eighteenth century, see Countryman, "'Out of the Bounds of the Law,'" in Young, *The American Revolution*.
9. See Smith, *The Dominion of Voice*, 44–45, for a discussion of representative government superseding the Whig theory of justified resistance; Alfred F. Young refers to this spate of postwar crowd action as "a radicalism of desperation." See Young, *Liberty Tree*, 226.
10. Mount Washington Petition, 80–81, quoted in Condon, *Shays's Rebellion*, 21; Condon, *Shays's Rebellion*,16, 13, 21, 6–7; Taylor, *American Revolutions*, 366–67; according to Donald Ratcliffe, the property requirement to vote likely disenfranchised very few people. Ratcliffe, "The Right to Vote and the Rise of Democracy," 228.
11. *Hampshire Herald*, September 19, 1786, quoted in Condon, *Shays's Rebellion*, 48; Massachusetts Archives, CLXXXIX, 1–5, quoted in Taylor, *Western Massachusetts in the Revolution*, 143; Condon, *Shays's Rebellion*, 44–57; for an argument that regulators drew on traditional methods of protest, see Nobles, "'Satan, Smith, Shattuck, and Shays,'" in Young, *Revolutionary Founders*, 223–24.

12. Adam Wheeler declaration, November 17, 1786, Shays's Rebellion Papers (American Antiquarian Society), quoted in Pencak, "'The Fine Theoretic Government,'" in Gross, *In Debt to Shays*, 126; Taylor, "Regulators and White Indians," in Gross, *In Debt to Shays*, 151–52.
13. Samuel Adams to Noah Webster, April 30, 1784, quoted in Smith, *The Freedoms We Lost*, 201.
14. Condon, *Shays's Rebellion*, 57–61, 65–72; Taylor, "Regulators and White Indians," 146–47; Taylor, *American Revolutions*, 368.
15. *Acts and Resolves, 1786–1787*, 102–3, quoted in Condon, *Shays's Rebellion*, 72; Condon, *Shays's Rebellion*, 65–72.
16. Condon, *Shays's Rebellion*, 73–104; Taylor, *American Revolutions*, 368.
17. Condon, *Shays's Rebellion*, 106–11, 114–18; Taylor, *American Revolutions*, 369.
18. William Moore, James Lawson, and William Jack, Westmoreland County, to Nicholson, December 1786, Records of the Office of the Comptroller General, Pennsylvania Historical and Museum Commission, Harrisburg, quoted in Bouton, *Taming Democracy*, 148; Bouton, *Taming Democracy*, 145–53, 156–57, 208.
19. Commissioners of Taxes, Northampton County, August 25, 1783, *Pennsylvania Archives*, series 1, vol. 10, 92, quoted in Bouton, *Taming Democracy*, 158; Bouton, *Taming Democracy*, 157–63, 166.
20. Hamilton to Fergusson, June 18, 1786, quoted in Lee, *The Price of Nationhood*, 235; Maganzin, "Economic Depression in Maryland and Virginia," 191–99; Holton, *Unruly Americans*, 10–12, 145–52; Lee, *The Price of Nationhood*, 232–39; Bellesiles, *Revolutionary Outlaws*, 246–48; Nadelhaft, *The Disorders of War*, 168; Taylor, *American Revolutions*, 368–69; for more on a pattern of backcountry resistance to proprietors, see Taylor, "Agrarian Independence," in *Beyond the American Revolution*, 221–45.
21. Conjectures about the New Constitution, [17–30 September 1787], *The Papers of Alexander Hamilton*, vol. 4, *January 1787–May 1788*, ed. Harold C. Syrett, New York: Columbia University Press, 1962, 275–77, Founders Online; Taylor, *American Revolutions*, 369–74; Bouton, *Taming Democracy*, 171–80.
22. James Lincoln quoted in Taylor, *American Revolutions*, 385; Taylor, *American Revolutions*, 383–93.
23. Green, *The Life of Ashbel Green*, 175–76; Waldstreicher, *In the Midst of Perpetual Fetes*, 90–93; Travers, *Celebrating the Fourth*, 70–83.
24. *Letters from a Federal Farmer*, quoted in Cornell, *The Other Founders*, 96; *Freeman's Journal*, March 18, 1788, quoted in Waldstreicher, *In the Midst of Perpetual Fetes*, 90; Cornell, *The Other Founders*, 110–11; Cornell, "Aristocracy Assailed," 1150–53.

25. Edgar, *South Carolina*, 252.
26. Bouton, *Taming Democracy*, 197–209.
27. Bouton, *Taming Democracy*, 197–200, 213–15.
28. Henry Johnson's deposition, February 15, 1808, Council Files, Massachusetts Historical Society, quoted in Taylor, *Liberty Men and Great Proprietors*, 120; Taylor, *Liberty Men and Great Proprietors*, 89–121; Taylor, "Regulators and White Indians," 145–46, 152–60.

## 3. Debating Dissent in the Whiskey Rebellion

1. Addison, *Reports of Cases*, 419–20.
2. Addison, *Reports of Cases*, 420, 126; in September 1795, Addison ruled that raising a liberty pole in a public space was illegal in *Pennsylvania v Morrison*. Addison, *Reports of Cases*, 275.
3. Ames, *Works of Fisher Ames: With a Selection from his Speeches and Correspondence* (1809), 174; Fennell, "From Rebelliousness to Insurrection," 44; for Washington's decision to make western Pennsylvania the test case for federal might, see Slaughter, *The Whiskey Rebellion*, 117–21; Bouton, *Taming Democracy*, 226–27.
4. Terry Bouton has called for a change in the name of the Whiskey Rebellion to the "Pennsylvania Regulation of 1794." See Bouton, *Taming Democracy*, 218.
5. Maier, *From Resistance to Revolution*, 5.
6. Johann N. Neem distinguishes between Federalists, Republican elites, and regulators in their approaches to legitimate political activity, see Neem, "Freedom of Association," 259–90; see also Owen, *Political Community in Revolutionary Pennsylvania*, 116. For examples of the Whiskey Rebellion as an economic protest, see Fennell, "From Rebelliousness to Insurrection"; Bouton, *Taming Democracy*; for an example of the rebellion as a regional conflict, see Slaughter, *The Whiskey Rebellion*.
7. Deposition of Daniel Rees, December 10, 1794, Deposition of Peter Faulkner, December 10, 1794, Deposition of James Jenkins, November 12, 1794, Rawle Family Papers; Notes of Testimony in U.S. vs Bonham, Rawle Family Papers; Brackenridge, *History of the Western Insurrection*, 17; Findley, *History of the Insurrection*, 41, 68; Baldwin, *Whiskey Rebels*, 25, 69, 72; Fennell, "From Rebelliousness to Insurrection," 56; Baldwin estimates that about one-quarter of operational stills in 1794 were located in Pennsylvania's western survey. Baldwin, *Whiskey Rebels*, 107.
8. Deposition of Daniel Rees, December 10, 1794, Deposition of Peter Faulkner, December 10, 1794, Deposition of James Jenkins, November 12, 1794,

Rawle Family Papers; Notes of Testimony in U.S. vs Bonham, Rawle Family Papers; Fennell, "From Rebelliousness to Insurrection," 38–39, 76–97; Slaughter, *The Whiskey Rebellion*, 94; Baldwin, *Whiskey Rebels*, 8–10, 71, 73; Sharp, "The Whiskey Rebellion and the Question of Representation," in Boyd, *The Whiskey Rebellion*, 121.

9. Deposition of James Jenkins, November 12, 1794, Rawle Family Papers; Findley, *History of the Insurrection*, 41; "Judge Alexander Addison on the Origin and History of the Whiskey Rebellion," in Boyd, *The Whiskey Rebellion*, 53; Fennell, "From Rebelliousness to Insurrection," 15–24; Baldwin, *Whiskey Rebels*, 58–60.

10. Brackenridge, *History of the Western Insurrection*, 39; Maier, *From Resistance to Revolution*, 4, 3–26; Bouton, *Taming Democracy*, 218–19; Neem, "Freedom of Association," 276–77; Taylor, "Regulators and White Indians," 145–60; David Bradford, a leader of the Whiskey Rebellion, had been brought up on charges for closing roads throughout the 1790s, see Bouton, *Taming Democracy*, 226.

11. Minutes of the Meeting at Pittsburgh, 1792, in *Pennsylvania Archives*, series 2, vol. 4, 30–31; The Secretary of the Treasury to President Washington, August 5, 1794, in *Pennsylvania Archives*, series 2, vol. 4, 92; Slaughter, *The Whiskey Rebellion*, 116; Baldwin, *Whiskey Rebels*, 86.

12. Charge of Chief Justice McKean and Reply of the Grand Jury, November 8, 1792, in *Pennsylvania Archives*, series 2, vol. 4; Address to the Officers of the Militia of the County of Lancaster, September 26, 1794, in *Pennsylvania Archives*, series 9, vol. 2, 877; Cornell, "'To Assemble Together," 931–32.

13. Governor Mifflin to the Judges of the Supreme Court, March 21, 1794, in *Pennsylvania Archives*, series 2, vol. 4, 58; Section 20, Article IX of Pennsylvania Constitution of 1790, in *Pennsylvania Archives*, series 3, vol. 10, 748; Judge Addison to Secretary Dallas, April 22, 1795, in *Pennsylvania Archives*, series 2, vol. 4, 530; Judge Addison to Secretary Dallas, April 22, 1795, in *Pennsylvania Archives*, series 2, vol. 4, 530; Addison, *Reports of Cases*, 49; Judge Addison's Charge to the Grand Jury of Allegheny, September 1, 1794, in *Pennsylvania Archives*, series 2, vol. 4, 244; Rowe, "Alexander Addison," 233–35; Addison allowed those writing resolutions against the excise to prepare them in his house, although he did not sign the eventual document, see Rowe, "Alexander Addison," 233; for Addison's Federalist-leaning views and later overt partisanship, see Rowe, "Alexander Addison," 221–50; for Federalist complaints about Addison's criticism of the excise, see George Clymer to Tench Coxe, April 21, 1794, Oliver Wolcott, Jr. Papers (Connecticut Historical Society).

14. Deposition of Daniel Rees, December 10, 1794, October 17, 1794, Deposi-

tion of Jonathan Walker, December 10, 1794, Deposition of John Mason, December 22, 1794, Rawle Family Papers.
15. Slaughter, *The Whiskey Rebellion*, 152–80, 185–88; Baldwin, *Whiskey Rebels*, 116–24, 138–39; for notices of banishment, see Resolves of the Committee of Pittsburgh, Respecting Gen. Gibson and Col. Neville, in *Pennsylvania Archives*, series 2, vol. 4, 158–59.
16. Kohn, "The Washington Administration's Decision," 575–76; Slaughter, *The Whiskey Rebellion* 196; Proclamation of President Washington, in *Pennsylvania Archives*, series 2, vol. 4, 123–27; Instructions to the United States Commissioners, August 8, 1794, in *Pennsylvania Archives*, series 2, vol. 4, 137–39; Brackenridge, *Incidents of the Insurrection*, 99, 102; Findley, *History of the Insurrection*, 115.
17. Brackenridge, *Incidents of the Insurrection*, 112–13, 116–17; Slaughter, *The Whiskey Rebellion*, 200–201; The U.S. Commissioners to the Committee of Conference, September 1, 1794, in *Pennsylvania Archives*, series 2, vol. 4, 233–37.
18. Willis Wilson to H. Lee, September 15, 1794, quoted in Slaughter, *The Whiskey Rebellion*, 212; Kohn, "The Washington Administration's Decision," 581; *Baltimore Daily Intelligencer*, September 8, 1794; *Gazette of the United States*, September 24, 1794, October 4, 1794; Slaughter, *The Whiskey Rebellion*, 210; Alexander Hamilton to Thomas Sim Lee, 6 September 1794, *The Papers of Alexander Hamilton*, vol. 17, *August 1794–December 1794*, ed. Harold C. Syrett, New York: Columbia University Press, 1972, 201–2, note 4, Founders Online; Secretary Dallas' Report to the Senate, September 10, 1794, in *Pennsylvania Archives*, series 2, vol. 4, 280–82; Bouton, *Taming Democracy*, 238–41; Kohn, "The Washington Administration's Decision," 581; Slaughter, *The Whiskey Rebellion*, 213–14; for a dramatic account of a militia unit refusing to march against the regulators by throwing down their weapons, see Examination of Mitchell Scott, February 2, 1795, Rawle Family Papers and Examination of John McKibbens, February 2, 1795, Rawle Family Papers.
19. Addison, *Reports of Cases*, 274–75; Slaughter, *The Whiskey Rebellion*, 203; Fennell, "From Rebelliousness to Insurrection," 118; *Carlisle Gazette*, September 17, 1794; for more accounts of violence and intimidation at the polls, see Baldwin, *Whiskey Rebels*, 210–14.
20. Deposition of Peter Faulkner, December 10, 1794, Deposition of Robert Lyon, December 12, 1794, Deposition of William Spring, December 12, 1794, Rawle Family Papers.
21. Deposition of Henry Lebo, January 7, 1795, Deposition of Peter Faulkner, December 10, 1794, Deposition of Rudolph Simmons, October 18,

1794, Rawle Family Papers; George Washington from Bernard Hubley, Jr., 8 October 1794, *The Papers of George Washington, Presidential Series*, vol. 17, *1 October 1794–31 March 1795*, ed. David R. Hoth and Carol S. Ebel, Charlottesville: University of Virginia Press, 2013, 27–32, Founders Online.

22. Deposition of Henry Lebo, January 7, 1795, Rawle Family Papers; George Washington from Bernard Hubley, Jr., 8 October 1794, *The Papers of George Washington, Presidential Series*, vol. 17, 27–32, Founders Online; Murdock, *Brady Family Reunion*, 67.

23. Deposition William P. Brady, October 15, 1794, Rawle Family Papers.

24. Deposition of John McGrath, December 22, 1794, Deposition of Robert Lyon, December 12, 1794, Deposition of James Allen, December 12, 1794, Deposition of William Spring, December 12, 1794, Rawle Family Papers; Bouton, *Taming Democracy*, 238.

25. Deposition of Benjamin F. Young, October 16, 1794, Deposition of Benjamin Young, December 9, 1794, Deposition of James Jenkins, November 12, 1794, Deposition of Rosewell Douty, December 27, 1794, Rawle Family Papers; Jasper Ewing, of Northumberland, to Charles Hall, of York, September 27, 1794, *Pennsylvania Archives*, series 2, vol. 4, 380.

26. Deposition of Flavel Roan, January 4, 1795, Deposition of William Wilson, October 20, 1794, Deposition of Rudolph Simmons, October 18, 1794, Rawle Family Papers.

27. Deposition of William Wilson, October 20, 1794, Deposition of William Wilson, November 29, 1794, Deposition of John MacPherson, December 20, 1794, Rawle Family Papers; Addison, *Reports of Cases*, 419; George Washington from Bernard Hubley, Jr., 8 October 1794, *The Papers of George Washington, Presidential Series*, vol. 17, 27–32.

28. Deposition of Rudolph Simmons, October 18, 1794, Rawle Family Papers; Jasper Ewing, of Northumberland, to Charles Hall, of York, September 27, 1794, *Pennsylvania Archives*, series 2, vol. 4, 380.

29. John Adams from Joseph Priestley, 13 November 1794, Founders Online; *United States Direct Tax of 1798: Tax Lists for the State of Pennsylvania*, M372, microfilm, 24 rolls, Records of the Internal Revenue Service, 1791–2006, Record Group 58, National Archives and Records Administration, Washington, D.C.; Records of the Office of the Comptroller General, RG-4, *Tax & Exoneration Lists, 1762–1794*, Microfilm Roll: 331, Pennsylvania Historical and Museum Commission, Harrisburg. Although Priestley insisted that "nothing can excuse an open opposition to the bringing of any tax laid by the representatives of the people," he questioned the wisdom of "[hazarding] the authority of government" by passing a "very unpopular" law.

"People will choose to do without government rather than pay so dear for it," he warned. Joseph Priestley to John Vaughan, August 1, 1794, Joseph Priestley Papers (American Philosophical Society); in Hagerstown, the *Baltimore Daily Intelligencer* reported that the town merchants refused to sell the pole-raisers gunpowder or flint. *Baltimore Daily Intelligencer,* September 8, 1794.

30. Messrs. Wilson and Hubley, of Northumberland, to Governor Mifflin, October 8, 1794, in *Pennsylvania Archives,* series 2, vol. 4, 402–3; George Eddy to Governor Mifflin, October 9, 1794, in *Pennsylvania Archives,* series 2, vol. 4, 404; Egle, *Notes and Queries,* 202. The governor agreed that Bowman should not ride on for Bedford until a peaceful submission to law and order prevailed throughout Northumberland. Once Bowman's troop left, they made their way to Bedford by way of several other towns with liberty poles, see Governor Mifflin to Capt. Ebenezer Bowman, October 10, 1794, *Pennsylvania Archives,* series 2, vol. 4, 407; George Eddy to Governor Mifflin, October 9, 1794, *Pennsylvania Archives,* series 2, vol. 4, 405.
31. Deposition of Jonathan Walker, October 18, 1794, Rawle Family Papers; Linn, *Annals of Buffalo Valley,* 291; for election results, see 288.
32. Executive Minutes, November 29, 1794, in *Pennsylvania Archives,* series 9, vol. 2, 888; Linn, *Annals of Buffalo Valley,* 290–91.
33. Deposition of William Wilson, October 20, 1794, November 29, 1794, Deposition of Daniel Montgomery, January 10, 1795, Rawle Family Papers; for copies of the complaints against Wilson, see Deposition of William Huffman, November 5, 1794, Deposition of William Cool, November 15, 1794, Rawle Family Papers; Addison, *Reports of Cases,* 419–20.
34. Findley, *History of the Insurrection,* 172–73, 178, 312.
35. *U.S. Circuit Court Criminal Case Files, 1790–1871,* Ancestry.com, https://www.ancestry.com/search/collections/1248/; Boyd, *The Whiskey Rebellion,* appendix A, 200–201; Linn, *Annals of Buffalo Valley,* 286; Findley, *History of the Insurrection,* 143–44; Brackenridge, *History of the Western Insurrection,* 268; *Gazette of the United States,* October 4, 1794; Ifft, "Treason in the Early Republic," in Boyd, *The Whiskey Rebellion,* 172; for examples of liberty poles, see Notes on the March from September 30, Until October 29, 1794, in *Pennsylvania Archives,* series 2, vol. 4, 429.
36. Addison, *Reports of Cases,* 419; El-Haj, "Changing the People," 123–24; see Cornell, "To Assemble Together," 930–33, for his argument that contemporaries understood the freedom to assemble not as an individual right, but as one linked to the common good. Wilson and MacPherson conducted most of the depositions for this case, despite the apparent conflict of interest.

37. Addison, *Reports of Cases*, 419–20; Jonathan Walker similarly argued to Bonham that the context of the rebellion made liberty poles illegitimate, see Deposition of Jonathan Walker, December 10, 1794, Rawle Family Papers.
38. Addison, *Reports of Cases*, 422.
39. *Baltimore Daily Intelligencer,* September 20, 1794.
40. Bell, *Party and Faction*, 47; Frank, *Constituent Moments*, 138; Fischer, *The Revolution of American Conservatism*, 4–5, 17.
41. Bouton, *Taming Democracy*, 218.
42. "Judge Alexander Addison on the Origin and History of the Whiskey Rebellion," in Boyd, *The Whiskey Rebellion*, 55.

## 4. The Federalist Popular Politics of Assent

1. *Farewell Address,* September 19, 1796, Founders Online.
2. For Federalist organizing, see Estes, *The Jay Treaty Debate;* Pasley, *The First Presidential Contest;* Cotlar, *Tom Paine's America*, 189; for Federalist popular celebrations, see Newman, *Parades and the Politics of the Street;* Waldstreicher, *In the Midst of Perpetual Fetes.*
3. Peter Van Schaack to Theodore Sedgwick, December 3, 1795, Sedgwick Family Papers (Massachusetts Historical Society).
4. Chauncey Goodrich to Oliver Wolcott, February 17, 1793, in Gibbs, *Memoirs of the administrations of Washington and John Adams*, 88; "The Bloody Buoy, Thrown Out as a Warning to the Political Pilots of All Nations" (1796), in Cobbett and Wilson, *Peter Porcupine in America*, 145 (American Philosophical Society); Sharp, *American Politics in the Early Republic*, 69–74; Cotlar, *Tom Paine's America*, 73; Taylor, *American Revolutions*, 415–16; Halperin, *Alien and Sedition Acts*, 14–15; for Republican celebrations of the French Revolution, see Newman, *Parades and the Politics of the Street*, 120–51; for more on the Haitian Revolution and its impact on American politics, see Dun, *Dangerous Neighbors;* White, *Encountering Revolution.*
5. *Spectator,* November 28, 1798; *Daily Advertiser,* July 21, 1798; Sharp, *American Politics in the Early Republic,* 74.
6. *Aurora General Advertiser,* December 19, 1796; Thomas Jefferson to Brissot de Warville, 8 May 1793, *The Papers of Thomas Jefferson*, vol. 25, *1 January–10 May 1793*, ed. John Catanzariti, Princeton: Princeton University Press, 1992, 679–80, Founders Online; Sharp, *American Politics,* 69–74; Cotlar, *Tom Paine's America*, 73, 98–101; Pasley, "The Tyranny of Printers," 79–104.
7. Alexander Hamilton to ———, [18 May 1793], *The Papers of Alexander*

*Hamilton*, vol. 14, *February 1793–June 1793*, ed. Harold C. Syrett, New York: Columbia University Press, 1969, 473–76, Founders Online.
8. Robertson, "'Look on This Picture,'" 1277; Waldstreicher, *In the Midst of Perpetual Fetes*; Hofstadter, *The Idea of a Party System*.
9. Robertson, "'Look on this Picture,'" 1277; Waldstreicher, *In the Midst of Perpetual Fetes*.
10. *Berkshire Gazette*, February 13, 1799; Austin, *An Oration, Pronounced at Worcester*, 35 (Library Company of Philadelphia); *Albany Gazette*, March 8, 1799; Newman, *Fries's Rebellion*, 165–67; Young, *Liberty Tree*, 368, 371; see also *Porcupine's Gazette*, March 22, 1798, July 14, 1798.
11. *Gazette of the United States*, August 28, 1793; Estes, *The Jay Treaty Debate*, 45–51; Ammon, "The Genet Mission," 732; Owen, *Political Community in Revolutionary Pennsylvania*, 158–61; for more on Federalist rituals of assent and the cult of Washington, see Waldstreicher, *In the Midst of Perpetual Fetes*, 117–26; Newman, *Parades and the Politics of the Street*, 44–68; Pasley, *The First Presidential Contest*, 132–81.
12. Sharp, *American Politics*, 113–37; Elkins and McKitrick, *The Age of Federalism*, 389.
13. Estes, *The Jay Treaty Debate*, 71–77; Sharp, *American Politics*, 113–37; Elkins and McKitrick, *The Age of Federalism*, 389; Robertson, "'Look on This Picture,'" 1271; Freeman, *Affairs of Honor*, xiii–xiv.
14. Benjamin Franklin Bache to Margaret Bache, July 8, 1795, Castle-Bache Collection (American Philosophical Society); *Aurora General Advertiser*, August 13, 1795; Estes, *The Jay Treaty Debate*, 134–38.
15. Ames, *Works of Fisher Ames, Compiled by a Number of his Friends*, 71 (New England Historic Genealogical Society); *Gazette of the United States*, August 21, 1795; Estes, *The Jay Treaty Debate*, 90–91; Pasley, *The First Presidential Contest*, 152–61.
16. Estes, *The Jay Treaty Debate*, 141–43.
17. Sharp, *American Politics*, 164–76; Elkins and McKitrick, *The Age of Federalism*, 537–88; Humphrey, *The Press of the Young Republic*, 57–58.
18. Cotlar, "The Federalists' Transatlantic Cultural Offensive," in Pasley et al., *Beyond the Founders*, 279–95; Newman, *Fries's Rebellion*, 75–77; Levine, "The Fries Rebellion," 242–43; Bouton, *Taming Democracy*, 245–49; Halperin, *Alien and Sedition Acts*, 53. For Federalist discussions of the effect of the dispatches on the public, see Thomas Dwight to Theodore Sedgwick, April 21, 1798, Sedgwick Family Papers (Massachusetts Historical Society); Theodore Sedgwick to Rufus King, May 1, 1798, July 1, 1798, Sedgwick Family Papers; Alexander Hamilton to Rufus King, [6 June 1798], *The*

*Papers of Alexander Hamilton*, vol. 21, April 1797–July 1798, ed. Harold C. Syrett, New York: Columbia University Press, 1974, 490–91, Founders Online; for the election of 1796 and the importance of foreign affairs on increasing partisanship, see Pasley, *The First Presidential Contest*.

19. Dwight, *An Oration Spoken at Hartford, in the State of Connecticut*, 20–21; Halperin, *Alien and Sedition Acts*, 35–37, 54–61; Bradburn, *The Citizenship Revolution*, 162–65; for an explanation of Federalist xenophobic views of citizenship and its relation to the Alien Law, see Bradburn, *The Citizenship Revolution*, 148–67.

20. *An Act for the punishment of certain crimes against the United States*, 5th Cong., 2nd sess., 112; *Annals of Congress*, 5th Cong., 2nd sess., 2098; *Annals of Congress*, 5th Cong., 2nd sess., 2096; Addison, *Charges to Grand Juries*, 286; Sharp, *American Politics*, 176–77; Taylor, *American Revolutions*, 423–24; Halperin, *Alien and Sedition Acts*, 61–71.

21. *Greenleaf's New York Journal*, July 7, 1798; Deposition of Henry Ohl, April 27, 1799, Rawle Family Papers; Bouton, *Taming Democracy*, 246–49; see chapter 5 for more on economic arguments against the Federalists.

22. *Stewart Kentucky Herald*, December 18, 1798, September 11, 1798.

23. *Albany Register*, November 5, 1798; Newman, *Parades and the Politics of the Street*, 174.

24. *Daily Advertiser*, July 21, 1798; for examples of liberty poles on private property, see *Porcupine's Gazette*, February 2, 1799; Newman, *Parades and the Politics of the Street*, 176.

25. Deposition of James Williamson, April 15, 1799, Rawle Family Papers; see chapter 5 for a discussion of pole-raisers charged under the Sedition Law.

26. *Middlesex Gazette*, February 22, 1799; see also *Spectator*, November 28, 1798.

27. *Newburyport Herald*, September 7, 1798; *Gazette of the United States*, July 24, 1798; *Aurora General Advertiser*, May 27, 1799; see chapter 6 for more examples.

28. *Oracle of Dauphin and Harrisburgh Advertiser*, February 6, 1799; *New York Gazette*, February 7, 1799. By the late 1790s, militias acted as political organizations and captains often doubled as local political leaders. Federalist militia units often led local Fourth of July celebrations and fraternized with other like-minded organizations, like the Society of the Cincinnati. In their local militias, Federalists found an association perfectly suited to attack liberty poles: a politicized group organized around the idea of defending the republic through the mobilization of collective force.

29. On August 10, 1798, the *Albany Centinel* circulated a rumor that the "patri-

otic ladies of German-Flatts ... intend[ed] to rise *en masse* and prostrate the poles of rebellion low in the dust."
30. Zagarri, "Gender and the First Party System," in Ben-Atar and Oberg, *Federalists Reconsidered*, 118–34; Zagarri, *Revolutionary Backlash*, 84–93; Waldstreicher, *In the Midst of Perpetual Fetes,*166–68, 232–36; Branson, *These Fiery Frenchified Dames*, 76–87; for women making liberty pole decorations, see Deposition of James Jackson, October 23, 1799, Rawle Family Papers. Although there is no definitive evidence that women attended most pole-raisings, the crowd sizes reported (often in the hundreds) indicate the extreme likelihood of female attendance. In addition, other scholars have emphasized female participation in similar political celebrations, see Zagarri, *Revolutionary Backlash*; Ryan, *Women in Public*.
31. *Independent Chronicle*, December 6, 1798; *Columbian Centinel*, December 5, 1798; *Massachusetts Spy*, December 12, 1798; *Federal Gazette*, December 19, 1798; *Columbian Centinel*, December 5, 1798; *Gazette of the United States*, December 17, 1798; *Commercial Advertiser*, December 8, 1798; for further examples of Federalist toasts after destroying a liberty pole, see *Albany Gazette*, August 27, 1798; *Porcupine's Gazette*, July 14, 1798.
32. Newman, *Parades and the Politics of the Street*, 176.
33. *Time Piece*, January 19, 1798; *Federal Gazette*, December 19, 1798.
34. *Otsego Herald*, May 3, 1798; *Albany Gazette*, March 8, 1799; see also *Gazette of the United States*, December 17, 1798; *Independent Chronicle*, December 6, 1798.
35. *Middlesex Gazette*, February 22, 1799; *Otsego Herald*, May 3, 1798; see also *Porcupine's Gazette*, March 22, 1798.
36. Addison, *Analysis of the Report of the Committee*, 42, 52 (Library Company of Philadelphia).
37. *Bee*, February 20, 1799; *Aurora General Advertiser*, May 3, 1798, August 18, 1798.
38. *Aurora Daily Advertiser*, April 25, 1799, August 23, 1798; *Centinel of Freedom*, April 17, 1798; *Commercial Advertiser*, August 22, 1798.
39. *Aurora General Advertiser*, August 18, 1798; *Centinel of Freedom*, November 13, 1798, August 21, 1798; *Bee*, September 5, 1798.
40. *Aurora General Advertiser*, May 24, 1799; *Greenleaf's New York Journal*, August 29, 1798; *Carey's United States Recorder*, August 25, 1798; *Massachusetts Spy*, August 29, 1798.
41. Matthew Lyon, "Colonel Lyon's Address to his Constituents ... ," quoted in Halperin, *Alien and Sedition Acts*, 82; Halperin, *Alien and Sedition Acts*, 73–96; Pasley, *"The Tyranny of Printers,"* 125; for a recent account of all of the

prosecutions made under the Alien and Sedition Acts, see Bird, *Criminal Dissent*.
42. See chapter 5.
43. Pasley, "The Tyranny of Printers," 408–9; see chapter 6 for an explanation of the electoral consequences of Federalist popular politics; Seth Cotlar argues that the Alien and Sedition Laws did succeed in their cultural project of demonizing extra-institutional politics as Jacobin, see Cotlar, "Federalists' Transatlantic Cultural Offensive," in Pasley et al., *Beyond the Founders*, 278–79, 295.

## 5. "Wandering Apostles of Sedition"

1. Fisher Ames to Christopher Gore, December 18, 1798, in Ames, *Works of Fisher Ames: With a Selection from his Speeches and Correspondence* (1854), 245–47.
2. For the history of Americans linking political and economic equality, see Bouton, *Taming Democracy*; Mandell, *The Lost Tradition of Economic Equality*.
3. Deposition of Henry Ohl, April 27, 1799, Rawle Family Papers.
4. Deposition of John Serfass, February 1, 1799, Rawle Family Papers.
5. Thomas Jefferson to James Madison, 30 January 1799, *The Papers of Thomas Jefferson*, vol. 30, *1 January 1798–31 January 1799*, ed. Barbara B. Oberg, Princeton: Princeton University Press, 2003, 665–67, Founders Online.
6. Manning, "The Key of Liberty (1799)," in Merrill and Wilentz, *The Key of Liberty*, 127, 138, 152; Merrill and Wilentz, "The Invention of American Politics," in *The Key of Liberty*, 4–6, 48.
7. Manning, "The Key of Liberty (1799)," 157, 134; Merrill and Wilentz, "The Invention of American Politics," 65–66.
8. Fisher Ames to Oliver Wolcott, November 14, 1796, Fisher Ames to Dwight Foster, January 4, 1796, in *Works of Fisher Ames, Compiled by a Number of his Friends*, 181–82; Ames, *Works of Fisher Ames, Compiled by a Number of his Friends*, 72; Ames, "Laocoon I," in *Works of Fisher Ames: With a Selection from his Speeches and Correspondence* (1809), 116–17; Hanson, *Dedham, Massachusetts, 1635–1800*, 168–70; in his eulogy of George Washington, Ames condemned the class-based language that Republicans learned from French Jacobins: "The leaders of the French revolution, from the beginning, excited the poor against the rich; this has made the rich poor, but it will never make the poor rich." Ames, *An Oration on the Sublime Virtues of General George Washington*, 21 (New England Historic Genealogical Society).
9. Fisher Ames to Oliver Wolcott, Jr., July 9, 1795, July 22, 1800, March 24, 1797, Oliver Wolcott, Jr. Papers; Ames, "Laocoon I," in *Works of Fisher*

Ames: With a Selection from his Speeches and Correspondence (1809), 116–17; see also Fisher Ames to Oliver Wolcott, Jr., January 12, 1800, Oliver Wolcott, Jr. Papers; Ames, An Oration on the Sublime Virtues of General George Washington, 23–24.
10. A Friend to Rational Liberty, "The Jacobin Looking-Glass," 18–19 (Massachusetts Historical Society); Thomas Dwight to Theodore Sedgwick, April 11, 1800, Sedgwick Family Papers (Massachusetts Historical Society); Peter Van Schaack to Theodore Sedgwick, December 25, 1799, Sedgwick Family Papers.
11. Daniel Dewey to Theodore Sedgwick, February 6, 1799, Sedgwick Family Papers.
12. Fisher Ames, Political Speech (ca. 1798), Papers of Fisher Ames and Fowler Families (Harvard University Archives); Fisher Ames to Timothy Pickering, July 1798, in Ames, Works of Fisher Ames (1854), 231.
13. Fisher Ames to Christopher Gore, December 18, 1798, in Works of Fisher Ames (1854), 247; Independent Chronicle, June 20, 1799; Records of the U.S. Circuit Court at Boston, 1799 (National Archives); for two historical accounts of Brown, the liberty pole, and the resulting court cases, see Anderson, "The Enforcement of the Alien and Sedition Laws," 122–26; Smith, "The Federalist 'Saints' versus 'The Devil of Sedition,'" 198–215; Brown never published his "Dissertations" and it no longer exists in manuscript form. However, the U.S. Circuit Court quoted from "Dissertations" extensively during Brown's sentencing. There are several David Browns who served in Connecticut regiments during the Revolutionary War. It is possible that the Brown in question served as a lieutenant in the 9th Connecticut Militia Regiment in Captain James Green's Company, where he suffered several injuries fighting in New York. It is also possible that he served in Captain Eleazer Hutchinson's Company of Militia and deserted for six weeks in the fall of 1776. Charles J. Hoadley, The Public Records of the State of Connecticut, from May, 1778, to April, 1780, inclusive (Hartford: The Case, Lockwood & Brainard Company, 1895), 328; Rolls and Lists of Connecticut Men in the Revolution, 1775–1783 (Hartford: Connecticut Historical Society, 1901), 161. I am grateful to Bill Ferraro for these sources.
14. Records of the U.S. Circuit Court at Boston, 1799; Independent Chronicle, June 20, 1799.
15. Records of the U.S. Circuit Court at Boston, 1799.
16. Records of the U.S. Circuit Court at Boston, 1799.
17. Records of the U.S. Circuit Court at Boston, 1799; Manning, "The Key of Liberty (1799)," 142, 131; Merrill and Wilentz, "The Invention of American Politics," 74; see chapter 3 for similar critiques made by William Bonham.

18. Warren, *Jacobin and Junto*, 105–6.
19. Warren, *Jacobin and Junto*, 105–6; *Massachusetts Mercury*, November 9, 1798; Fisher Ames to Christopher Gore, December 18, 1798, Fisher Ames to Jeremiah Smith, November 22, 1798, Fisher Ames to Timothy Pickering, November 22, 1798, in *Works of Fisher Ames* (1854), 247, 240, 242; *Courier of New Hampshire*, November 10, 1798; *The Diary of William Bentley*, 289 (Massachusetts Historical Society); Smith, "The Federalist 'Saints,'" 203; for an example of John Lowell's Federalism, see Lowell, *An Oration Pronounced July 4, 1799* (New England Historic Genealogical Society).
20. *Salem Gazette*, March 29, 1799; *Columbian Centinel*, November 7, 1798, November 10, 1798; *Oracle of the Day*, April 6, 1799; Warren, *Jacobin and Junto*, 106.
21. *Independent Chronicle*, June 20, 1799; Ames declined to act as Fairbanks's lawyer for the case, stating that "considering my local situation, and other obvious circumstances, . . . it would be unbecoming and improper for me to appear as his advocate."
22. *Independent Chronicle*, June 20, 1799.
23. *Independent Chronicle*, June 20, 1799; Smith, "The Federalist 'Saints,'" 211; unable to afford a lawyer, Brown represented himself in court.
24. *Independent Chronicle*, June 20, 1799; Smith, "The Federalist 'Saints,'" 212–14; Brown twice petitioned Adams for clemency to no avail. Jefferson granted him a full pardon on March 12, 1801; Anderson, "The Enforcement," 124–25; Pardon for David Brown, 12 March 1801, *The Papers of Thomas Jefferson*, vol. 33, *17 February–30 April 1801*, ed. Barbara B. Oberg, Princeton: Princeton University Press, 2006, 251–52, Founders Online.
25. *Independent Chronicle*, January 13, 1799, August 15, 1799, February 25, 1799; *Aurora General Advertiser*, November 22, 1798.
26. Fisher Ames to Timothy Dwight, December 22, 1799, Fisher Ames Papers (Dedham Historical Society). In May 1801, Jason Fairbanks, a relative of Benjamin's, was sentenced to death for the murder of Elizabeth Fales. That August, Fairbanks escaped from jail. The *Columbian Centinel* blamed the pole-raisers of 1798 for the prison break. "We learn that JASON FAIRBANKS, under sentence of death for murder, and confined in *Dedham* jail, was liberated therefrom on *Monday*, night last, by a banditti of the liberty-pole gentry of that part of the country." *Columbian Centinel*, August 19, 1801; Hanson, *Dedham*, 176–85.
27. Newman, *Fries's Rebellion*, xi, 13, 110, 121; for more details of this opposition, see the depositions in boxes 5 and 6 of the Rawle Family Papers at the Historical Society of Pennsylvania; James Roger Sharp describes Fries's Rebellion as "the missing piece of evidence—the Rosetta Stone—

that served to confirm the Federalists' most terrifying fears." Sharp, *The Deadlocked Election of 1800*, 64.
28. Deposition of Henry Ohl, April 27, 1799, Rawle Family Papers; Bouton, *Taming Democracy*, 247; Newman, *Fries's Rebellion*, 35, 32, 4–5; for more on the economic grievances of eastern Pennsylvanians, see Bouton, "'No Wonder the Times were Troublesome,'" 21–42; for an explanation of the link between landowning and political independence in the American consciousness, see Bouton, *Taming Democracy*, 17–18.
29. *The Oracle of Dauphin and Harrisburgh Advertiser*, January 23, 1799; Examination of Henry Ohl, April 27, 1799, Rawle Family Papers; Newman, *Fries's Rebellion*, 35–36.
30. Deposition of John Jarett, April 10, 1799, Deposition of Jacob Gorr, October 7, 1799, Deposition of Andrew Schlechter, April 6, 1799, Rawle Family Papers; Newman, *Fries's Rebellion*, 84; for a detailed description of the creating and raising of a liberty pole, see Deposition of James Jackson, October 23, 1799, Rawle Family Papers; for a discussion of the militia's centrality to the tax resistance, see Newman, *Fries's Rebellion*, 94.
31. Deposition of John Serfass, February 1, 1799, Rawle Family Papers; *The Two Trials of John Fries*, 222; Deposition of John Snyder, October 7, 1799, Examination of Jacob Eyerman, June 14, 1799, Rawle Family Papers; Newman, *Fries's Rebellion*, 103.
32. Deposition of John Serfass, February 1, 1799, Deposition of Conrad Kroesy, February 1, 1799, Deposition of John Snyder, October 7, 1799, Rawle Family Papers; *The Two Trials of John Fries*, 222; for an explanation of regulators' arguments that the Direct Tax was unconstitutional, see Newman, *Fries's Rebellion*, 119.
33. Deposition of Philip Wesco, undated, Deposition of John Fogel, Jr., January 29, 1799, Deposition of Michael Bapot, April 10, 1799, Deposition of Jacob Gorr, October 7, 1799, Rawle Family Papers; for examples of threats to tie officials to the liberty pole, see Examination of Samuel Clark, undated, Deposition of Jacob Brown, February 11, 1799, Deposition of Philip Kremer, February 13, 1799, Rawle Family Papers; Jarret even traveled to Upper Milford to campaign for the opposition, see "Loose unlabeled notes," in Rawle Family Papers, box 6, folder 3; these associations included the boycott of assessors' businesses, see Newman, *Fries's Rebellion*, 20; upon learning that his community's petition did not contain a section on the whiskey excise, one man declared, "then [throw] the petition into the fire and erect a Liberty Pole and let us fight." See Deposition of Frederick Seiberling, January 28, 1799, Rawle Family Papers.
34. For a more general discussion of liberty poles in 1798 and 1799, see chapter 4.

35. Chauncey Goodrich to John Treadwell, February 6, 1799, John Treadwell Papers (Connecticut Historical Society); *Annals of Congress*, 5th Cong., 3rd sess., February 25, 1799, 2990–92, quoted in Newman, *Fries's Rebellion*, 122; *The Two Trials of John Fries*, 40; Henderson, "Treason, Sedition, and Fries' Rebellion," 310; Newman, *Fries's Rebellion*, 109, 125, 138–40.

36. Deposition of Phillip Schlough, April 15, 1799, Rawle Family Papers; *The Two Trials of John Fries*, 221, 26, 41; Newman, *Fries's Rebellion*, ix; *Constitutional Diary and Philadelphia Evening Advertiser*, December 13, 1799; for more information on John Fries, see Newman, *Fries's Rebellion*, 114–19.

37. *Gazette of the United States*, March 11, 1799; *Oracle of Dauphin and Harrisburgh Advertiser*, April 10, 1799; Steiner, *The Life and Correspondence of James McHenry*, 437; Newman, *Fries's Rebellion*, 142–43.

38. Thomas Jefferson to Archibald Stuart, 13 February 1799, *The Papers of Thomas Jefferson*, vol. 31, *1 February 1799–31 May 1800*, ed. Barbara B. Oberg, Princeton: Princeton University Press, 2004, 33–36, Founders Online; Thomas Jefferson to Edmund Pendleton, 14 February 1799, *The Papers of Thomas Jefferson*, vol. 31, 36–39; *Aurora General Advertiser*, March 22, 1799; Newman, *Fries's Rebellion*, 150–51; see also Thomas Jefferson to Edmund Pendleton, 14 February 1799, *The Papers of Thomas Jefferson*, vol. 31, 36–39.

39. *American State Papers, Miscellaneous*, 185–86, quoted in Newman, *Fries's Rebellion*, 143; *Aurora General Advertiser*, March 22, 1799, March 15, 1799; Newman, *Fries's Rebellion*, 143–44.

40. Steiner, *The Life and Correspondence of James McHenry*, 433–34; Alexander Hamilton from James McHenry, 15 March 1799, *The Papers of Alexander Hamilton*, vol. 22, *July 1798–March 1799*, ed. Harold C. Syrett, New York: Columbia University Press, 1975, 539–42, Founders Online; Newman, *Fries's Rebellion*, 145–56.

41. Chauncey Goodrich to Oliver Wolcott, Jr., April 1799, Oliver Wolcott, Jr. Papers (Connecticut Historical Society); William MacPherson, *William MacPherson, Brigadier General in the Army of the United States* (Library Company of Philadelphia).

42. MacPherson's forces cut down one pole in Millerstown and four poles in Reading. They likely cut down more, but these instances went unrecorded. *Aurora General Advertiser*, April 13, 1799, May 24, 1799. See chapter 6 for a more detailed examination of troops' attacks on liberty poles and the political repercussions.

43. Note of Information from Colonel Valentine Eckhart, April 12, 1799, MacPherson Family Papers (Historical Society of Pennsylvania); William

MacPherson to Mahlon Ford, March 27, 1799, April 15, 1799, MacPherson Family Papers; *Aurora General Advertiser,* April 11, 1799; see also *Aurora General Advertiser,* April 13, 1799, April 16, 1799, May 21, 1799; the reports to the *Aurora* came from Thomas Leiper's Fourth Troop of Philadelphia City Cavalry, a Republican unit. Leiper and his troop are discussed in chapter 6. Koschnik, "Let a Common Interest Bind Us Together," 127–28.

44. Timothy Pickering to John Jay, May 21, 1799, Timothy Pickering Papers (Massachusetts Historical Society); Timothy Pickering to John Sloss Hobart, May 21, 1799, June 8, 1799, Timothy Pickering Papers; see Rawle Family Papers, box 6, folder 3, for Eÿermann's arrest warrant.
45. *The Two Trials of John Fries,* 220–22; Newman, *Fries's Rebellion,* 175–76.
46. Deposition of John Snyder, October 7, 1799, Rawle Family Papers; *The Two Trials of John Fries,* 223–24; see also Deposition of John Serfass, February 1, 1799, Rawle Family Papers.
47. *The Two Trials of John Fries,* 224–26; *Commercial Advertiser,* October 22, 1799; Bird, *Criminal Dissent,* 194–97.
48. John Adams from Jacob Eÿermann, 5 June 1800, Founders Online; John Adams to James Lloyd, 31 March 1815, Founders Online; *The Two Trials of John Fries,* 226; Newman, *Fries's Rebellion,* 180–83; several women also petitioned the president, see Woodrow et al., To the President of the United States, Miscellaneous Manuscripts Collection, 1668–1983 (American Philosophical Society); Fries received two trials. Judge Iredell threw out the guilty verdict in the first after Fries's attorney presented evidence that one of the jurors had publicly stated that Fries should be hanged, see *The Two Trials of John Fries,* appendix 2; Newman, *Fries's Rebellion,* 173.
49. George Washington from James McHenry, 30 March 1799, *The Papers of George Washington, Retirement Series,* vol. 3, *16 September 1798–19 April 1799,* ed. W. W. Abbot and Edward G. Lengel, Charlottesville: University Press of Virginia, 1999, 451–52, Founders Online; John Adams from Oliver Wolcott, Jr., 25 May 1799, Founders Online; William MacPherson to Mahlon Ford, April 15, 1799, William MacPherson Papers; John Adams to Abigail Smith Adams, 11 March 1799, Founders Online; Abigail Smith Adams to John Quincy Adams, 30 July 1799, Founders Online.
50. *Bee,* January 8, 1800; *Aurora General Advertiser,* July 15, 1799.
51. Since both Brown and Eÿermann were itinerants, neither of them owed any money under the Direct Tax. For an emphasis on this point with regard to Eÿermann, see Philanthropist, "Something Respecting the Parson Eyermann," October 20, 1799, in Rawle Family Papers.
52. *Columbian Centinel,* March 27, 1799.

## 6. From Poles to Polls

1. *Centinel of Freedom,* March 12, 1799.
2. I derived this number from evidence contained in the Rawle Family Papers (Historical Society of Pennsylvania) and contemporary newspapers; for more on the 1799 regulation, see chapter 5.
3. Deposition of James Jackson, October 23, 1799, Rawle Family Papers; Newman, *Fries's Rebellion,* 3; for Federalists' attempted prosecution of those involved in the Hembolts' pole-raising, see Bird, *Criminal Dissent,* 191–93.
4. Hand, "Circular" (Library Company of Philadelphia); *Circular Letter* (Library Company of Philadelphia); "Circular," *Philadelphia Gazette and Universal Daily Advertiser,* April 11, 1799; *Kline's Carlisle Weekly Gazette,* April 17, 1799; "Circular," *Universal Gazette,* May 23, 1799; Harris, *A Biographical History of Lancaster County;* Rupp, *History of Lancaster County;* there is no complete muster or payroll list for the Lancaster Troop of 1799. As constable for Reading, George Shoemaker identified John Frey, Adam Reigart, and Tobias Cryder as involved in the whipping of Schneider, see *Aurora General Advertiser,* May 24, 1799; for all other names, I have used the 1794 Payroll obtained from the Lancaster Historical Society.
5. We have the names of five of the Reading pole-raisers, since they offered sworn accounts of their treatment at the hands of the Lancaster Troop. Jacob Gossin had emigrated from Germany in 1788 with his wife and two children. John Strohecker, Isaac Feather, and Jacob Epler were Revolutionary War veterans of German descent. No records exist for Rudolph Sample. *Aurora General Advertiser,* May 24, 1799; *The Universal Gazette,* May 30, 1799; *Herald of Liberty,* June 10, 1799; Egle, *Names of Foreigners who took the Oath of Allegiance,* 533; Roberts, *Biographical Annals of Montgomery County,* 187; *Laws enacted in the third sitting of the eleventh General Assembly,* 320; Montgomery, *History of Berks County, Pennsylvania,* 207; *Lineage Book—National Society of the Daughters of the American Revolution,* vol. 50, 189; *Lineage Book—National Society of the Daughters of the American Revolution,* vol. 53, 126–27; *Free Press,* September 30, 1820; *State of the accounts of Jacob Morgan,* 15; Epler volunteered for multiple Republican committees of correspondence and served in the state Assembly in 1804; *Oracle of Dauphin and Harrisburgh Advertiser,* October 20, 1804; *Aurora General Advertiser,* June 18, 1806, November 24, 1807.
6. These details are taken from Gossin, Strohecker, Sample, Feather, Epler, and Schneider's sworn testimony printed in the *Aurora General Advertiser,* May 24, 1799.
7. *Aurora General Advertiser,* May 24, 1799.

8. *Aurora General Advertiser,* May 24, 1799.
9. *Aurora General Advertiser,* May 24, 1799.
10. *Aurora General Advertiser,* May 24, 1799.
11. *Aurora General Advertiser* May 13, 1799 (translated from the *Reading Adler,* April 9, 1799); see Newman, *Fries's Rebellion,* 80, for more information on the *Reading Adler;* for Pickering's aim to prosecute Schneider under the Sedition Law, see Bird, *Criminal Dissent,* 199–203.
12. Cox, *Champion of Southern Federalism,* 145–56; Sommerville, "Robert Goodloe Harper," 10–13; Newman, *Fries's Rebellion,* 162; Steiner, *The Life and Correspondence of James McHenry,* 433–34.
13. *Herald of Liberty,* May 20, 1799 (translated from the *Reading Adler,* April 23, 1799); *Aurora General Advertiser,* May 24, 1799 (translated from the *Reading Adler,* April 23, 1799). Leiper, a wealthy tobacco merchant, had served as a sergeant during the War of Independence and later belonged to the First Troop of Philadelphia City Cavalry, a Federalist volunteer unit. In 1794, the troop elected Leiper as a lieutenant. However, Leiper resigned that October due to an "indisposition." His resignation coincided with the First Troop's participation in quashing the Whiskey Rebellion, suggesting that Leiper left the troop for ideological reasons. Indeed, Leiper had criticized the whiskey excise since its passage in 1791. Soon after leaving the First Troop, Leiper established his own Republican Philadelphia City Cavalry. During the late 1790s, he became a financial backer of the *Aurora,* a regular chair of Republican meetings, and corresponded with Jefferson. In their 1799 Fourth of July toasts, Leiper's Fourth Troop endorsed Republican candidate Thomas McKean for governor. They also criticized the Lancaster Troop by insisting that militia should "be conspicuous for discipline and respect for the laws" and so, they implied, avoid trespassing, destroying property, and harassing civilians. *By-Laws, Muster-Roll, and Papers Selected from the Archives,* 16, 55; Koschnik, *"Let a Common Interest Bind Us Together,"* 99, 134; Shankman, *Crucible of American Democracy,* 47–48; *Aurora General Advertiser,* July 9, 1799.
14. *Aurora Daily Advertiser,* May 21, 1799.
15. *Weekly Advertiser of Reading,* April 6, 1799, April 27, 1799, May 25, 1799.
16. *Aurora General Advertiser,* May 13, 1799; *Universal Gazette,* May 16, 1799.
17. *Philadelphia Gazette and Universal Daily Advertiser,* May 13, 1799; *Porcupine's Gazette,* May 15, 1799.
18. *Aurora General Advertiser,* May 14, 1799.
19. *Herald of Liberty,* August 12, 1799; *Aurora General Advertiser,* May 6, 1799; for MacPherson's remarks, see *Universal Gazette,* May 16, 1799.
20. *Aurora General Advertiser,* May 13, 1799 (translated from *Reading Adler,* April 9, 1799).

21. *Aurora General Advertiser,* May 16, 1799, April 11, 1799, April 13, 1799, April 16, 1799, May 21, 1799; Koschnik, "*Let a Common Interest Bind Us Together,*" 127–29; *Gazette of the United States,* May 15, 1799; *Herald of Liberty,* June 3, 1799; *Philadelphia Gazette and Universal Daily Advertiser,* May 15, 1799; *Universal Gazette,* May 23, 1799; *Minutes of Examination, taken in short notes on the trial of the rioters;* some details of Duane's account were refuted by the *Philadelphia Gazette and Universal Daily Advertiser,* May 16, 1799.
22. *Aurora General Advertiser,* May 21, 1799; *Minutes of Examination,* 1–6; Daniel, *Scandal and Civility,* 261–64.
23. *Aurora General Advertiser,* May 16, 1799, May 21, 1799; for the links between Fries's Rebellion and the 1799 gubernatorial election, see Owen, *Political Community in Revolutionary Pennsylvania,* 170–71.
24. *Aurora General Advertiser,* April 30, 1799; for Republican descriptions of McKean and Ross, see, for example, A Citizen, "To the Electors of Cumberland County" (Library Company of Philadelphia).
25. Freneau, *Letters on Various Interesting and Important Subjects,* 30 (Library Company of Philadelphia); *Aurora General Advertiser,* April 30, 1799, July 30, 1799.
26. "Philadelphia Circular," May 27, 1799 (Library Company of Philadelphia); Postlethwaite, "Circular Letter," March 6, 1799 (Historical Society of Pennsylvania); for more of Addison's campaign activities, see, for example, Addison, "Copy of a Letter from Alexander Addison . . . to the Reverend Nathaniel Grier" (Historical Society of Pennsylvania).
27. *Aurora General Advertiser,* May 6, 1799; *Herald of Liberty,* August 12, 1799; see also *Aurora General Advertiser,* May 21, 1799; see *Aurora General Advertiser,* May 14, 1799, for the accusation that the Lancaster Troop acted like Jacobins.
28. Elijah Griffiths to Thomas Jefferson, August 4, 1799, *The Papers of Thomas Jefferson Digital Edition,* ed. Barbara B. Oberg and J. Jefferson Looney, Charlottesville, 2015, 151–53, Founders Online; George Washington to Jonathan Trumbull, Jr., 21 July 1799, *The Papers of George Washington, Retirement Series,* vol. 4, *20 April 1799–13 December 1799,* ed. W. W. Abbot, Charlottesville: University Press of Virginia, 1999, 201–4, Founders Online.
29. Lampi Collection of American Electoral Returns, 1788–1825, American Antiquarian Society, 2007; Keller, *Rural Politics and the Collapse of Pennsylvania Federalism,* 40–41; Gans and Mulling, *Voter Turnout in the United States,* 44–57; since Thomas Mifflin ran with bipartisan support in the two preceding gubernatorial elections, I did not use those statistics as reliable indicators of Republican strength. In the 1802 gubernatorial election,

Reading voted 88 percent Republican. In 1805, this number dropped to 71 percent, and it continued to decline thereafter. The Federalists received a 53 percent majority in Reading in 1814.

30. Examination of Francis Gibson, September 29, 1794, Rawle Family Papers; for more on McKean during the Whiskey Rebellion, see chapter 3.
31. James Monroe to Thomas McKean, July 12, 1800, Thomas McKean Papers (Historical Society of Pennsylvania); Thomas McKean to Samuel Adams, March 31, 1800, Samuel Adams Papers (David Library of the American Revolution).
32. *Aurora General Advertiser*, November 8, 1799; *Herald of Liberty*, November 24, 1800; see Weisberger, *America Afire*, 232–33, for Pennsylvania as an accurate predictor of national trends; for the links between local and national elections, see Waldstreicher, *In the Midst of Perpetual Fetes*, 184–85.
33. *Herald of Liberty*, December 1, 1800; *Aurora General Advertiser*, October 20, 1800.
34. *Centinel of Freedom*, March 12, 1799, March 25, 1800.
35. *Constitutional Telegraphe*, March 15, 1800; Thomas Jefferson to Edmund Pendleton, 29 January 1799, *The Papers of Thomas Jefferson*, vol. 30, 661–63, Founders Online; *Centinel of Freedom*, March 12, 1799.
36. *Centinel of Freedom*, December 23, 1800; Bishop, *Connecticut Republicanism*, 40 (Library Company of Philadelphia); Bishop, *Oration Delivered in Wallingford*, 37 (Library Company of Philadelphia).
37. Samuel Sitgreaves to Theodore Sedgwick, December 8, 1799, Sedgwick Family Papers (Massachusetts Historical Society); Charles L. Ogden to David Meredith, May 3, 1800, Meredith Family Papers (Historical Society of Pennsylvania); *Porcupine's Gazette*, October 19, 1799.
38. Black, *Address to the Federal Republicans of Burlington County*, 29 (Library Company of Philadelphia); Ames, "Laocoon No. II," in *Works of Fisher Ames* (1854), 127; Smith, "The Federalist 'Saints,'" 207–9.
39. Worcester, *An Election Sermon, delivered at Concord, June 4, 1800*, 13 (Library Company of Philadelphia); Peregrine Foster to Dwight Foster, May 21, 1798, Dwight Foster Papers (Massachusetts Historical Society); see also Daniel Dewey to Theodore Sedgwick, July 27, 1798, Sedgwick Family Papers.
40. Lee, *The Tree of Knowledge of Political Good and Evil*, 29 (Library Company of Philadelphia); Herrick, *An Oration, Delivered at Deerfield, on the Fourth of July, 1800*, 18 (Library Company of Philadelphia); *Columbian Centinel*, October 18, 1800.
41. Linn, *Serious Considerations on the Election of a President*, 19, 24 (American Philosophical Society); Worcester, *An Election Sermon*, 13; for an explo-

ration of the public images of Jefferson and Adams during the election of 1796, see Pasley, *The First Presidential Contest*, 224–306.
42. Young, *Liberty Tree*, 246; Sharp, *The Deadlocked Election of 1800*, 117, 119, 126, 128; Dunn, *Jefferson's Second Revolution*, 192–95; election data taken from the House of Representatives returns in Lampi Collection of American Electoral Returns.
43. *Aurora General Advertiser*, March 9, 1801, quoted in Newman, *Parades and the Politics of the Street*, 81; *Guardian of Liberty*, January 3, 1801; Newman, *Parades and the Politics of the Street*, 80–81.
44. Thomas Jefferson, Inaugural Address, March 4, 1805, American Presidency Project; Dunn, *Jefferson's Second Revolution*, 222–23; for a detailed discussion of Jefferson's First Inaugural Address, see Weisberger, *America Afire*, 279–84.
45. James Madison from Thomas Jefferson, 16 August 1803, *The Papers of James Madison, Secretary of State Series*, vol. 5, *16 May–31 October 1803*, ed. David B. Mattern, J. C. A. Stagg, Ellen J. Barber, Anne Mandeville Colony, and Bradley J. Daigle, Charlottesville: University Press of Virginia, 2000, 314–15, Founders Online; *Gazette of the United States*, March 11, 1801; Cotlar, *Tom Paine's America*, 211–14; Cotlar, "The Federalists' Transatlantic Cultural Offensive," in Pasley et al., *Beyond the Founders*, 276; Cotlar, "Joseph Gales and the Making of the Jeffersonian Middle Class," in *The Revolution of 1800*, 352–55; Daniel, *Scandal and Civility*, 282; Young, *Liberty Tree*, 247–48; Smith, *The Press, Politics, and Patronage*, 43–47; see the appendix in Stewart, *The Opposition Press of the Federalist Period*, for a list of newspapers and their partisan affiliations; for more on Duane's struggle to receive financial rewards from the Jefferson administration, see Cunningham, *The Jeffersonian Republicans in Power*, 268–74; for an argument that Jefferson retained the administrative apparatus designed by the Federalists, see Morone, *The Democratic Wish*, 70–73; for the post-1800 taming of Republican Fourth of July celebrations and partisan symbols, see Newman, *Parades and the Politics of the Street*, 116, 163–65.
46. Thomas Jefferson to Thomas McKean, 19 February 1803, *The Papers of Thomas Jefferson*, vol. 39, *13 November 1802–3 March 1803*, ed. Barbara B. Oberg, Princeton: Princeton University Press, 2012, 552–55, Founders Online; Thomas Jefferson from Thomas McKean, 7 February 1803, *The Papers of Thomas Jefferson*, vol. 39, 471–74; Levy, *Jefferson and Civil Liberties*, 58–67; Dunn, *Jefferson's Second Revolution*, 235; for a discussion of scholars' accusations that Jefferson acted hypocritically, see Sharp, *American Politics in the Early Republic*, 279–82.

47. Green, *An Address delivered before the Washington Benevolent Societies,* 21 (American Philosophical Society); Raguet, *Oration delivered before the Washington Benevolent Society,* 18 (American Philosophical Society); Harper, *A letter from Robert Goodloe Harper, of South Carolina, to his Constituents,* 3 (Library Company of Philadelphia); Fisher Ames to Oliver Wolcott, March 9, 1803, Oliver Wolcott, Jr. Papers; for more on this subject see Kerber, *Federalists in Dissent;* Fischer, *The Revolution of American Conservatism,* 25–26.
48. Taylor, *The Civil War of 1812,* 110–18; Jennings, "The Agitation for the Repeal of the Embargo Act," 220–24.
49. *Columbian Centinel,* January 6, 1808; *Boston Gazette,* March 18, 1808, quoted in Jennings, "The Agitation for the Repeal of the Embargo Act," 223; for an account of smuggling, see Jennings, "The Agitation for the Repeal of the Embargo Act," 231, 237–41; for an examination of the impulses within Federalism that constrained opposition, see Siegel, "'Steady Habits' under Siege," in Ben-Atar and Oberg, *Federalists Reconsidered,* 212–13.
50. Thomas Jefferson to Albert Gallatin, 19 April 1808, Founders Online; Sharp, *American Politics in the Early Republic,* 281–82; Thomas Jefferson to Thomas Lehré, 8 November 1808, Founders Online; Jennings, "The Agitation for the Repeal of the Embargo Act," 241.
51. *American Mercury,* July 1, 1802; *Centinel of Freedom,* March 15, 1803; *Public Advertiser,* June 22, 1808; see also *Eastern Argus,* July 4, 1812, *Saratoga Patriot,* October 19, 1813, *American Watchman and Delaware Republican,* November 17, 1813; on the disappearance of radicalism in Republican political culture, see Newman, *Parades and the Politics of the Street,* 186–92.
52. *Green-Mountain Farmer,* June 22, 1812; quoted in Strum, "New York Federalists and Opposition to the War of 1812," 171; Thomas Jefferson to James Madison, 29 June 1812, *The Papers of Thomas Jefferson, Retirement Series,* vol. 5, *1 May 1812 to 10 March 1813,* ed. J. Jefferson Looney, Princeton: Princeton University Press, 2008, 191–92, Founders Online; Strum, "New York Federalists and Opposition to the War of 1812," 171, 173; Taylor, *Civil War of 1812,* 125–37.
53. *Buffalo Gazette,* October 6, 1812, quoted in Taylor, *Civil War of 1812,* 179; Taylor, *Civil War of 1812,* 125–37, 177–78; Strum, "New York Federalists and Opposition to the War of 1812," 173.
54. Otis, *Letters Developing the Character and Views of the Hartford Convention,* by "One of the Convention," 21 (Connecticut Historical Society); *Amendments to the Constitution Proposed by the Hartford Convention: 1814,* Avalon Project; Banner, *To the Hartford Convention,* vii–ix, 294–350.

55. For Republicans channeling dissent into calls for a change in people, not systems, see Taylor, "Agrarian Independence," in *Beyond the American Revolution*, 235–37.

## 7. Partisan Politics and Poles in the Nineteenth Century

1. For examples of hickory poles, see *Daily National Journal*, June 7, 1828, *United States' Telegraph*, July 2, 1828, *New Orleans Argus*, July 14, 1828, *Connecticut Mirror*, November 17, 1828, *Enquirer*, March 17, 1829.
2. *Hudson River Chronicle*, December 25, 1838.
3. Thomas Jefferson to Destutt de Tracy, 26 January 1811, *The Papers of Thomas Jefferson, Retirement Series*, vol. 3, *12 August 1810 to 17 June 1811*, ed. J. Jefferson Looney, Princeton: Princeton University Press, 2006, 334–39, Founders Online. For more on the different views on partisanship from the First Party System to the Second, see Hofstadter, *The Idea of a Party System*.
4. Keyssar, *The Right to Vote*, 24–25; Grinspan, *The Virgin Vote*, 6–8; Altschuler and Blumin, *Rude Republic*, 14–17, 57–69; Watson, *Liberty and Power*, 232; for a useful summary of the legal, institutional, and cultural changes to the political landscape during this period, see Huston, "Rethinking the Origins of Partisan Democracy," in Peart and Smith, *Practicing Democracy*, 56–65; for a contextualization of these statistics, see Robertson, "Jeffersonian Parties, Politics, and Participation," in *Practicing Democracy*, 99–122.
5. Cotlar, *Tom Paine's America*, 206–9; Smith, *The Freedoms We Lost*, 183–210; Zagarri, *Revolutionary Backlash*, 148–80; for the exclusion of minorities in Republican popular culture post-1800, see Newman, *Parades and the Politics of the Street*, 186–92; for Republican celebrations as a form of electioneering, see Waldstreicher, *In the Midst of Perpetual Fetes*, 187; for an argument that elections replaced the more democratic system of regulation, see Bouton, "William Findley, David Bradford, and the Pennsylvania Regulation of 1794," in Young, *Revolutionary Founders*, 250. For more on the Second Party System, see Gienapp, "'Politics Seem to Enter into Everything,'" in Maizlish, *Essays on American Antebellum Politics*; Altschuler and Blumin, *Rude Republic*; "Political Engagement and Disengagement in Antebellum America: A Roundtable," 833–54; Pasley, "Party Politics, Citizenship, and Collective Action," 39–54; McGerr, *The Decline of Popular Politics*; Bensel, *The American Ballot Box in the Mid-Nineteenth Century*.
6. Neem, "Two Approaches to Democratization," in Peart and Smith, *Practicing Democracy*, 253–55; for female reformers denying their activities were political, see Zagarri, *Revolutionary Backlash*, 140–47.
7. Johnson, *Transportation of the mail on the Sabbath . . . ; Boston Statesmen*,

April 18, 1835, quoted in Neem, *Creating a Nation of Joiners*, 158; *Christian Examiner*, 1829, quoted in Peter Dobkin Hall, "The Decline, Transformation, and Revival of the Christian Right in the United States," in Bring and Schroedel, *Evangelicals and Democracy in America*, 253; Neem, *Creating a Nation of Joiners*,156; Volk, *Moral Minorities*, 28–29.

8. Volk, *Moral Minorities*, 172; Smith, *The Dominion of Voice*, 68; Varon, *Disunion!*, 102–3; Grimstead, *American Mobbing*, 13.
9. Davis, *Parades and Power*, 73–111.
10. Formisano, *For the People*, 72–77.
11. *Freeholder*, March 25, 1846, quoted in Huston, "Popular Movements and Party Rule," in Pasley et al., *Beyond the Founders*, 364; Formisano, *For the People*, 176–89; Huston, "Popular Movements and Party Rule," 361–65. For more on "playing Indian," see Deloria, *Playing Indian*.
12. Huston, "Popular Movements and Party Rule," 360–75.
13. Smith, *The Dominion of Voice*, 82, 53, 77; Gilje, *The Road to Mobocracy*, 200–205.
14. Watson, *Liberty and Power*, 87–95, 77; Holt, *Political Parties and American Political Development*, 34–36.
15. *Delaware Journal*, quoted in *Daily National Journal*, June 7, 1828; Watson, *Liberty and Power*, 94.
16. Watson, *Liberty and Power*, 113–27.
17. President Jackson's Proclamation Regarding Nullification, December 10, 1832, Avalon Project; Watson, *Liberty and Power*, 122, 127–31.
18. *United States' Telegraph*, July 20, 1831; *Greenville Mountaineer*, March 2, 1833; Huff, *Greenville*, 105; Holt, *The Political Crisis of the 1850s*, 7; for South Carolina's anti-party tradition, see Banner, "The Problem of South Carolina," in Elkins and McKitrick, *The Hofstadter Aegis*, 60–93; nullifiers also used palmetto trees as symbols, see, for example, *Niles Weekly Register*, April 20, 1833; I am very grateful to Brian Neumann for these sources and his helpful explanation of nullification and South Carolina politics.
19. *Baltimore Republican*, December 11, 1839, quoted in Watson, *Liberty and Power*, 215; Watson, *Liberty and Power*, 205–17; Holt, *Political Parties and American Political Development*, 152–53; Holt, *The Rise and Fall of the American Whig Party*, 31–32; for more on the growing acceptance of partisanship by 1840, see Silbey, *The American Political Nation*, 33–72.
20. *Madisonian*, March 9, 1840, May 28, 1840; see also *Haverhill Gazette*, July 4, 1840, *Madisonian*, October 6, 1840, *Daily National Intelligencer*, April 1, 1840, *Pennsylvania Inquirer and Daily Courier*, April 6, 1840, *Scioto Gazette*, May 28, 1840.
21. *Hudson River Chronicle*, July 9, 1839, September 15, 1840, December 25,

1838; *Daily National Intelligencer,* October 7, 1840; *Daily Herald and Gazette,* December 27, 1838.

22. *Ohio Statesman,* June 12, 1844, July 17 1844; *Ohio State Journal,* June 19, 1844; *Pittsfield Sun,* August 1, 1844; *Hudson River Chronicle,* August 6, 1844; *New Hampshire Patriot and State Gazette,* September 26, 1844, October 10, 1844; *Emancipator and Weekly Chronicle,* September 25, 1844; Watson, *Liberty and Power,* 229–30; for Whigs' purposeful reuse of the Harrison poles in 1844, see *Cleveland Herald,* March 15, 1844; *Daily Ohio Statesman,* July 27, 1852, *Bangor Daily Whig & Courier,* August 10, 1852, *Daily Atlas,* August 12, 1852, *New Hampshire Patriot and State Gazette,* September 29, 1852, October 6, 1852, September 3, 1856, *Arkansas Whig,* October 21, 1852, *Farmer's Cabinet,* July 17, 1856, August 7, 1856.

23. *Baltimore Patriot,* August 30, 1834; *North American and Daily Advertiser,* September 3, 1842; *North American,* October 16, 1846; *Log Cabin,* August 8, 1840; *Mississippi Free Trader and Natchez Gazette,* August 3, 1844; *Daily Ohio Statesman,* July 27, 1852; see also *North American and Daily Advertiser,* August 7, 1844; *Boston Daily Atlas,* November 7, 1844; *North American,* October 16, 1846; *Milwaukee Daily Sentinel,* September 14, 1852, September 18, 1852; papers also reported on poles destroyed by weather as signs of divine disfavor, see, for example, *Cleveland Herald,* June 26, 1844; *Boston Daily Atlas,* August 26, 1844; *Weekly Ohio Statesman,* September 11, 1844; *Fayetteville Observer,* October 23, 1844. Occasionally, fatal accidents occurred while raising poles, see, for example, *North American and Daily Advertiser,* October 10, 1842, October 3, 1844; *Daily National Advertiser,* August 19, 1844, September 30, 1844; October 1, 1844; *Boston Daily Atlas,* October 19, 1844.

24. *Ohio Statesman,* September 4, 1844; *Macon Weekly Telegraph,* June 25, 1844; *Log Cabin,* August 8, 1840; *Mississippi Free Trader and Natchez Gazette,* August 3, 1844; *Daily Ohio Statesman,* July 27, 1852, September 6, 1852.

25. *Ohio Statesman,* August 12, 1840; see also *Daily National Intelligencer,* November 6, 1844; *Daily Ohio Statesman,* September 25, 1852.

26. *Ohio Statesman,* June 5, 1844; see also *Daily Atlas,* July 11, 1844.

27. *Baltimore Patriot,* October 17, 1834; *New Hampshire Gazette,* October 21, 1834; *Daily Atlas,* October 17, 1834, October 18, 1834; *Newport Mercury,* October 18, 1834; *Portsmouth Journal of Literature and Politics,* October 25, 1834; *Rhode-Island Republican,* October 29, 1834; *Daily National Intelligencer,* October 17, 1834; the Whig candidates of Moyamensing won the election by about two hundred votes, despite the area being previously Democratic; see *Haverhill Gazette,* October 11, 1834.

28. *Sun,* November 4, 1840.

29. *Vermont Patriot*, July 29, 1839; *United States' Telegraph*, September 2, 1834; see also *New Hampshire Gazette*, October 8, 1844, *New Hampshire Statesman and State Journal*, May 24, 1834; *Cleveland Daily Herald*, June 8, 1840, June 18, 1840; *Weekly Ohio Statesman*, April 3, 1844.
30. *United States' Telegraph*, September 27, 1834.
31. *Connecticut Courant*, October 28, 1837; see also *Vermont Patriot*, July 5, 1839.
32. *Ohio Statesman*, August 12, 1840, August 21, 1840, August 26, 1840, January 14, 1845.
33. For the transition of rhetorical explanations for riots from institutional failures to individual moral defects, see Smith, *The Dominion of Voice*, 53.
34. Cotlar, *Tom Paine's America*, 206–9; for arguments that elections constituted a carnivalesque social inversion that legitimized the power of elites by marking the power of "the people" as temporary, see Morgan, *Inventing the People*, 197–208; Robertson, "Voting Rites," 62.
35. October 9, 1860; *Wisconsin Patriot*, July 21, 1860; McPherson, *Battle Cry of Freedom*, 213–33; the election of 1860 witnessed the formation of the Wide Awakes, a paramilitary political group of young men who campaigned for Lincoln and the Republicans. The Wide Awakes offer another example of popular political organizing focused on electoral victories. For more on the Wide Awakes, see Grinspan, "'Young Men for War,'" 357–78.
36. *New York Herald*, July 27, 1860, July 29, 1860, July 30, 1860.
37. *Charleston Courier*, November 20, 1860; *Philadelphia Inquirer*, November 19, 1860; McPherson, *Battle Cry of Freedom*, 232–35.
38. *New York Herald*, January 20, 1861; *Sun*, November 17, 1860; *New Hampshire Statesman*, November 24, 1860; *Houston Tri-Weekly Telegraph*, November 27, 1860.
39. *Philadelphia Inquirer*, January 1, 1861; *Macon Daily Telegraph*, February 9, 1861; *New York Herald*, December 24, 1860; McPherson, *Battle Cry of Freedom*, 254.
40. *Hartford Daily Courant*, April 30, 1861; *Bangor Daily Whig & Courier*, May 2, 1861; *Freedom's Champion*, May 11, 1861; *Wisconsin State Register*, May 11, 1861; *Sun*, April 20, 1861; see also *Bangor Daily Whig & Courier*, May 4, 1861, *Columbus Journal*, quoted in *Wisconsin State Register*, May 18, 1861, *Daily Evening Bulletin*, May 27, 1861, *New York Herald*, June 7, 1861, *Milwaukee Morning Sentinel*, June 28, 1861; for partisan poles during the war, see *Newark Advocate*, November 28, 1862; see also *Newark Advocate*, August 14, 1863, September 23, 1864; *Bangor Daily Whig & Courier*, September 4, 1863; *New Hampshire Statesman*, September 2, 1864; for a discussion of wartime partisan politics in the North, see Furniss, "States of the Union"; for Unionism and its links to the Revolution, see Gallagher, *The Union War*.

41. Jefferson Davis's Farewell Address, January 21, 1861, *The Papers of Jefferson Davis*, vol. 7, 18–23. Transcribed from the *Congressional Globe*, 36th Cong., 2nd sess., 487; Speech to the One Hundred Sixty-Fourth Ohio Regiment, August 18, 1864, *Collected Works of Abraham Lincoln*, vol. 7, Ann Arbor: University of Michigan Digital Library Production Services, 2001, 505.
42. *Vermont Watchman and State Journal*, July 17, 1863; *North American and United States Gazette*, November 2, 1863; *Ripley Bee*, June 27, 1861; *Daily Evening Bulletin*, April 11, 1862; *Freedom's Champion*, August 16, 1862; *Bangor Daily Whig & Courier*, July 23, 1863; *New Haven Daily Palladium*, April 13, 1865.
43. Holt, *The Political Crisis of the 1850s*, 220–59.
44. *Daily Cleveland Herald*, September 7, 1868; *Newark Advocate*, August 14, 1868; *Daily National Intelligencer*, August 19, 1868, August 22, 1868, August 24, 1868, August 29, 1868, September 17, 1868; *Boston Daily Advertiser*, September 9, 1868; *Lowell Daily Citizen and News*, September 22, 1868; *Bangor Daily Whig & Courier*, May 27, 1872; *Cleveland Morning Daily Herald*, August 8, 1872; *Milwaukee Sentinel*, August 15, 1872, September 23, 1872; *St. Louis Globe—Democrat*, August 23, 1876; *Inter Ocean*, September 4, 1876.
45. For examples of Centennial commemorations, see *Boston Daily Advertiser*, April 20, 1875, July 15, 1876; *Congregationalist*, April 22, 1875; *Bangor Daily Whig & Courier*, May 18, 1875; *Milwaukee Daily Sentinel*, July 4, 1876, July 22, 1876; *Arizona Weekly Miner*, July 21, 1876.
46. Waldstreicher, Pasley, and Robertson, "Introduction: Beyond the Founders," in Pasley et al., *Beyond the Founders*, 2–3; Peart and Smith, "Introduction," in Peart and Smith, *Practicing Democracy*, 7–8; Mandell, *The Lost Tradition of Economic Equality*, 164–91; Waldstreicher, *In the Midst of Perpetual Fetes*, 177–245; for an argument that electioneering rituals in the early republic were more inclusive than in the antebellum era, see Robertson, "Voting Rites," in Pasley et al., *Beyond the Founders*; for an argument that nineteenth-century elections were masculine spaces, see Grimstead, *American Mobbing*.

## Epilogue

1. Robert H. Kelby, Meeting Minutes, November 5, 1919, "Liberty Pole—Documents Concerning the 1922 Rededication" (New York Historical Society); the bottom two-thirds of the pole consisted of Douglas fir from Oregon and the top third was wood from Maine, "joining the East and the West as contributors to the completion of the pole." Joint Committee of Historical Society and Sons of the Revolution to George A. Zabriskie, July 14, 1820,

"Liberty Pole—Documents Concerning the 1922 Rededication" (New York Historical Society).
2. Goold, "Liberty Poles—Symbols of Freedom," 20.
3. Kristin LaFratta, "Bedford 'Pole Capping' Ceremony: The Massachusetts Tradition You've Probably Never Heard Of," *MassLive,* April 8, 2017. Some examples of street names include Liberty Pole Road in Hingham, Massachusetts, and Springwater, New York, Liberty Pole Way in Rochester, New York, and Liberty Pole Point in Stonington, Maine. For further examples, see Young, *Liberty Tree,* 374.
4. Perry Stein, "Marijuana and Statehood Activists Are Chaining Themselves to 'Liberty Pole' on the Mall," *Washington Post,* April 15, 2015.
5. Diana Nelson Jones, "Rebel History Makes for Spirited Tour in Washington County," *Pittsburgh Post-Gazette,* June 9, 2018; Celine Roberts, "Distillery in Washington, Pa., looks to history," *Pittsburgh City Paper,* July 6, 2016; Katherine Mansfield, "Give me Liberty (Pole Spirits)," *Observer Reporter,* May 17, 2022.
6. Young, *The Shoemaker and the Tea Party,* 113; Alan Taylor, "Our Feuding Founding Fathers," *New York Times,* October 17, 2016; for more on the Declaration of Independence in popular memory, see Maier, *American Scripture.*
7. Skinner, *Liberty Before Liberalism,* 117–20.

❖ ESSAY ON SOURCES ❖

### Primary Sources

Like many twenty-first-century scholars, I began my research with a keyword search. To my delight, the term "liberty pole" returned hundreds of hits in the *American Historical Newspapers* database. As I read the articles, I was captivated by the stories that I found—a whipping in Reading, a near-riot in Northumberland, a mock funeral in Hackensack, a trial in Dedham. A world of grassroots political activity opened to me, and my project began to take shape. Newspapers form the bedrock of this book, revealing not only reports of specific incidents, but also the geographic spread of liberty poles, how news of their raisings and destructions traveled over space and time, and how partisans reacted to these events. These reports range from full pages of firsthand testimony to just a few words noting locations where poles had been sighted. This wide spectrum of detail is why some poles form the basis of certain chapters and others are barely mentioned.

For other sources, especially those that offer firsthand accounts, I scoured numerous archives. The Rawle Family Papers at the Historical Society of Pennsylvania (HSP) is a treasure trove of information on liberty poles raised during the Whiskey Rebellion and Fries's Rebellion. William Rawle was the United States district attorney for Pennsylvania between 1791 and 1799, and his papers contain scores of depositions from those events, almost all of which focus on liberty pole conflicts. The depositions attest to the centrality of liberty poles to those regulations and provide a window into community dynamics as neighbors blamed, defended, and accused each other. They enabled me to piece together the events of my Pennsylvania case studies in Carlisle, Northumberland, and Hamilton. They also revealed heretofore unstudied local political leaders, like William Bonham and Jacob Eÿermann.

I searched through many collections of other personal papers at several different archives looking for liberty poles. This exercise felt like searching for a needle in a haystack, if both the needle and haystack had messy handwriting. But my labors were rewarded, sometimes handsomely. For instance, in the MacPherson Family Papers at the HSP, I discovered General William MacPherson's instructions to cut down liberty poles, lest they serve as rallying points for the regulators—the only official order to destroy liberty poles that my research unearthed. Other Federalist papers, like the Dwight Foster Papers and the Sedgwick Family Papers at the Massachusetts Historical Society, contain firsthand accounts and opinions on liberty poles.

Court records provide information about those occasions when pole-raisers faced formal justice. The trial transcripts contain the arguments each side used to either criminalize or legitimize liberty pole-raisings. They also demonstrate how courts often offered leniency to community members and harshly punished outsiders, as illustrated in the trials of Benjamin Fairbanks and David Brown. In addition, at Brown's sentencing, the court quoted extensively from his unpublished "Dissertations," and so the Records of the U.S. Circuit Court at Boston at the National Archives contain the only surviving fragments of Brown's writings.

To better understand the communities and individuals that populated my case studies, I relied on published local histories, sermons, toasts, speeches, diaries, tax and census data, electoral results, and militia records. In particular, the Direct Tax lists of 1798 reveal the economic statuses of the various players and wider communities in several pole-raisings. As I panned out from the particulars of pole-raisings and destructions to the state and national political scenes, I relied on a primary source base familiar to all historians of early American political culture: newspapers, pamphlets, broadsides, circulars, correspondence, resolutions, remonstrances, orations, toasts, sermons, and congressional records, to name but a few.

## Secondary Sources

This is the first book-length study of liberty poles, but a handful of scholars have explored the phenomenon in a more limited fashion. Some historians of the American Revolution have examined New York City's liberty poles and Boston's Liberty Tree together, as well as the spread of both symbols throughout the colonies. See Arthur M. Schlesinger, "Liberty Tree: A Genealogy," *New*

*England Quarterly* 25, no. 4 (Dec. 1952): 435–58; David Hackett Fischer, *Liberty and Freedom: A Visual History of America's Founding Ideas* (New York: Oxford University Press, 2005); Alfred F. Young, *Liberty Tree: Ordinary People and the American Revolution* (New York: New York University Press, 2006). For an analysis of the New York City liberty poles as political markers of space and their destructions as a form of iconoclasm, see Wendy Bellion, "Mast Trees, Liberty Poles, and the Politics of Scale in Late Colonial New York," in *Scale*, ed. Jennifer L. Roberts, Terra Foundation Essays, Volume 2 (Chicago: University of Chicago Press, 2016), 218–49. Lee R. Boyer's work on Revolutionary New York City and the Battle of Golden Hill offers helpful insight into the economic tensions between New York pole-raisers and British soldiers. See Lee R. Boyer, "Lobster Backs, Liberty Boys, and Laborers in the Streets: New York's Golden Hill and Nassau Street Riots," *New York Historical Society Quarterly* 57 (1973).

There are two articles on the Dedham liberty pole, both of which focus on the ensuing trials as evidence of Federalists' political prosecution of Republicans: James Morton Smith, "The Federalist 'Saints' versus 'The Devil of Sedition': The Liberty Pole Case of Dedham, Massachusetts 1798–1799," *New England Quarterly* 28, no. 2 (June 1955): 198–215; Frank Maloy Anderson, "The Enforcement of the Alien and Sedition Laws," *Annual Report of the American Historical Association for the Year 1912* (Washington, 1914), 115–26.

Simon P. Newman briefly explores liberty poles in his analysis of partisan symbols in *Parades and the Politics of the Street: Festive Culture in the Early American Republic* (Philadelphia: University of Pennsylvania Press, 1997). Newman draws interesting connections between Republican liberty poles, European maypoles, and French liberty poles, emphasizing especially how the latter two imbued the former with connotations of social and political inversion. These insights helped me see how these transnational symbolic connections informed Federalist reactions.

In short, the existing scholarship offers some scattered, tantalizing mentions of liberty poles, but no sustained and significant analysis. In filling this gap, this book demonstrates the centrality of liberty poles to early American politics and so deepens our understandings of Federalist popular action, Republican intra-party tensions, and the contested place of resistance and regulation as American political culture evolved. Liberty poles force us to revise, challenge, and deepen previous understandings of the early American political landscape.

As a result, this book relies on the excellent work of the past several decades on that topic. Many superb studies have broken important ground by expanding "the political" and exploring power, organizing, and leadership in a diverse array of contexts. This scholarship has had an immeasurable impact on my thinking and laid the foundation for my study of extra-institutional politics. Although not an exhaustive list, below is a discussion of some of the work most critical to the formation of this project.

Joanne Freeman and Stephanie M. H. Camp illustrate the broad range of political activity found at both ends of the social spectrum when one looks beyond just elections and legislatures. Freeman's analysis of elite dueling and honor culture and Camp's exploration of everyday plantation resistance enriched and expanded my understanding of who and what count as political history. See Joanne Freeman, *Affairs of Honor: National Politics in the New Republic* (New Haven: Yale University Press, 2001); Stephanie M. H. Camp, *Closer to Freedom: Enslaved Women and Everyday Resistance in the Plantation South* (Chapel Hill: University of North Carolina Press, 2004). Likewise, Jeffrey L. Pasley's and Richard S. Newman's arguments for widening the category of political leadership informed my reading of local political activists as grassroots partisan leaders. See Jeffrey L. Pasley, *"The Tyranny of Printers": Newspaper Politics in the Early American Republic* (Charlottesville: University of Virginia Press, 2001); Richard S. Newman, *Freedom's Prophet: Bishop Richard Allen, the AME Church, and the Black Founding Fathers* (New York: New York University Press, 2008). Both Doron Ben-Atar and Barbara B. Oberg, eds., *Federalists Reconsidered* (Charlottesville: University of Virginia Press, 1998) and Jeffrey L. Pasley, Andrew W. Robertson, and David Waldstreicher, eds., *Beyond the Founders: New Approaches to the Political History of the Early American Republic* (Chapel Hill: University of North Carolina Press, 2004) are valuable collections that illustrate the wide-ranging possible avenues of analysis in the field of political culture.

The work on festive culture has been foundational to the field of early American popular politics. Newman, *Parades and the Politics of the Street*; David Waldstreicher, *In the Midst of Perpetual Fetes: The Making of American Nationalism, 1776–1820* (Chapel Hill: University of North Carolina Press, 1997); Len Travers, *Celebrating the Fourth: Independence Day and the Rites of Nationalism in the Early Republic* (Amherst: University of Massachusetts Press, 1997) are the key works on how rituals, symbols, and celebrations, as well as their coverage in the press, shaped the First Party System. This scholarship has proved invaluable to me in its exploration of grassroots Federalist political action. Waldstreicher, Newman, and Travers have shown how Federalists used festive culture to demonstrate popular approval of the federal government. Waldstreicher's explanation of nationalism as "partisan antipartisanship" has been particularly helpful in understanding how both Federalists and Republicans viewed and legitimized their actions.

Others have looked specifically at how Federalists organized counter-demonstrations to combat the growing Republican opposition movement. See Todd Estes, *The Jay Treaty Debate, Public Opinion, and the Evolution of Early American Print Culture* (Amherst: University of Massachusetts Press, 2006); Jeffrey L. Pasley, *The First Presidential Contest: 1796 and the Founding of American Democracy* (Lawrence: University Press of Kansas, 2013). Estes, in particular, shows how Federalists used crowd action and the press to shape popular opinion. This work has laid an important foundation for my study of Federalist popular politics of assent, which reveals how Federalist crowd action grew more confrontational and violent in the face of Republican liberty poles.

There is a wealth of interesting and important work on regulation and popular dissent. For early regulators, I relied on Marjoleine Kars, *Breaking Loose Together: The Regulator Rebellion in Pre-Revolutionary North Carolina* (Chapel Hill: University of North Carolina Press, 2002); Sean Condon, *Shays's Rebellion: Authority and Distress in Post-Revolutionary America* (Baltimore: John Hopkins University Press, 2015); Robert A. Gross, ed., *In Debt to Shays: The Bicentennial of an Agrarian Rebellion* (Charlottesville: University of Virginia Press, 1993); Alan Taylor, *Liberty Men and Great Proprietors: The Revolutionary Settlement of the Maine Frontier, 1760–1820* (Chapel Hill: The Omohundro Institute of Early American History and Culture by the University of North Carolina Press, 1990).

In *Taming Democracy: The People, the Founders, and the Troubled Ending of the American Revolution* (Oxford: Oxford University Press, 2007), Terry Bouton exposes lesser-known decentralized regulations in Pennsylvania during the 1780s and draws a through line between these events and the regulations of 1794 and 1799. Bouton establishes important connections between grassroots economic grievances from the Revolutionary period and the opposition politics of the early republic. This book builds on Bouton's findings by looking beyond just Pennsylvania and interrogating the local divides over regulations and resistance practices.

Likewise, in *Political Community in Revolutionary Pennsylvania, 1774–1800* (Oxford: Oxford University Press, 2018), Kenneth Owen explores political organizing and resistance in Pennsylvania and makes a compelling case for the influence of popular politics on the state's political culture, parties, and institutions. However, Owen's analysis ends in 1800 and so does not grapple with the reverses that I and others have observed in the antebellum era.

Both Owen and Bouton look at the connections between the events of 1794 and 1799 and their deeper roots in Pennsylvania's popular political culture. Other important work on the Whiskey Rebellion includes Thomas P. Slaughter, *The Whiskey Rebellion: Frontier Epilogue to the American Revolution* (New York: Oxford University Press, 1986); Dorothy Elaine Fennell, "From Rebelliousness to Insurrection: A Social History of the Whiskey Rebellion, 1765–1802," PhD diss., University of Pittsburgh, 1981; Johann N. Neem, "Freedom of Association in the Early Republic: The Republican Party, the Whiskey Rebellion, and the Philadelphia and New York Cordwainers' Cases," *Pennsylvania Magazine of History and Biography* 127, no. 3 (July 2003): 259–90; Steven R. Boyd, ed., *The Whiskey Rebellion: Past and Present Perspectives* (Westport: Greenwood Press, 1985). Paul Douglas Newman's *Fries's Rebellion: The Enduring Struggle for the American Revolution* (Philadelphia: University of Pennsylvania Press, 2004) remains the definitive work on Fries's Rebellion. Saul Cornell provides the best guide to Anti-Federalism; see Saul Cornell, *The Other Founders: Anti-Federalism and the Dissenting Tradition in America, 1788–1828* (Chapel Hill: University of North Carolina Press, 1999).

A handful of scholars have used studies of popular politics to rethink ideas of democratization and political participation. I have been greatly influenced by Seth Cotlar, *Tom Paine's America: The Rise and Fall of Transatlantic Radicalism in the Early Republic* (Charlottesville: University of Virginia Press, 2011), and Rosemarie Zagarri, *Revolutionary Backlash: Women and Politics in the Early Republic* (Philadelphia: University of Pennsylvania Press, 2008). Both books argue that the antebellum embrace of partisanship and electoral politics sacrificed the more democratic and inclusive popular politics of the early republic. My study of the liberty pole's transition from a resistance to a campaign symbol aligns with their analyses. Other works make a similar argument, although they locate the shift earlier. Barbara Clark Smith argues that the transition occurred immediately after the American Revolution, and Bouton states that it took place during the 1780s and 1790s. See Barbara Clark Smith, *The Freedoms We Lost: Consent and Resistance in Revolutionary America* (New York: New Press, 2010). However, the arc of the liberty pole suggests that the elections of 1799 and 1800 are a more accurate pivot point.

Several key books on the Revolutionary period have informed my understanding of Patriot resistance practices and their relationship to colonial traditions. In addition to Smith, I have especially relied on Young, *Liberty Tree;* Alfred F. Young, ed., *The American Revolution: Explorations in the History of American Radicalism* (DeKalb: Northern Illinois University Press, 1976); Paul A. Gilje, *The Road to Mobocracy: Popular Disorder in New York City, 1763–1834* (Chapel Hill: University of North Carolina Press, 1987).

There is a wealth of important work on the early republic's popular politics, partisanship, and political culture. For partisan division over ideas of citizenship, participation, and tactics, I found especially helpful Albrecht Koschnik, *"Let a Common Interest Bind Us Together": Associations, Partisanship, and Culture in Philadelphia, 1775–1840* (Charlottesville: University of Virginia Press, 2007); Douglas Bradburn, *The Citizenship Revolution: Politics and the Creation of the American Union, 1774–1804* (Charlottesville: University of Virginia Press, 2009). Some useful syntheses of the period include Carol Berkin, *A Sovereign People: The Crises of the 1790s and the Birth of American Nationalism* (New York: Basic Books, 2017); James Roger Sharp, *American Politics in the Early Republic: A New Nation in Crisis* (New Haven: Yale University Press, 1993).

For insight into early Americans who linked political and economic power, I relied on the excellent work of Bouton, Cotlar, and Andrew Shankman, *Crucible of American Democracy: The Struggle to Fuse Egalitarianism & Capitalism in Jeffersonian Pennsylvania* (Lawrence: University of Kansas Press, 2004). For a recent work that traces this ideological tenet from its English origins through Reconstruction, see Daniel R. Mandell, *The Lost Tradition of Economic Equality in America, 1600–1870* (Baltimore: Johns Hopkins University Press, 2020). For a study of William Manning and *The Key of Libberty*, see Michael Merrill and Sean Wilentz, eds., *The Key of Liberty: The Life and Democratic Writings of William Manning, 'A Laborer,' 1747–1814* (Cambridge: Harvard University Press, 1993). All of these studies provided important background for my analysis of Brown and Eÿermann and the underground cohort of itinerant activists that they represent.

There is an abundance of fascinating scholarship on the antebellum era's political culture, too much to name. I have relied primarily on work concerned with extra-institutional political action and partisan organizing. Both Susan G. Davis, *Parades and Power: Street Theatre in Nineteenth Century Philadelphia* (Philadelphia: Temple University Press, 1986), and David Grimstead, *American Mobbing, 1828–1861: Toward Civil War* (Oxford: Oxford University Press, 2003), explore how different classes, groups, and regions used street politics and how those tactics changed over time. Although I disagree with Glenn C. Altschuler's and Stuart Blumin's thesis about disengagement, their work was supremely helpful in thinking through the distance antebellum partisanship created between people and politics. See *Rude Republic: Americans and Their Politics in the Nineteenth Century* (Princeton: Princeton University Press, 2000). In *Moral Minorities and the Making of American Democracy* (Oxford: Oxford University Press, 2014), Kyle G. Volk provides a clear, persuasive guide to moral reform movements and their impact on shifting ideas of minority rights and majority rule. Volk's book helped me clarify the differences between institutional advocacy and extra-institutional protest in the antebellum era. The essays in *Practicing Democracy: Popular Politics in the United States from the Constitution to the Civil War*, eds. Daniel Peart and Adam I. P. Smith (Charlottesville: University of Virginia Press, 2015), reinforce this book's contention that partisanship, participation, and political practice are interrelated yet distinct entities, and that conflating them obscures both the continuities and the differences between the early republic and antebellum eras.

For a theoretical approach to American political thought and action, especially as it pertains to the slipperiness of "the people," I utilized Jason A. Frank, *Constituent Moments: Enacting the People in Postrevolutionary America* (Durham: Duke University Press, 2010); James A. Morone, *The Democratic Wish: Popular Participation and the Limits of American Government*, revised edition (New Haven: Yale University Press, 1998). Similarly, Kimberly K. Smith, *The Dominion of Voice: Riot, Reason, and Romance in Antebellum Politics* (Lawrence: University Press of Kansas, 1999), offers a helpful study of American concepts of the right to resistance and how they evolved over time.

As should be evident by now, this book is deeply embedded in the scholarship of early American political history. But it is also informed by the historical moment in which I wrote it. Current tensions over the relationship between citizens and elected officials, the legitimacy of protest, the efficacy of elections, the restrictions of partisanship, and the role of media shaped my questions and analysis. Some may criticize this as presentism, but I am steadfast in my belief that history is better when it speaks to the present and best when it implores us toward a better future.

## ❖ BIBLIOGRAPHY ❖

### Primary Sources

*Manuscript and Archival Sources*

#### AMERICAN PHILOSOPHICAL SOCIETY, PA
Castle-Bache Collection
Joseph Priestley Papers
Miscellaneous Manuscripts Collection, 1668–1983

#### CONNECTICUT HISTORICAL SOCIETY
John Treadwell Papers
Oliver Wolcott, Jr. Papers

#### DAVID LIBRARY OF THE AMERICAN REVOLUTION, MA
Samuel Adams Papers

#### DEDHAM HISTORICAL SOCIETY, MA
Fisher Ames Papers

#### HARVARD UNIVERSITY ARCHIVES
Papers of Fisher Ames and Fowler Families

#### HISTORICAL SOCIETY OF PENNSYLVANIA
Alexander Addison, "Copy of a Letter from Alexander Addison . . . to the Reverend Nathaniel Grier"

MacPherson Family Papers
Meredith Family Papers
Rawle Family Papers
Samuel Postlethwaite, "Circular Letter," March 6, 1799
Thomas McKean Papers

### LANCASTER HISTORICAL SOCIETY, PA

Lancaster Troop of Horse, Payroll, 1794

### LIBRARY COMPANY OF PHILADELPHIA

A Citizen, "To the Electors of Cumberland County," Philadelphia, 1799
Brutus, "To the Public," January 15, 1770, New York City
*Circular Letter*, Philadelphia, April 4, 1799
Edward Hand, "Circular," Lancaster, 1799
"Philadelphia Circular," May 27, 1799
William MacPherson, *William MacPherson, Brigadier General in the Army of the United States, Commanding the troops destined to act against the Insurgents in the Counties of Northampton, Montgomery, and Bucks, in the State of Pennsylvania*, Philadelphia, 1799

### MASSACHUSETTS HISTORICAL SOCIETY

Dwight Foster Papers
Sedgwick Family Papers
Timothy Pickering Papers

### NATIONAL ARCHIVES

Records of the Office of the Comptroller General. RG-4. *Tax & Exoneration Lists, 1762–1794*. Microfilm Roll: 331
Records of the U.S. Circuit Court at Boston, 1799
*United States Direct Tax of 1798: Tax Lists for the State of Pennsylvania*. M372, microfilm, 24 rolls. Records of the Internal Revenue Service, 1791–2006. Record Group 58

### NEW YORK HISTORICAL SOCIETY

Liberty Pole—Documents Concerning the 1922 Rededication
"To the Sons of Liberty in this City," February 3, 1770, New York City

PENNSYLVANIA STATE ARCHIVES

Record Group LC-3, Berks County, Board of Commissioners, Reading Township, Roll 522, Courtesy of Pennsylvania Historical and Museum Commission

## Newspapers

*Albany (NY) Centinel*
*Albany (NY) Gazette*
*Albany (NY) Register*
*American Mercury* (Hartford, CT)
*American Watchman and Delaware Republican* (Wilmington)
*Arizona Weekly Miner* (Prescott)
*Arkansas Whig* (Little Rock)
*Aurora Daily Advertiser* (Philadelphia)
*Aurora General Advertiser* (Philadelphia)
*Baltimore Daily Intelligencer*
*Baltimore Patriot*
*Bangor (ME) Daily Whig & Courier*
*Bee* (Hudson, NY)
*Berkshire Gazette* (Pittsfield, MA)
*Boston Daily Advertiser*
*Boston Daily Atlas*
*Boston Gazette*
*Carey's United States Recorder* (Philadelphia)
*Carlisle (PA) Gazette*
*Centinel of Freedom* (Newark, NJ)
*Charleston (SC) Courier*
*Cleveland Daily Herald*
*Cleveland Herald*
*Cleveland Morning Daily Herald*
*Columbian Centinel* (Boston)
*Commercial Advertiser* (New York City)
*Congregationalist* (Boston)
*Connecticut Courant* (Hartford)
*Connecticut Mirror* (Hartford)
*Constitutional Diary and Philadelphia Evening Advertiser*
*Constitutional Telegraphe* (Boston)
*Courier of New Hampshire* (Concord)

*Daily Atlas* (Boston)
*Daily Cleveland Herald*
*Daily Evening Bulletin* (Philadelphia)
*Daily Herald and Gazette* (Cleveland)
*Daily National Intelligencer* (Washington, DC)
*Daily National Journal* (Washington, DC)
*Daily Ohio Statesman* (Columbus)
*Dunlap and Claypoole's American Advertiser* (Philadelphia)
*Eastern Argus* (Portland, ME)
*Emancipator and Weekly Chronicle* (Boston)
*Farmer's Cabinet* (Amherst, NH)
*Fayetteville (NC) Observer*
*Federal Gazette* (Philadelphia)
*Freedom's Champion* (Atchison, KS)
*Free Press* (Charleston, SC)
*Gazette of the United State* (New York City)
*Greenleaf's New York Journal* (New York City)
*Green-Mountain Farmer* (Bennington, VT)
*Greenville (SC) Mountaineer*
*Guardian of Liberty* (Newport, RI)
*Hartford (CT) Daily Courant*
*Haverhill Gazette* (MA)
*Herald* (New York City)
*Herald of Liberty* (Washington)
*Houston Tri-Weekly Telegraph*
*Hudson River Chronicle* (Westchester, NY)
*Independent Chronicle* (Boston)
*Inter Ocean* (Chicago)
*Kline's Carlisle (PA) Weekly Gazette*
*Log Cabin* (New York City)
*Lowell (MA) Daily Citizen and News*
*Macon (GA) Daily Telegraph*
*Macon (GA) Weekly Telegraph*
*Madisonian* (Washington, DC)
*Massachusetts Mercury* (Boston)
*Massachusetts Spy* (Boston)
*Middlesex (CT) Gazette*
*Milwaukee Daily Sentinel*
*Milwaukee Morning Sentinel*
*Milwaukee Sentinel*

*Mississippi Free Trader and Natchez Gazette*
*Newark (OH) Advocate*
*Newburyport (MA) Herald*
*New Hampshire Gazette* (Portsmouth)
*New Hampshire Patriot and State Gazette* (Concord)
*New Hampshire Statesman* (Concord)
*New Hampshire Statesman and State Journal* (Concord)
*New Haven (CT) Daily Palladium*
*New Orleans Argus*
*Newport (RI) Mercury*
*New-York Gazette* (New York City)
*New York Gazette, and Weekly Mercury* (New York City)
*New York Gazette, or Weekly Post Boy* (New York City)
*New York Herald* (New York City)
*New York Journal* (New York City)
*New York Mercury* (New York City)
*Niles Weekly Register* (Baltimore)
*North American* (Philadelphia)
*North American and Daily Advertiser* (Philadelphia)
*North American and United States Gazette* (Philadelphia)
*Ohio State Journal* (Columbus)
*Ohio Statesman* (Columbus)
*Oracle of Dauphin and Harrisburgh (PA) Advertiser*
*Oracle of the Day* (Portsmouth, NH)
*Otsego (NY) Herald*
*Pennsylvania Chronicle* (Philadelphia)
*Pennsylvania Inquirer and Daily Courier* (Philadelphia)
*Pennsylvania Telegraph* (Harrisburg)
*Philadelphia Gazette and Universal Daily Advertiser*
*Pittsfield (MA) Sun*
*Porcupine's Gazette* (Philadelphia)
*Portsmouth (NH) Journal of Literature and Politics*
*Public Advertiser* (New York City)
*Rhode-Island Republican* (Newport)
*Ripley (OH) Bee*
*Salem (MA) Gazette*
*Saratoga (NY) Patriot*
*Scioto Gazette* (Chillicothe, OH)
*Spectator* (New York City)
*Stewart Kentucky Herald* (Lexington)

*St. Louis Globe—Democrat*
*Sun* (New York City)
*Time Piece* (New York City)
*United States' Telegraph* (Washington, DC)
*Universal Gazette* (Philadelphia)
*Vermont Patriot* (Montpelier)
*Vermont Watchman and State Journal* (Montpelier)
*Weekly Advertiser of Reading (PA)*
*Wisconsin Patriot* (Madison)
*Wisconsin State Register* (Columbia)

## Published Primary Sources

A Friend to Rational Liberty. "The Jacobin Looking-Glass." Worcester: Leonard Worcester, 1795.

Addison, Alexander. *Analysis of the Report of the Committee of the Virginia Assembly, on the Proceedings of Sundry of the Other States in Answer to their Resolutions.* Raleigh: Hodge & Boylan, 1800.

———. *Charges to Grand Juries of the County Courts of the Fifth Circuit, of the state of Pennsylvania.* Vergennes: Printed by Samuel Chipman, Jr., 1799.

———. *Reports of Cases in the County Courts of the Fifth Circuit and in the High Court of Errors and Appeals in the State of Pennsylvania.* Philadelphia: Kay & Brother, 1883.

*American State Papers, Miscellaneous,* Volume 1. Washington, D.C.: Gales and Seaton, 1834.

Ames, Fisher. *An Oration on the Sublime Virtues of General George Washington.* Boston: Young & Minns, 1800.

———. *Works of Fisher Ames, Compiled by a Number of his Friends.* Boston: T. B. Wait, 1809.

———. *Works of Fisher Ames: With a Selection from his Speeches and Correspondence.* Boston: Everett and Monroe, 1809.

———. *Works of Fisher Ames: With a Selection from his Speeches and Correspondence.* Edited by Seth Ames. Boston: Little, Brown and Company, 1854.

Austin, Samuel. *An Oration, Pronounced at Worcester, on the Fourth of July, 1798.* Worcester: Leonard Worcester, 1798.

Bishop, Abraham. *Connecticut Republicanism: An Oration, on the Extent and Power of Political Delusion.* Philadelphia: Matthew Carey, 1800.

———. *Oration Delivered in Wallingford.* New Haven: William W. Morse, 1801.

Black, John, et al. *Address to the Federal Republicans of Burlington County.* Trenton: Sherman, Mershon & Thomas, 1800.

Brackenridge, H. H. *Incidents of the Insurrection in the Western Parts of Pennsylvania, in the year 1794.* Philadelphia: Printed by John McCulloch, 1795.

Brackenridge, H. M. *History of the Western Insurrection Commonly Called the Whiskey Insurrection, 1794.* Pittsburgh: W. S. Haven, 1859.

*By-Laws, Muster-Roll, and Papers Selected from the Archives of the First Troop Philadelphia City Cavalry, from November 17, 1774 to March 1, 1856.* Philadelphia: J. B. Smith and Co., 1856.

Cobbett, William, and David A. Wilson, ed. *Peter Porcupine in America: Pamphlets on Republicanism and Revolution.* Ithaca: Cornell University Press, 1994.

*The Colden Letter Books.* Volume 2. New York: Printed for the New York Historical Society, 1878.

*The Correspondence of General Thomas Gage with the Secretaries of State, 1763–1775.* Edited by Clarence Edwin Carter. New Haven: Yale University Press, 1931.

*The Correspondence of John Jay.* Edited by Henry P. Johnston. New York: Knickerbocker Press, 1891.

*The Diary of William Bentley, D. D., Pastor of the East Church, Salem, Massachusetts,* Volume 2. Salem: Essex Institute, 1907.

Dwight, Theodore. *An Oration Spoken at Hartford, in the State of Connecticut, on the Anniversary of American Independence, July 4th, 1798.* Hartford: Hudson and Goodwin, 1798.

Findley, William. *History of the Insurrection in the Four Western Counties in the Year M;DCC;XCIV.* Philadelphia: Samuel Harrison Smith, 1796.

Gibbs, George. *Memoirs of the administrations of Washington and John Adams, edited from the papers of Oliver Wolcott.* New York: W. Van Norden, 1846.

Green, Ashbel. *The Life of Ashbel Green.* New York: R. Carter & Bros., 1849.

Green, James S. *An Address delivered before the Washington Benevolent Societies of Cranberry and Princeton, in the state of New-Jersey, on the 22nd of February, 1815.* New-Brunswick: Lewis Deare, 1815.

Freneau, Philip Morin. *Letters on Various Interesting and Important Subjects.* Philadelphia: D. Hogan, 1799.

Harper, Robert Goodloe. *A letter from Robert Goodloe Harper, of South Carolina, to his Constituents.* Providence: John Carter, 1801.

*Historical Sketches of North Carolina, from 1584 to 1851.* Edited by John H. Wheeler. Philadelphia: Lippincott, Grambo and Co., 1851.

Herrick, Claudius. *An Oration, Delivered at Deerfield, on the Fourth of July, 1800.* Greenfield: Thomas Dickman, 1800.

Johnson, Richard M. *Transportation of the mail on the Sabbath . . .* Frankfort, 1829.

*Laws enacted in the third sitting of the eleventh General Assembly of the Commonwealth of Pennsylvania.* Philadelphia: T. Bradford, 1787.

Lee, Chauncey. *The Tree of Knowledge of Political Good and Evil.* Bennington: T. Collier, 1800.

Linn, William. *Serious Considerations on the Election of a President: Addressed to the Citizens of the United States.* New York: Jay Furman, 1800.

Lowell, John, Jr. *An Oration Pronounced July 4, 1799, At the Request of the Inhabitants of the town of Boston, in Commemoration of the Anniversary of American Independence.* Boston: Manning & Loring, 1799.

Manning, William. "The Key of Liberty (1799)." In Michael Merrill and Sean Wilentz, eds. *The Key of Liberty: The Life and Democratic Writings of William Manning, 'A Laborer,' 1747–1814.* Cambridge: Harvard University Press, 1993.

*Minutes of the Common Council of the City of New York, 1784–1831,* Volume 7. New York: M. B. Brown Printing and Binding, 1917.

*Minutes of Examination, taken in short notes on the trial of the rioters, for a riot and assault on William Duane, on the 15 May, 1799, trial 28 April, 1801.* Philadelphia, 1801.

Montresor, James Gabriel, and John Montresor. *The Montresor Journals.* Edited by G. D. Scull. New York: Printed for the New York Historical Society, 1882.

Otis, Harrison Gray. *Letters Developing the Character and Views of the Hartford Convention, by "One of the Convention."* Washington, 1820.

*Pennsylvania Archives,* Series 2. Volume 4. Edited by John B. Linn and William Henry Egle. Harrisburg: B. F. Meyers, 1876.

*Pennsylvania Archives,* Series 3. Volume 10. Edited by William Henry Egle. Harrisburg: Clarence M. Buseh, 1896.

*Pennsylvania Archives,* Series 9. Volume 2. Edited by Gertrude MacKinney. Harrisburg: Department of Property and Supplies, 1931.

Raguet, Condy. *Oration delivered before the Washington Benevolent Society at their Second Anniversary Meeting on the Twenty-Second of February, 1814.* Philadelphia: William Fry, 1814.

Rush, Benjamin. "Address to the People of the United States." *American Museum,* January 1787.

*State of the accounts of Jacob Morgan, Senior, late lieutenant of Berks County, from March 1777 to March 1780.* Philadelphia: Robert Aitken, 1783.

Steiner, Bernard C. *The Life and Correspondence of James McHenry: Secretary of War under Washington and Adams.* Cleveland: The Burrows Brothers Company, 1907.

*The Two Trials of John Fries.* Philadelphia: William W. Woodward, 1800.

Worcester, Noah. *An Election Sermon, delivered at Concord, June 4, 1800.* Concord: Elijah Russell, 1800.

## Secondary Sources

Altschuler, Glenn C., and Stuart Blumin. *Rude Republic: Americans and Their Politics in the Nineteenth Century.* Princeton: Princeton University Press, 2000.

Ammon, Harry. "The Genet Mission and the Development of American Political Parties." *Journal of American History* 52, no. 4 (1966): 725–41.

Anderson, Frank Maloy. "The Enforcement of the Alien and Sedition Laws." *Annual Report of the American Historical Association for the Year 1912* (Washington, 1914): 115–26.

Baldwin, Leland D. *Whiskey Rebels: The Story of a Frontier Uprising.* Pittsburgh: University of Pittsburgh Press, 1968.

Banner, James M., Jr. *To the Hartford Convention: The Federalists and the Origins of Party Politics in Massachusetts, 1789–1815.* New York: Alfred A. Knopf, 1970.

Bell, Rudolph. *Party and Faction in American Politics: The House of Representatives, 1789–1801.* Westport: Greenwood Press, 1973.

Bellesiles, Michael A. *Revolutionary Outlaws: Ethan Allen and the Struggle for Independence on the Early American Frontier.* Charlottesville: University Press of Virginia, 1993.

Ben-Atar, Doron, and Barbara B. Oberg, eds. *Federalists Reconsidered.* Charlottesville: University of Virginia Press, 1998.

Bensel, Richard. *The American Ballot Box in the Mid-Nineteenth Century: Law, Identity, and the Polling Place.* New York: Cambridge University Press, 2004.

Berkin, Carol. *A Sovereign People: The Crises of the 1790s and the Birth of American Nationalism.* New York: Basic Books, 2017.

Bird, Wendell. *Criminal Dissent: Prosecutions Under the Alien and Sedition Acts of 1798.* Cambridge: Harvard University Press, 2020.

Bouton, Terry. "'No Wonder the Times Were Troublesome': The Origins of Fries Rebellion, 1783–1799." *Pennsylvania History* 67, no. 1 (Winter 2000): 21–42.

———. *Taming Democracy: The People, the Founders, and the Troubled Ending of the American Revolution.* Oxford: Oxford University Press, 2007.

Boyd, Steven R., ed. *The Whiskey Rebellion: Past and Present Perspectives.* Westport: Greenwood Press, 1985.

Boyer, Lee R. "Lobster Backs, Liberty Boys, and Laborers in the Streets: New York's Golden Hill and Nassau Street Riots." *New York Historical Society Quarterly* 57 (1973): 281–308.

Bradburn, Douglas. *The Citizenship Revolution: Politics and the Creation of the American Union, 1774–1804.* Charlottesville: University of Virginia Press, 2009.

Branson, Susan. *These Fiery Frenchified Dames: Women and Political Culture in Early National Philadelphia*. Philadelphia: University of Pennsylvania Press, 2001.

Bring, Steven, and Jean Reith Schroedel, eds. *Evangelicals and Democracy in America: Volume II, Religion and Politics*. New York: Russell Sage Foundation, 2009.

Camp, Stephanie M. H. *Closer to Freedom: Enslaved Women and Everyday Resistance in the Plantation South*. Chapel Hill: University of North Carolina Press, 2004.

Chandler, Abby. "'Unawed by the Laws of their Country': Local and Imperial Legitimacy in North Carolina's Regulator Rebellion." *North Carolina Historical Review* 92, no. 2 (April 2016): 119–46.

Colley, Linda. *Britons: Forging the Nation, 1707–1837*. New Haven: Yale University Press, 1992.

Condon, Sean. *Shays's Rebellion: Authority and Distress in Post-Revolutionary America*. Baltimore: John Hopkins University Press, 2015.

Conway, Stephen. *War, State, and Society in Mid-Eighteenth Century Britain and Ireland*. New York: Oxford University Press, 2006.

Cornell, Saul. "Aristocracy Assailed: The Ideology of Backcountry Anti-Federalism." *Journal of American History* 76, no. 4 (Mar. 1990): 1148–72.

———. *The Other Founders: Anti-Federalism and the Dissenting Tradition in America, 1788–1828*. Chapel Hill: University of North Carolina Press, 1999.

———. "'To Assemble Together for their Common Good': History, Ethnography, and the Original Meanings of the Rights of Assembly and Speech." *Fordham Law Review* 84, no. 3 (2015): 914–34.

Cotlar, Seth. *Tom Paine's America: The Rise and Fall of Transatlantic Radicalism in the Early Republic*. Charlottesville: University of Virginia Press, 2011.

Cox, Joseph W. *Champion of Southern Federalism: Robert Goodloe Harper of South Carolina*. Port Washington: Kennikat Press, 1972.

Cunningham, Noble E., Jr. *The Jeffersonian Republicans in Power: Party Operations, 1801–1809*. Chapel Hill: University of North Carolina Press, 1963.

Daniel, Marcus. *Scandal and Civility: Journalism and the Birth of American Democracy*. Oxford: Oxford University Press, 2009.

Davis, Susan G. *Parades and Power: Street Theatre in Nineteenth Century Philadelphia*. Philadelphia: Temple University Press, 1986.

Deloria, Philip J. *Playing Indian*. New Haven: Yale University Press, 1998.

Dun, James Alexander. *Dangerous Neighbors: Making the Haitian Revolution in Early America*. Philadelphia: University of Pennsylvania Press, 2016.

Dunn, Susan. *Jefferson's Second Revolution: The Election Crisis of 1800 and the Triumph of Republicanism*. Boston: Houghton Mifflin, 2004.

Edgar, Walter B. *South Carolina: A History.* Columbia: University of South Carolina Press, 1998.

Egle, William Henry. *Names of Foreigners who took the Oath of Allegiance to the Province and State of Pennsylvania, 1727–1775, with the foreign arrivals, 1786–1808.* Baltimore: Genealogical Publishing Co., 1967.

———. *Notes and Queries Historical, Biological, and Genealogical Relating Chiefly to Western Pennsylvania.* Harrisburg: Harrisburg Publishing Company, 1898.

El-Haj, Tabatha Abu. "Changing the People: Transformations in American Democracy, 1880–1930." PhD diss., New York University, 2008.

Elkins, Stanley, and Eric McKitrick. *The Age of Federalism: The Early American Republic, 1788–1800.* Oxford: Oxford University Press, 1995.

———, eds. *The Hofstadter Aegis: A Memorial.* New York: Alfred A. Knopf, 1974.

Estes, Todd. *The Jay Treaty Debate, Public Opinion, and the Evolution of Early American Print Culture.* Amherst: University of Massachusetts Press, 2006.

Fennell, Dorothy Elaine. "From Rebelliousness to Insurrection: A Social History of the Whiskey Rebellion, 1765–1802." PhD diss., University of Pittsburgh, 1981.

Fischer, David Hackett. *Liberty and Freedom: A Visual History of America's Founding Ideas.* New York: Oxford University Press, 2005.

———. *The Revolution of American Conservatism: The Federalist Party in the Era of Jeffersonian Democracy.* Chicago: University of Chicago Press, 1975.

Fitz, Caitlin. *Our Sister Republics: The United States in an Age of American Revolutions.* New York: Liveright Publishing Corporation, 2016.

Frank, Jason A. *Constituent Moments: Enacting the People in Postrevolutionary America.* Durham: Duke University Press, 2010.

Freeman, Joanne. *Affairs of Honor: National Politics in the New Republic.* New Haven: Yale University Press, 2001.

Formisano, Ronald P. *For the People: American Populist Movements from the Revolution to the 1850s.* Chapel Hill: University of North Carolina Press, 2008.

Fuentes, Yvonne, and Mark R. Malin, eds. *Protest in the Long Eighteenth Century.* New York: Routledge, 2021.

Furniss, Jack. "States of the Union: The Rise and Fall of the Political Center in the Civil War North." PhD diss., University of Virginia, 2018.

Gallagher, Gary W. *The Union War.* Cambridge: Harvard University Press, 2011.

Gans, Curtis, and Matthew Mulling. *Voter Turnout in the United States, 1788–2009.* Washington, D.C.: CQ Press, 2011.

Gilje, Paul A. *The Road to Mobocracy: Popular Disorder in New York City, 1763–1834.* Chapel Hill: University of North Carolina Press, 1987.

Goold, Roy D. "Liberty Poles—Symbols of Freedom." *Sons of the American Revolution Magazine* 78, no. 2 (Fall 1983).

Greene, James M. "Ethan Allen and Daniel Shays: Contrasting Models of Political Representation in the Early Republic." *Early American Literature* 48, no. 1 (2013): 125–51.

Grimstead, David. *American Mobbing, 1828–1861: Toward Civil War.* Oxford: Oxford University Press, 2003.

Grinspan, Jon. *The Virgin Vote: How Young Americans Made Democracy Social, Politics Personal, and Voting Popular in the Nineteenth Century.* Chapel Hill: University of North Carolina Press, 2016.

———. "'Young Men for War': The Wide Awakes and Lincoln's 1860 Presidential Campaign." *Journal of American History* 96 (Sept. 2009): 357–78.

Gross, Robert A., ed. *In Debt to Shays: The Bicentennial of an Agrarian Rebellion.* Charlottesville: University of Virginia Press, 1993.

Halperin, Terri Diane. *Alien and Sedition Acts of 1798: Testing the Constitution.* Baltimore: John Hopkins University Press, 2016.

Hanson, Robert Brand. *Dedham, Massachusetts, 1635–1800.* Dedham: Dedham Historical Society, 1976.

Harden, J. David. "Liberty Caps and Liberty Trees." *Past & Present*, no. 146 (Feb. 1995): 66–102.

Harris, Alexander. *A Biographical History of Lancaster County.* Lancaster, 1872.

Henderson, Dwight F. "Treason, Sedition, and Fries' Rebellion." *American Journal of Legal History* 14, no. 4 (Oct. 1970): 308–18.

Hofstadter, Richard. *The Idea of a Party System: The Rise of Legitimate Opposition in the United States, 1780–1840.* Berkeley: University of California Press, 1969.

Hole, Christina. *British Folk Customs.* London: Hutchinson & Co., 1976.

Holt, Michael F. *The Political Crisis of the 1850s.* New York: W. W. Norton & Company, 1983.

———. *Political Parties and American Political Development from the Age of Jackson to the Age of Lincoln.* Baton Rouge: Louisiana State University Press, 1992.

———. *The Rise and Fall of the American Whig Party: Jacksonian Politics and the Onset of the Civil War.* New York: Oxford University Press, 1999.

Holton, Woody. *Unruly Americans and the Origins of the Constitution.* New York: Hill & Wang, 2007.

Hoock, Holger. *Empires of Imagination: Politics, War, and the Arts in the British World, 1750–1850.* London: Profile Books, 2010.

Horn, James J., et al., eds. *The Revolution of 1800: Democracy, Race and the New Republic.* Charlottesville: University of Virginia Press, 2002.

Huff, Archie Vernon, Jr. *Greenville: The History of the City and County in the South Carolina Piedmont.* Columbia: University of South Carolina Press, 1995.

Humphrey, Carol Sue. *The Press of the Young Republic, 1783–1883.* Westport: Greenwood Press, 1996.

Hutchins, Zachary McLeod, ed. *Community Without Consent: New Perspectives on the Stamp Act*. Hanover: Dartmouth College Press, 2016.

Irvin, Benjamin H. *Clothed in Robes of Sovereignty: The Continental Congress and the People Out of Doors*. Oxford: Oxford University Press, 2011.

———. "Tar, Feathers, and the Enemies of American Liberties, 1768–1776." *New England Quarterly* 76, no. 2 (2003): 197–238.

Jacob, Margaret, and James Jacob, eds. *The Origins of Anglo-American Radicalism*. London: George Allen & Unwin, 1984.

Jennings, Walter W. "The Agitation for the Repeal of the Embargo Act." *Social Science* 3, no. 2 (1928): 217–46.

Kars, Marjoleine. *Breaking Loose Together: The Regulator Rebellion in Pre-Revolutionary North Carolina*. Chapel Hill: University of North Carolina Press, 2002.

Keller, Kenneth W. "Rural Politics and the Collapse of Pennsylvania Federalism." *Transactions of the American Philosophical Society* 72, no. 6 (1982): 1–73.

Kerber, Linda K. *Federalists in Dissent: Imagery and Ideology in Jeffersonian America*. Ithaca: Cornell University Press, 1970.

Keyssar, Alexander. *The Right to Vote: The Contested History of Democracy in the United States*. New York: Basic Books, 2000.

Kohn, Richard H. "The Washington Administration's Decision to Crush the Whiskey Rebellion." *Journal of American History* 59, no. 3 (1972): 567–84.

Koschnik, Albrecht. *"Let a Common Interest Bind Us Together": Associations, Partisanship, and Culture in Philadelphia, 1775–1840*. Charlottesville: University of Virginia Press, 2007.

Lee, Jean B. *The Price of Nationhood: The American Revolution in Charles County*. New York: W. W. Norton & Company, 1994.

Levine, Peter. "The Fries Rebellion: Social Violence and the Politics of the New Nation." *Pennsylvania History* 40, no. 3 (1973): 240–58.

Levy, Leonard W. *Jefferson and Civil Liberties: The Darker Side*. Cambridge: Belknap Press of Harvard University Press, 1963.

"The Liberty Pole on the Commons." *New York Historical Society Quarterly Bulletin* 3, no. 4 (Jan. 1920).

*Lineage Book—National Society of the Daughters of the American Revolution*. Volumes 50 and 53. Washington, D.C.: Judd & Detweiler, Inc., 1922.

Linn, John Blair. *Annals of Buffalo Valley, Pennsylvania, 1755–1855*. Harrisburg: Lane S. Hart, 1877.

Lurie, Shira. "Liberty Poles and the Fight for Popular Politics in the Early Republic." *Journal of the Early Republic* 38, no. 4 (Winter 2018): 673–97.

Maganzin, Louis. "Economic Depression in Maryland and Virginia, 1783–1787." PhD diss., Georgetown University, 1967.

Maier, Pauline. *American Scripture: Making the Declaration of Independence.* New York: Knopf, 1997.

———. *From Resistance to Revolution: Colonial Radicals and the Development of American Opposition to Britain, 1765–1766.* New York: W. W. Norton & Company, 1991.

Maizlish, Stephen E., ed. *Essays on American Antebellum Politics, 1840–1860.* Arlington: Texas A&M University, 1982.

Mandell, Daniel R. *The Lost Tradition of Economic Equality in America, 1600–1870.* Baltimore: Johns Hopkins University Press, 2020.

McConville, Brendan. "Pope's Day Revisited, 'Popular' Culture Reconsidered." *Explorations in Early American Culture* 4 (2000): 258–80.

McGerr, Michael E. *The Decline of Popular Politics: The American North, 1865–1928.* New York: Oxford University Press, 1986.

McPherson, James M. *Battle Cry of Freedom: The Civil War Era.* New York: Oxford University Press, 1988.

Merrill, Michael, and Sean Wilentz, eds. *The Key of Liberty: The Life and Democratic Writings of William Manning, 'A Laborer', 1747–1814.* Cambridge: Harvard University Press, 1993.

Montgomery, Morton L. *History of Berks County, Pennsylvania, in the Revolution, from 1774 to 1783.* Reading: C. F. Haage, 1894.

Morgan, Edmund S. *Inventing the People: The Rise of Popular Sovereignty in England and America.* New York: W. W. Norton & Company, 1989.

Morone, James A. *The Democratic Wish: Popular Participation and the Limits of American Government*, revised edition. New Haven: Yale University Press, 1998.

Murdock, William Gray. *Brady Family Reunion and Fragments of Brady History and Biography.* Milton, 1909.

Nadelhaft, Jerome J. *The Disorders of War: The Revolution in South Carolina.* Orono: University of Maine at Orono Press, 1981.

Neem, Johann N. *Creating a Nation of Joiners: Democracy and Civil Society in Early National Massachusetts.* Cambridge: Harvard University Press, 2008.

———. "Freedom of Association in the Early Republic: The Republican Party, the Whiskey Rebellion, and the Philadelphia and New York Cordwainers' Cases." *Pennsylvania Magazine of History and Biography* 127, no. 3 (July 2003): 259–90.

Newman, Paul Douglas. *Fries's Rebellion: The Enduring Struggle for the American Revolution.* Philadelphia: University of Pennsylvania Press, 2004.

Newman, Simon P. *Parades and the Politics of the Street: Festive Culture in the Early American Republic.* Philadelphia: University of Pennsylvania Press, 1997.

Owen, Kenneth. *Political Community in Revolutionary Pennsylvania, 1774–1800*. Oxford: Oxford University Press, 2018.

Palmer, Bryan D. "Discordant Music: Charivaris and White Capping in Nineteenth-Century North America." *Labour/Le Travailleur* 3 (1978): 5–62.

Pasley, Jeffrey L. *The First Presidential Contest: 1796 and the Founding of American Democracy*. Lawrence: University Press of Kansas, 2013.

———. "Party Politics, Citizenship, and Collective Action in Nineteenth-Century America: A Response to Stuart Blumin and Michael Schudson." *Communication Review* 4 (2000): 39–54.

———. *"The Tyranny of Printers": Newspaper Politics in the Early American Republic*. Charlottesville: University of Virginia Press, 2001.

Pasley, Jeffrey L., Andrew W. Robertson, and David Waldstreicher, eds. *Beyond the Founders: New Approaches to the Political History of the Early American Republic*. Chapel Hill: University of North Carolina Press, 2004.

Peart, Daniel, and Adam I. P. Smith, eds. *Practicing Democracy: Popular Politics in the United from the Constitution to the Civil War*. Charlottesville: University of Virginia Press, 2015.

Pencak, William, et al., eds. *Riot and Revelry in Early America*. University Park: Pennsylvania State University Press, 2002.

"Political Engagement and Disengagement in Antebellum America: A Roundtable." *Journal of American History* 84, no. 3 (Dec. 1997): 855–909.

Ratcliffe, Donald. "The Right to Vote and the Rise of Democracy, 1787–1828." *Journal of the Early Republic* 33 (Summer 2013): 219–54.

Ridner, Judith. *A Town In-Between: Carlisle, Pennsylvania, and the Early Mid-Atlantic Interior*. Philadelphia: University of Pennsylvania Press, 2011.

Roberts, Ellwood. *Biographical Annals of Montgomery County, Pennsylvania*. Montgomery County: T. S. Benham, 1904.

Roberts, Jennifer L., ed. *Scale*. Terra Foundation Essays, Volume 2. Chicago: University of Chicago Press, 2016.

Robertson, Andrew W. "'Look on This Picture . . . And on This!' Nationalism, Localism, and Partisan Images of Otherness in the United States, 1787–1820." *American Historical Review* 106 (Oct. 2001): 1263–80.

Rowe, G. S. "Alexander Addison: The Disillusionment of a 'Republican Schoolmaster.'" *Western Pennsylvania Historical Magazine* 62, no. 3 (July 1979): 221–50.

Rupp, I. Daniel. *History of Lancaster County*. Lancaster, 1844.

Ryan, Mary P. *Women in Public: Between Banners and Ballots, 1825–1880*. Baltimore: Johns Hopkins University Press, 1992.

Schlesinger, Arthur M. "Liberty Tree: A Genealogy." *New England Quarterly* 25, no. 4 (Dec. 1952): 435–58.

Shankman, Andrew. *Crucible of American Democracy: The Struggle to Fuse Egalitarianism & Capitalism in Jeffersonian Pennsylvania*. Lawrence: University of Kansas Press, 2004.

Shapiro, Darline. "Ethan Allen: Philosopher-Theologian to a Generation of American Revolutionaries." *William and Mary Quarterly* 21, no. 2 (Apr. 1964): 236–55.

Sharp, James Roger. *American Politics in the Early Republic: A New Nation in Crisis*. New Haven: Yale University Press, 1993.

———. *The Deadlocked Election of 1800: Jefferson, Burr, and the Union in the Balance*. Lawrence: University Press of Kansas, 2010.

Shaw, Peter. *American Patriots and the Rituals of Revolution*. Cambridge: Harvard University Press, 1981.

Shy, John W. *Toward Lexington: The Role of the British Army in the Coming of the American Revolution*. Princeton: Princeton University Press, 1965.

Silbey, Joel H. *The American Political Nation, 1838–1893*. Stanford: Stanford University Press, 1991.

Skinner, Quentin. *Liberty Before Liberalism*. Cambridge: Cambridge University Press, 1998.

Slaughter, Thomas P. *The Whiskey Rebellion: Frontier Epilogue to the American Revolution*. New York: Oxford University Press, 1986.

Smith, Barbara Clark. *The Freedoms We Lost: Consent and Resistance in Revolutionary America*. New York: New Press, 2010.

Smith, Culver H. *The Press, Politics, and Patronage: The American Government's Use of Newspapers, 1789–1875*. Athens: University of Georgia Press, 1977.

Smith, Kimberly K. *The Dominion of Voice: Riot, Reason, and Romance in Antebellum Politics*. Lawrence: University Press of Kansas, 1999.

Smith, James Morton. "The Federalist 'Saints' versus 'The Devil of Sedition': The Liberty Pole Case of Dedham, Massachusetts 1798–1799." *New England Quarterly* 28, no. 2 (June 1955): 198–215.

Sommerville, C. W. "Robert Goodloe Harper." PhD Diss., Johns Hopkins University, 1899.

Stewart, Donald H. *The Opposition Press of the Federalist Period*. Albany: State University of New York Press, 1969.

Strum, Harvey. "New York Federalists and Opposition to the War of 1812." *World Affairs* 142, no. 3 (1980): 169–87.

Taylor, Alan. *American Revolutions: A Continental History*. New York: W. W. Norton & Company, 2016.

———. *The Civil War of 1812: American Citizens, British Subjects, Irish Rebels, & Indian Allies*. New York: Vintage Books, 2010.

———. *Liberty Men and Great Proprietors: The Revolutionary Settlement of the*

*Maine Frontier, 1760–1820*. Chapel Hill: The Omohundro Institute of Early American History and Culture by the University of North Carolina Press, 1990.

Taylor, Robert J. *Western Massachusetts in the Revolution*. Providence: Brown University Press, 1954.

Thompson, E. P. "The Moral Economy of the English Crowd in the Eighteenth Century." *Past and Present* 50 (Feb. 1971): 76–136.

Travers, Len. *Celebrating the Fourth: Independence Day and the Rites of Nationalism in the Early Republic*. Amherst: University of Massachusetts Press, 1997.

Underdown, David. *Revel, Riot, and Rebellion: Popular Politics and Culture in England, 1603–1660*. New York: Oxford University Press, 1985.

Varon, Elizabeth R. *Disunion!: The Coming of the American Civil War, 1789–1859*. Chapel Hill: University of North Carolina Press, 2008.

Volk, Kyle G. *Moral Minorities and the Making of American Democracy*. Oxford: Oxford University Press, 2014.

Waldstreicher, David. *In the Midst of Perpetual Fetes: The Making of American Nationalism, 1776–1820*. Chapel Hill: University of North Carolina Press, 1997.

Warren, Charles. *Jacobin and Junto, or Early American Politics as viewed in the Diary of Dr. Nathaniel Ames, 1758–1822*. Cambridge: Harvard University Press, 1931.

Watson, Harry L. *Liberty and Power: The Politics of Jacksonian America*. New York: Hill and Wang, 2006.

Weisberger, Bernard A. *America Afire: Jefferson, Adams, and the First Contested Election*. New York: Harper Collins, 2001.

White, Ashli. *Encountering Revolution: Haiti and the Making of the Early Republic*. Baltimore: Johns Hopkins University Press, 2010.

Young, Alfred F. *Liberty Tree: Ordinary People and the American Revolution*. New York: New York University Press, 2006.

———. *The Shoemaker and the Tea Party: Memory and the American Revolution*. Boston: Beacon Press, 1999.

Young, Alfred F., ed. *The American Revolution: Explorations in the History of American Radicalism*. DeKalb: Northern Illinois University Press, 1976.

Young, Alfred F., et al., eds. *Revolutionary Founders: Rebels, Radicals, and Reformers in the Making of the Nation*. New York: Vintage Books, 2012.

Zagarri, Rosemarie. *Revolutionary Backlash: Women and Politics in the Early Republic*. Philadelphia: University of Pennsylvania Press, 2008.

## ❖ INDEX ❖

Adams, Abigail, 101
Adams, John, 9, 56, 64, 72, 82, 86, 96, 98–101, 106, 111, 116, 118–19, 174n24, 182n41
Adams, John Quincy, 130–31
Adams, Samuel, 36, 87, 115
Addison, Alexander, 47, 51, 53, 61, 164n13
*Albany Gazette,* 69
Alien and Sedition Laws, 65, 73–79, 81–82, 84, 86, 91–93, 99, 106, 109, 112, 115–16, 170n25, 172n43
American militia, 6, 33–34, 36–37, 39, 52–53, 57, 77–78, 81, 94, 96, 98, 105–12, 121, 129, 165n18, 170n28, 173n13, 175n30, 179n13, 192
American Revolution, 2, 4–5, 7, 10, 15–16, 18–20, 22–30, 32, 36, 38, 40, 41,42, 43, 48, 50, 53, 68, 74, 80, 91, 106, 118, 135–36, 139, 140, 143–46
Ames, Fisher, 48, 84, 87–89, 91–93, 117, 120, 174n21
Anti-Federalists, 40–41, 114
Anti-Rent Wars (New York), 129–30
*Aurora General Advertiser,* 71, 80, 93, 98–99, 101, 109–13, 136, 177n43

Baltimore, 122, 135
*Baltimore Daily Intelligencer,* 61, 167
*Baltimore Patriot,* 133, 135
*Baltimore Sun,* 135

Battle of Golden Hill, 27–28, 193
Berks County, 77, 94, 107, 114
Berkshire County, 35
*Berkshire Gazette,* 69
Bonham, William, 49–59, 168n37, 191
Boston, 17–18, 21, 29, 35, 37, 71–72, 91
*Boston Gazette,* 121
Boston Massacre, 28
Boston Tea Party, 18, 29
Boude, Thomas, 107
Bowdoin, James, 36–38
Brady, John, 57
Brady, William Perry, 54, 56–57, 59–60
British Army, 2, 15–16, 19–20, 23, 29, 31, 80, 193
British Empire, 20, 28–29, 35. *See also* empire of liberty
British Navy, 22, 70
Brown, David, 84–87, 89–93, 95, 101–2, 173n13, 174nn23–24, 192
Bucks County, 93, 133

Calhoun, John C., 131
Carlisle (Pennsylvania), 1–4, 10, 41, 53, 63, 191
*Carlisle Gazette,* 2
celebration, 7, 9, 17–19, 21, 24, 30, 40, 65, 70, 77, 119, 125, 136, 144, 146, 158n11, 168n2, 168n4, 170n28, 171n30, 182n45, 184n5, 194
*Centinel of Freedom,* 80, 105, 116

Charles County, 39
Civil War, 5, 127, 138–40
Clay, Henry, 131, 133–34
Congress, 10, 50, 52–53, 65, 72, 76, 87–88, 90, 94–96, 98–99, 107, 121–23, 128, 131, 146
Connecticut, 20, 29, 75, 89, 120, 122, 136, 139, 173n13
Constitutional Convention, 39–42, 48
Continental Congress, 20
crowd action: and the American Revolution, 35; during the colonial era, 16–19, 32; and Federalists, 5, 10, 97, 117, 195; legitimacy of, 38; and liberty poles, 8, 16; and police force, 130; and radicalism, 161n9; and Republicans, 6; and resistance, 4, 30, 43, 48; rites of, 29, 32, 157n3; and violence, 128

*Daily Advertiser,* 67, 133
Dauphin County, 94
Dedham (Massachusetts), 84–85, 87, 89–93, 102, 191, 193
Democrats, 125, 129, 130–40
Direct Tax Law, 35, 73, 75, 84–85, 87, 90, 93–96, 100, 106, 116, 175n32, 177n51, 192
dissent, 3, 6, 8–10, 47, 54, 58, 60, 71, 74, 106, 113, 121–24, 128, 141, 184n55; Republican popular politics of dissent, 6, 9, 10, 66
Dwight, Thomas, 88

embargo, 121–22
empire of liberty, 16, 19
extra-institutional politics, 48, 51, 59, 68, 87, 127, 137, 172n43, 194
extra-institutional processes, 7–8, 18, 58, 70, 106, 123, 130
extra-institutional resistance, 11, 85, 117, 127, 129–30, 197–98
Eÿermann, Jacob, 85–87, 95–97, 99–101, 177n51, 191, 197

federal government: approval of, 9, 195; and William Bonham, 50; and the Constitution, 39; critics of, 4–5, 92–94, 107; and Federalists, 69, 73, 76, 80; and Thomas Jefferson, 119; and New Jersey, 97; and nullification, 131; and political parties, 130; and regulations, 65, 109; and resistance, 61; and treason, 60; and the whiskey excise, 1
Federalist Papers, 70, 192
Federalists: administrations, 84; and anarchy, 64–66; and the election of 1800, 115, 118–20, 127; and the First Party System, 10, 67–68, 123–24; and grassroots activity, 9–10, 70–71, 105–6, 194–95; and ideology, 4–6, 40, 64–66, 82, 85–91, 101–2, 121–24, 128, 141; and the Jay Treaty, 72; and John Brady, 57; and legislation, 6, 73, 81–82, 85, 91, 119; and liberty poles, 4–5, 66, 75–82, 84, 96, 111–12, 116, 137; and popular politics, 5, 10–11, 40, 64–66, 69–72, 76–78, 97, 99, 105–12, 120, 123, 156n19, 168n2, 172n43, 193–95; popular politics of assent, 9–10, 65–67, 69–72, 76–80, 82, 111–12, 169n11, 195; printers, 78–79, 110, 117–18, 121–22; ratification, 40–41; and representative government, 93, 98; and Republicans, 8–10, 67–70, 74–76, 80, 89–90, 98, 106, 113–16, 163n6; and tax legislation, 73–74, 85–88, 95, 99; and violence, 136; and Whigs, 136; and the Whiskey Rebellion, 113
federal law, 8, 49, 53, 131
Findley, William, 58
"Founders Chic," 146
France, 7, 21, 23, 66–70, 72–74, 82, 88, 90, 97, 120, 193; Francophobia, 68, 109; French Revolution, 67, 81, 118, 168n4, 172n8; French West Indies, 70; trade with the United States, 71

freedom. *See* liberty
Fries, John, 96–98, 100–101
Fries's Rebellion, 6, 93–101, 106–12, 113, 191

Gage, Thomas, 20, 25–26, 28, 159n30
grassroots activism, 5, 8–10, 65–66, 70, 76, 81, 84–86, 88, 102, 105–6, 115, 119–24, 191, 194–95
Greenbrier County, 39

Hamilton, Alexander, 9, 39–40, 48, 50, 68, 71, 95, 100, 102, 191
Hampshire County, 36
Harper, Robert Goodloe, 98–99, 108–11, 120
Harrison, William Henry, 132
Hartford Convention, 122–23
Henry, Patrick, 53
Heydrick, Jacob, 1–2
hickory poles, 125, 130–36, 138, 140, 184n1
Huntingdon County, 41
Hutchinson, Thomas, 18, 29

Imperial Crisis, 1, 4, 6, 18, 28, 30, 32, 75, 96, 143
insurrection, 59, 69, 91, 95, 97–98, 101, 111, 113

Jackson, Andrew, 125, 130–31, 135, 140
Jarret, Henry, 96
Jay, John, 5, 70–72
Jay Treaty, 70–72, 76
Jefferson, Thomas, 8, 65, 68, 85, 97, 114–22, 124–26, 139, 179n13, 182n41, 182n45
Jenkins, Robert, 107
justice, 18, 27, 54–55, 75, 109, 112, 192
justice of the peace, 47, 55, 58–59, 77, 96

Kentucky Relief Wars, 129

Labouring Society, 87
Lamb, John, 20, 26
Lancaster County, 94, 113
Lancaster Troop of Horse, 107–13, 137, 178nn4–5, 179n13, 180n27
law and order, 33, 36, 43, 48, 53, 59, 61, 86, 98–99, 109, 111, 141, 167n30
Leiper, Thomas, 109, 111, 177n43, 179n13
liberty, 4, 6, 16, 18, 20, 21–26, 29–30, 39–41, 43, 52–55, 59, 63, 65–66, 68, 71–72, 74–75, 80–82, 87, 91, 95–96, 99, 102, 108, 111, 114–15, 117, 119, 130, 134, 136–37, 139, 143–44, 146, 156n15, 167n36
liberty caps, 7, 20, 66, 69, 78, 81, 91, 105–6, 116, 144
Liberty Men, 42
liberty trees, 21–22, 29, 192–93
Lowell, John, 91
Luzerne County, 57

MacPherson, William, 98–99, 108, 110–11, 167n36, 176n42, 192
Madison, James, 8, 65, 85, 119, 122, 124, 155n7
Manning, William, 86–87, 90, 197
Massachusetts, 29, 35–38, 70, 75, 84, 86, 88–90, 117, 121, 144
Massachusetts Constitution, 35
maypoles, 20–21, 25, 193
McHenry, James, 98
McKean, Thomas, 51, 112, 114–15, 117, 120, 137, 179n13
*Middlesex Gazette*, 76
Mifflin, Thomas, 51, 57–58, 112, 180
Monroe, James, 115
Montgomery, Daniel, 47, 55, 57–60
Montgomery, William, 107, 109–13
Montgomery County, 106, 115

Neutrality Proclamation, 70, 76
New Hampshire, 17, 34, 37, 39, 71

New Jersey, 7, 39, 58, 75, 78, 81, 97–98, 105, 116–17, 122
New York City, 15–23, 27–30, 35, 71, 125, 143–44, 192–93
*New York Gazette*, 15, 24–25
New York Historical Society, 143
Nichols, William, 96–98, 100
Northampton County, 96–98
North Carolina, 75, 122
North Carolina Regulation, 32–36
Northumberland County, 47, 49, 63
Nullification Crisis, 127, 131–32, 140, 185n18

Ohio, 52, 134, 140
*Ohio Statesman*, 134, 136–37
Orange County, 33–34

parades, 9, 75, 126
Parliament, 2–3, 16, 18–24
partisanship, 5, 9–10, 61, 64–67, 69, 83, 85, 96, 105, 113, 116, 119, 122, 125–27, 130, 132–35, 137–41, 164n13, 170n18, 180n29, 182n45, 184n3, 185n19, 187n40, 191, 193–98
Patriots, 16, 28–30, 34–35, 89, 140, 144, 146, 160n34, 197
Pennsylvania, 1–2, 20, 38–39, 41–42, 47–50, 52–53, 57–59, 74–77, 79, 81–82, 85, 93–99, 101–2, 105–6, 111–17, 120, 133–34, 146, 163n7, 191, 195–96
Pennsylvania State Constitution, 31, 38
Philadelphia, 39–40, 49, 52, 54, 71, 95–99, 109–10, 112–14, 134–35
*Philadelphia Gazette*, 110
*Philadelphia Inquirer*, 138
Pitt, William, 20
pole-raisers, 2, 5, 7–8, 10–11, 15–16, 20, 24, 29–30, 34, 53–56, 58–60, 66, 75–77, 79, 93, 105, 114, 125–26, 133–34, 137–38, 140, 147, 167n29, 170n25, 174n26, 178n5, 192–93
political culture: antebellum, 11, 127, 133, 197; colonial, 35, 157n3; and Federalists, 74, 80, 82, 106; and the First Party System, 5, 130; and the Imperial Crisis, 30; and Kentucky, 129; and liberty poles, 141, 147, 193; and media, 192; and Pennsylvania, 196; and popular will, 155n8; and Republicans, 6, 65–66, 102, 106, 137, 183n51; and the Revolution, 43; and the Second Party System, 126, 130; and violence, 11
political expression, 3–4, 7, 11, 17, 21, 30, 47, 59–61, 65, 74, 79–80, 106, 109, 111, 113, 127–28, 134, 146
Polk, James K., 133
Pope's Day, 17–18, 157n5
popular politics, 194, 196–98; and Anti-Federalists, 41; colonial, 38; Federalist popular politics of assent, 9–10, 65–67, 69–72, 76–80, 82, 111–12, 169n11, 195; and moral reform, 127; Republican popular politics of dissent, 6, 9, 10, 66. *See also* Federalists; Republicans
popular sovereignty, 3–4, 38, 73, 87, 137, 141, 146
popular will, 3, 9, 70, 72–73, 76, 78, 85, 110, 123, 126, 130, 155n8
*Porcupine's Gazette*, 110
power: abuse of, 50, 65; check on, 58, 64; colonists', 33, 36; economic, 85; federal, 65, 74, 123, 130, 137, 140; and Federalists, 89–91, 115; foreign, 69; government, 7, 17–19, 42, 71, 80, 91, 98, 127, 130, 146; imperial, 24, 28, 35; people's, 1, 3–5, 19, 23, 31, 38, 43, 48, 74, 86–87, 106, 113; redcoats, 30; and Republicans, 117, 123; state, 39; structures, 16, 140; symbolic power, 10, 24, 40, 56, 110; taxing, 99; transitions of, 126
presidential election of 1796, 114
presidential election of 1800, 82, 102, 106, 115–19
presidential election of 1824, 131

presidential election of 1828, 125, 130
presidential election of 1840, 132, 135–36
presidential election of 1860, 137
property, 17–18, 24, 34–35, 39–40, 50, 56, 73, 86, 94–95, 102, 108–9, 126, 128, 138, 161n10, 170n24, 179n13
public justice, 8, 17–19, 22, 30, 33 60, 96, 157n4
public space, 7–8, 66, 75, 78, 156n15, 163n2
public sphere, 5, 40, 66, 78–79

Queen's County, 77

Rawle, William, 100, 191
Reading (Pennsylvania), 77, 81, 105, 107–11, 113–14, 136, 176n42, 191
Reconstruction, 140
regulation, 8, 10, 31–39, 41–43, 48, 50–53, 58, 61, 65, 75, 82, 85, 87, 89–90, 94–102, 106, 115, 121, 124–25, 127, 129–31, 137, 141, 156n17, 161n11, 163n6, 165n18, 175n32, 178n2, 184n5, 192–93, 195
representative government, 4, 10, 32, 36, 38, 49–52, 58, 61, 64, 66, 71, 76, 85–86, 88–89, 93, 95, 98, 101, 110, 126, 140, 161n9
Republicans, 4–5, 91; and the Alien and Sedition Laws, 74, 78; and the election of 1800, 115–20; elites, 8, 102, 163n6; and the French Revolution, 168n4, 172n8; and liberty poles, 70, 74–82, 91, 96, 106–9, 119, 121–22, 193, 195; opposition movement, 87–88, 98, 107, 119–22, 195; party, 65–66, 69, 106; and Pennsylvania, 99, 109, 111–12; and political culture, 6; politicians, 86, 93–94, 97–98, 102, 116, 179n13; and popular politics, 5–6, 9–10, 57, 65–68, 72, 77–78, 81–83, 89, 102, 105–6, 110, 123, 136, 139, 178n5, 184n5; popular politics of dissent, 6, 9, 10, 66; press, 8, 66, 68, 71, 80, 82, 86, 93, 98, 101, 108, 111, 113–16; and protest, 11, 69–70, 78, 89; radicalism, 86, 120; victories, 105–6, 117–18, 119–20, 123–24
Republicans (Third Party System), 133, 137–38, 140, 187n35
resistance: activities, 8, 11, 31, 48, 51, 53, 61, 65, 70–71, 76, 85, 95, 109, 119, 195; community, 22, 141; and Andrew Jackson, 125; and liberty poles, 19, 30, 58, 122, 196; movements, 10, 33, 49, 56; and New Yorkers, 25; and Northumberland, 52; and Pennsylvania, 39, 48, 82, 93, 196; plantation, 194; popular, 4, 16, 29, 38–39, 50, 54, 73, 82, 87–88, 90, 96–97, 121, 124, 126–27, 130, 134, 137–38, 197; and redcoats, 24; Republican, 69, 89, 193; right to, 198; and Sons of Liberty, 27; suppressing, 37, 52; tax, 94, 99, 101–2, 106, 175n30; to unjust laws, 4; and Whigs, 17, 161n9
Ross, James, 107, 112–13, 137
Rush, Benjamin, 4

*Salem Gazette*, 91
secession, 131, 138–40
sedition, 27, 61, 76, 84, 92–93, 159n26. *See also* Alien and Sedition Laws
sedition poles, 10, 77, 80, 99, 110–11
Shays, Daniel, 36–38
Shays's Rebellion, 35–38, 87
slavery, 29, 75, 128, 138
Sons of Liberty, 15, 20, 22–23, 25–29, 33, 41, 143, 160nn30–31
South Carolina, 22, 39–41, 71, 75, 108–9, 126, 131–32, 138, 185n18. *See also* Nullification Crisis
suffrage, 7, 28, 126

Tammany Society, 21
tarring and feathering, 18, 22, 50, 54, 55
taverns, 7, 15, 23, 26, 39, 54–55, 58, 63, 75, 96–97, 135, 143

taxation, 2, 31–35, 38–39, 48–52, 61, 65, 73–74, 82, 85, 88–90, 94–95, 100, 117, 122
Tryon, William, 28, 33–34
two-party system, 11, 126

Ulster County, 76
U.S. Constitution, 3, 33, 39, 51, 76, 95, 99, 106–7, 114, 118, 120, 122–23, 128, 139, 146; and ratification, 9, 31, 40–42, 87
violence, 5, 15, 26–27, 40, 48, 50, 53, 56, 60, 67–68, 76, 94, 97, 107–13, 121–22, 128, 136, 139, 141, 165n19

Virginia, 1, 39, 48, 52–53, 58, 62–63, 70, 75, 118, 132, 138–39

War of 1812, 122–23, 125, 127
Washington, Bushrod, 100
Washington, D.C., 132
Washington, George, 9, 48–49, 52–53, 58–59, 64, 70, 105, 114, 158n12, 169n11, 172n8
*Washington Advertiser*, 120
Washington County, 39, 63

Wayne County, 76
*Weekly Advertiser of Reading*, 109
Westmoreland County, 38, 63
Whigs, 125, 129, 132–36, 161n9, 186n27
whiskey excise (1791), 1, 3, 47–51, 54, 56, 60–61, 71, 114, 121–22, 175n33, 179n13
Whiskey Rebellion, 1–3, 6–7, 43, 47–63; and David Bradford, 164n10; and Terry Bouton, 163n4; and dissent, 47, 60–61; and Federalists, 97, 113; and the Imperial Crisis, 96; and Thomas Leiper, 179n13; and liberty poles, 43, 47–48, 52–54, 63, 69, 75, 146, 191; and political participation, 49, 64; and regulations, 87
Williams, Jonathan, 110–11
Williams, Samuel, 120
Wilson, William, 47, 55, 57–60
women, 7, 20, 77, 81, 94, 108, 127–28, 158n14, 171n30, 177n48
Worcester County, 36

XYZ Affair, 72, 84

York County, 94

THE REVOLUTIONARY AGE

*European Friends of the American Revolution*
Andrew J. O'Shaughnessy, John A. Ragosta, and
Marie-Jeanne Rossignol, editors

*The Tory's Wife: A Woman and Her Family in Revolutionary America*
Cynthia A. Kierner

*Writing Early America: From Empire to Revolution*
Trevor Burnard

*Spain and the American Revolution: New Approaches and Perspectives*
Gabriel Paquette and Gonzalo M. Quintero Saravia, editors

*The American Revolution and the Habsburg Monarchy*
Jonathan Singerton

*Navigating Neutrality: Early American Governance in the Turbulent Atlantic*
Sandra Moats

*Ireland and America: Empire, Revolution, and Sovereignty*
Patrick Griffin and Francis D. Cogliano, editors

www.ingramcontent.com/pod-product-compliance
Lightning Source LLC
Chambersburg PA
CBHW021606140725
29581CB00025B/555